"I fell absolutely in love with Russell W charming sense of wry humor, the quest to understand family and find roots, the deeply moving search for meaning in the face of mortality, the sharp insights, the keen eye, the vicarious peeks into life on the Gold Rush Trail of 1849, the road trip with a purpose — all of it makes for delightful company. What a ride! I'd follow this literary voice anywhere." — Angie Abdou, author of *This One Wild Life*

"Russell Wangersky is a natural-born storyteller, and he weaves together two starkly different, yet oddly complimentary journeys — past and present, home and away — and does so with great aplomb. Less a travel book than a palimpsest, *Same Ground* overlays the Gold Rush Trail of '49 with its modern equivalent, featuring cowboys and cardsharps, dodgy motels and tatty roadside attractions, the 'natural beauty' of a slag pour, and towns that died of thirst. A thoughtful, meditative look at the open road and where it can lead us." — Will Ferguson, Giller Award–winning author of *419* and *The Finder*

"Russell Wangersky weaves the diary of his ancestor's trek in 1849 with his own pursuit along the California Gold Rush Trail in a seamless tapestry that melds space and time. His theme is connection: his own lost family, the families he and his wife Leslie meet on the blue highways of America, the moms and pops who run the motels and the diners. *Same Ground* takes us on a wild chase into the uncharted territories of the heart." — Wayne Grady, author of *The Good Father*

"Overlaid like a stereoscope, past and present give Wangersky's pilgrimage along the Gold Rush Trail vivid three-dimensional reality. His great-great-grandfather's diary is packed with fascinating detail, and the quest to see what he saw opens the old and the new west to our eyes. As the modern couple scuffles around in the desert, the road also reveals the anatomy of a marriage — as all the best journeys do. A thoroughly enjoyable book." — Marina Endicott, author of *The Difference*

Praise for Russell Wangersky

"Read him: Cross of Ishmael Reed and Lou Reed. Here be expert experimentalism: The dictionary exploded and reloaded; the canon fired and melted down." — George Elliott Clarke, author of *I & I*

"[Russell] has a gift for astute observation, wisely chosen detail and characterization that nods in certain directions without forcing or pushing." — Joan Barfoot for *London Free Press*

"With sympathy for both males and females, *Whirl Away* explores romance, disillusionment, money worries, infidelity, layoffs, and tipping points, quiet conflicts like butter simmering on a stove and about to angrily turn color and burn." — Mark Jarman for *Globe and Mail* on Giller Prize–shortlisted *Whirl Away*

"A master storyteller with a keen eye for the critical details that bring his written descriptions to life as cinematic scenes." — *What's on Winnipeg* on *Burning Down the House*

"One of the most unsettling crime novels I've read this year . . . Wangersky can write extraordinarily well in a number of disciplines, so it's only reasonable to expect that, when turning his attention to psychological suspense, he'd excel at this, too." — Sarah Weinman for *National Post* on *Walt*

Same Ground

Same Ground

Chasing Family down the California Gold Rush Trail

By Russell Wangersky

This book is also available as a Global Certified Accessible™ (GCA) ebook. ECW Press's ebooks are screen reader friendly and are built to meet the needs of those who are unable to read standard print due to blindness, low vision, dyslexia, or a physical disability.

Purchase the print edition and receive the eBook free. For details, go to ecwpress.com/eBook.

Published by ECW Press
665 Gerrard Street East
Toronto, Ontario, Canada M4M 1Y2
416-694-3348 / info@ecwpress.com

Editor for the Press: Susan Renouf
Copy editor: Shannon Parr
Cover design: Michel Vrana
Mapmaker: Rhys Davies

LIBRARY AND ARCHIVES CANADA CATALOGUING IN PUBLICATION

Title: Same ground : chasing family down the Gold Rush trail / by Russell Wangersky.

Names: Wangersky, Russell, 1962- author.

Identifiers: Canadiana (print) 20220186855 | Canadiana (ebook) 20220186960

ISBN 978-1-77041-654-3 (softcover)
ISBN 978-1-77852-020-4 (ePub)
ISBN 978-1-77852-021-1 (PDF)
ISBN 978-1-77852-022-8 (Kindle)

Subjects: LCSH: Wangersky, Russell, 1962——Travel—West (U.S.) | LCSH: Wangersky, Russell, 1962——Family. | CSH: Authors, Canadian (English)—21st century—Biography. | LCGFT: Autobiographies.

Classification: LCC PS8645.A5333 Z46 2022 | DDC C818/.603—dc23

We acknowledge the support of the Canada Council for the Arts. *Nous remercions le Conseil des arts du Canada de son soutien.* This book is funded in part by the Government of Canada. *Ce livre est financé en partie par le gouvernement du Canada.* We acknowledge the support of the Ontario Arts Council (OAC), an agency of the Government of Ontario, which last year funded 1,965 individual artists and 1,152 organizations in 197 communities across Ontario for a total of $51.9 million. We also acknowledge the support of the Government of Ontario through the Ontario Book Publishing Tax Credit, and through Ontario Creates.

PRINTED AND BOUND IN CANADA

PRINTING: MARQUIS   5   4   3   2   1

MIX
Paper from responsible sources
FSC® C103567
www.fsc.org

For my father, Peter John Wangersky

I wish you were still here to read this

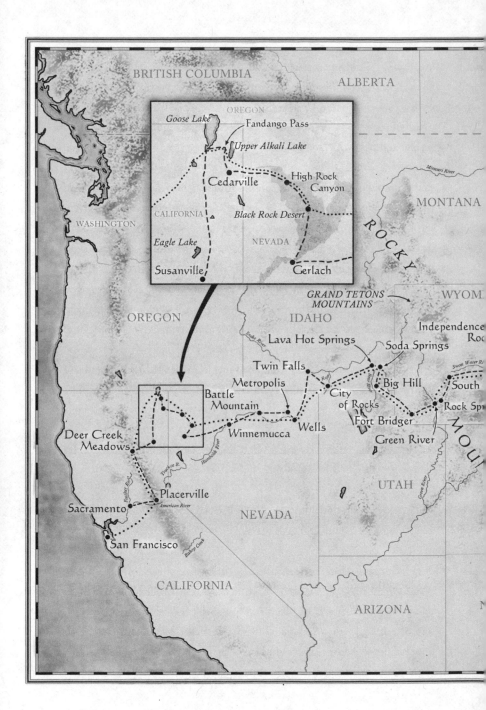

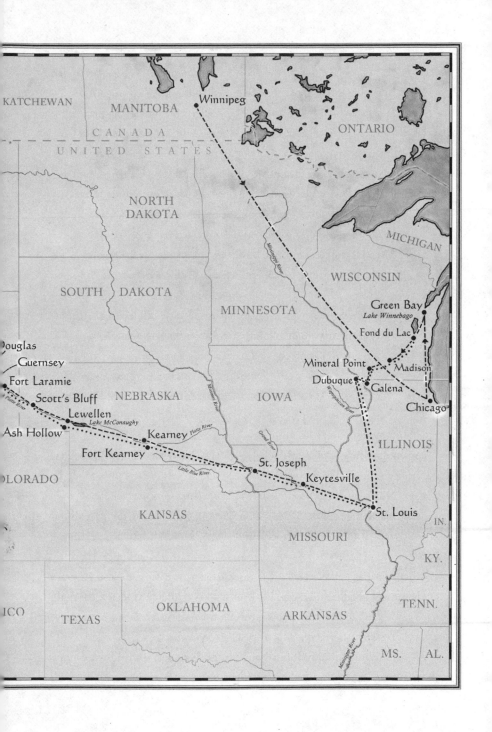

Table of Contents

Introduction	1
Wisconsin	11
Along the Mississippi	28
St. Louis, Missouri	40
Omaha, Nebraska	58
St. Joseph, Missouri	63
Kearny (or Kearney), Nebraska	79
Lewellen, Nebraska	119
Heading for Independence Rock	144
The Continental Divide	173
The Stories of Soda Springs	201
Lava Hot Springs	215
The Road to Wells, Nevada	230
Winnemucca and the Start of Real Desert	243
The Western Desert	252
Night Falls	283
Into California	299
Across the Continent	341
Afterword	345
Acknowledgements	349

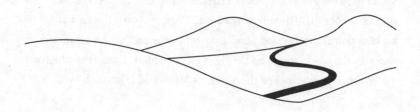

I t's like watching dominoes fall, like a science fiction movie, every member of my mother's side of the family toppling over and turning to dust. No, less than dust — to nothing, as if they'd never been.

It's all because of the simplest of things: my wife saying, "If William Dodge had died out here, none of you would ever even have been born."

And we wouldn't: if he'd been bitten by a rattlesnake (he almost was) or shot (he almost was) or died of influenza (he almost did), that would have been it right there. That whole side of my family, and me — and my children — simply would never have been.

But he wasn't. So we were, and we are.

She says it to me first as we sit deep in the blazing High Rock Canyon in Nevada, in the heat-shimmer and dust and scarcity of it, and she says it again as we pass beside the big blue bowl of Walker Lake, heading south toward Vegas.

We drive through an artillery base, the ground on both sides of the road hummocked with row after row of ammunition bunkers — the Hawthorne Army Depot, 2,400 ammunition bunkers — the ground pimpled with mounds of high explosives all around us. I can't help but suddenly feel just as unsafe as my great-great-grandfather must have felt in 1849.

I've been thinking a lot about risk, about how we're all just binary switches in the great computer of the universe. Ones and zeros, switches that are either turned on or turned off. That, if North Korea wanted to make a point, the 147,000 acres that comprise the largest ammunition depot in the world might be the right place to start. Ironic that the road we're driving on is named the Veterans Memorial Highway.

There isn't any safe ground out here.

Road crews work in the crushing heat, laying down asphalt that runs to the very horizon. Tanker trucks spread water to hold the dust down. We pass a massive array of solar mirrors, directing the bright sun to a collector atop a tower at the centre of the mirrored circle, a tower looking for all the world like the Eye of Sauron.

We pass the eerie Clown Motel on the high ground at Tonopah.

This may feel like the beginning of a story.

It's actually the end.

The beginning is next.

Introduction

I wrote these few paragraphs at the very beginning of a trip that would carry me across much of the United States, retracing a trail that is sometimes invisible, other times etched distinctly as a set of wheel ruts.

My parents didn't so much cut down the family tree as they cut it down and pulled the stump right up from the ground, moving us far north to another country, leaving behind the family universe of uncles, aunts, and cousins. They did it for opportunity, for sure, and to escape the yoke that families often are. Then, work undone it seems, our nuclear family — three boys, two parents — split again, spread right across the northern hemisphere of North America.

When I go to others' family gatherings, I circle the edges like Pluto, out there on the very edge of the solar system. I can't help but feel the gravitational attraction, the sense that I am missing something integral.

Now I find myself on an airplane, heading south to a country I was born in but have no claim to, in search of a relative tantalizingly close, if in no other way than by his words. And words? I know that family well.

My father, Peter John Wangersky, had told me for years that I should read my great-great-grandfather William Castle Dodge's gold rush diary. Dad had taken the time to not just read the diary but to correct a decades-old typed version and make a new copy. He'd made that effort, though Dodge was my mother's great-grandfather, not his own. Perhaps like me, my father — an only child whose parents had emigrated from a small village that Stalin soon razed — had the desire to find roots in familial connection, no matter how tenuous. To track backwards through that most-constant of human pursuits — picking up the path of those who've moved on, en route to better opportunities.

Dad wanted me to find a way for others to read it, but I didn't start until after he died.

That is how regrets are made.

Dodge was only 22: born in New York, he had gone to Fond du Lac, Wisconsin to study law. Halting his studies midstream, he teamed up with a group of other young men, who named themselves "The New York Company" to go west in the 1849 gold rush. Dodge would later write that there were nine members of the company, but he doesn't ever identify them completely, using primarily surnames or initials for surnames.

The 1849 gold rush brought thousands of eager neophyte gold miners, like Dodge and his partners, onto the California Trail. In late 1848, when word spread to the eastern states of a gold strike at Sutter's Mill in Coloma, California, thousands of people made plans to head west as soon as the weather broke in the spring.

In 1849 alone, some 35,000 people set out to find their fortunes in the goldfields, most travelling overland from the eastern states. William Castle Dodge was just one of them. Many found hardship, disease, and poverty. They died of cholera, of typhoid fever, of drowning, of exposure, of accidental and intentional gunshot wounds. Some went mad on the journey — many returned with no fortunes, but with lingering health issues that would follow them for the rest of their lives.

They started with heavily laden wagons, but the difficult trip killed livestock and pack animals, saw expensive provisions and equipment discarded and scattered for hundreds of miles along the route, and reduced many hopeful miners-to-be to packing on foot, and later desperate for whatever food and other materials they could scavenge.

Much of the route between Missouri and California was unmapped wilderness: miners and settlers — as well as army units "protecting" these American emigrants from the Indigenous inhabitants — travelled along different portions of the California Trail. The army was exploring and mapping this new territory as they went but the only established marking points in 1849 were natural features and the occasional frontier fort. There were less than five of those forts — some barely more than trappers' stockades — for the entire 3,000-mile trail. Their appearance was keenly anticipated, because they were often the only solid evidence that travellers were on the right path. Some of the travellers were part of guided parties — most were not, trusting directions as simple as word of mouth or tattered guidebooks that other settlers wrote out and shared or sold.

The great migration west built the state of California, but it also destroyed peace with the Native American Peoples and set the stage for the Indian Wars, as settlers heading west killed game, strayed from agreed-upon routes of travel, and introduced disease that swept through the Indigenous populations.

Some, especially among the first miners and certainly among those who sold supplies, made fortunes in the goldfields; a lucky miner could make a year's wages in mere days.

Most did not.

And the great migration? It continues, today, tomorrow, and every day. Towns grow around natural resources and economic needs, then shrink and fail alongside those diminishing needs. We move, and if we do not, if we're safely and comfortably settled, we resist those who do. Often, forcefully.

My wife, Leslie Vryenhoek, and I started our trip toward Dodge's trail from Manitoba, where Leslie's roots are.

We met up with four generations of the matrilineal Urquhart line on a small flatland farm framed by trees near Cypress River, two hours west of Winnipeg.

Past Rathwell and Treherne and Holland. You turn right on a dirt road just past the weather recording station on Highway 2, if that's any help.

It's Valerie and Marc's farm, the place they and their son Isaac — and their horses, pigs, and chickens — call home. It's a small acreage, a corner cut off huge blocks of open, industrial-farmed land that's planed flat for ease in planting. Theirs is a more traditional island in a tilled sea.

And on that island, the disparate family gathers.

The younger cousins spool around in packs, brought together from Manitoba, from Saskatchewan, even from Newfoundland, individuals not always in regular physical contact with one another but somehow able to pick up the pieces and slip into their familiar places as easily as putting on a sweater.

The adults spread out more, less concentrated but every bit as connected. Relatives picking up where they last left off. Family and familiar: words with the same root.

Marc has built a massive pile of wood for a bonfire when night falls, a pile easily 25 feet high in the centre of a field by the chicken coop. The chickens run around. A sheep named Gordon Ramsay, more pet than livestock, moves through the throng, occasionally butting people with its hornless head. The younger cousins feed the three huge pigs with windfall apples, laugh at the pigs' snorting delight. The horses — along with the pigs and the special chickens that have names — are family, too.

The bonfire whooshes to life after a barbeque, the flames huge and devouring, with showers of sparks shooting into the sky as a half-circle of lawn chairs is formed up on the windward side. Cool September night wind on your back, but your face flush with the heat.

The air is full of shared stories . . . stories started by one cousin, corrected by a sister, completed by another. The definitive version of each story is a conglomerate: an accepted mash of different perceptions of the same events. The night runs late, very late, and we toss our beer cans and bottles deep into the lava-red centre of the fire, where the glass crackles explosively and the cans wrinkle and disappear.

Leslie and I are sleeping in a pop-up tent trailer where the absolutely most important, final duty of the night is to kill the last of the whining, hungry mosquitoes before turning off our flashlight. Later, a distant prairie thunderstorm will grumble and flash its way across the horizon, and the skin of the tent trailer will light up and darken, light up and darken, while I ponder the excellent conductivity of its aluminum structural frame.

I think about something else: about the loneliness of being outside this big comfortable family, of watching it tick through all of its remembered processes in a way that's novel to me, familiar to everyone else. Or so I believe. I essentially stopped living at home at 16, when I left Halifax, Nova Scotia, for high school in another province. The family home became a visit — lengthy, sometimes, but a visit just the same. Leslie misses her extended family keenly when she's away from them. (We lived almost half the continent away from the largest collection of them then.)

I don't feel the same tug and wonder about its absence.

Leslie and I had originally planned to hitch a lift from Winnipeg to Green Bay with the three oldest members of her family, all in their eighties, the two Urquhart sisters, Leslie's mother, Billie, and her aunt, Margaret, and Ian, Margaret's husband. They had an aged van with a leaking gas tank, bad brakes, and, when I was last in it, an empty propane cylinder rolling around behind the back seat. The trio had planned to make their way to North Carolina and leave us behind along the way. But Ian, the driver, had broken his right foot, and despite dogged efforts to master the pedals with his left, he hadn't managed well enough for such a long haul. (For the assembled family, it will be just one small chapter in a huge volume of quirky but loving family lore that I will only ever know in fragments.)

In the morning, the huge fire will be a gently smoking circle of ash, the beer bottles and cans reduced to shapeless blobs.

The family will wake up as it always does. Familiar in a way where even offhand comments have history. Familiar with which cousin is a morning person, and which one needs two cups of coffee before they are even human.

It's a familiarity that makes me wonder where my people are, and where I have to look to find them. I've spent my life feeling like I'm on the outside of things: often uncomfortable at parties and get-togethers, always on the edges watching all the other people who seem to interact seamlessly. I miss that: in my family, uncles and aunts are rarely more than names that pop up in obituaries. The cousins? They're out there, I know. I know a few names, I've even met some of them, and occasionally get added to email chains, but those relatives are all carried far away, like dandelion seeds on the wind.

I am, I guess, looking: looking for my great-great-grandfather's route, for his wins and losses and doubts on the trail. For signs of the great overarching family story in all that dust and sage. In a way, looking for my father, too.

Looking for that thing called family that so many other people seem to have found almost effortlessly. Looking for my spot in the world.

I don't even know where to begin.

William Castle Dodge's diary begins in Fond du Lac, Wisconsin.

I discovered that Dodge was in Fond du Lac to study law in his obituary in the *Washington Post*, which ran on January 4 and 5, 1914 (and appears in its entirety in this book's appendices). The obituary begins with the headline "Inventor Dodge is Dead" and offers the facts of that death at age 86 — of pneumonia, at home, sudden and unexpected. It then details what the obituary writer called "a most eventful life." His work, his inventions, his marriages and children — but for me, everything I have questions about is in a single, short sentence of that obituary: "When the rush for gold was made to California in 1849, Mr. Dodge was among the first to cross the prairies in quest of the precious metal."

In Dodge's own words, it wasn't a sentence: it was 52,000 words, the gold rush diary of a 22-year-old crossing a wide continent, much of it on foot and much of it not yet the United States. (A word of warning: Dodge was a product of his times, and you can expect to be offended by some of his language and his characterizations. I don't abridge the diary to avoid that; I can't sugarcoat it either. But he might surprise you from time to time.)

I admit right now that I'm breaking faith with the dead: Dodge never intended the diary for publication: "It is intended as a mere private record of the journey and what I saw and felt, expressly for my own especial benefit in afterlife."

He started the diary with this entry written on April 4, 1849.

<><><><><>

"The following is a journal of my trip among hundreds of others, to the 'El Dorado' or gold regions of California; during the memorable excitement of 1849. It is intended as a mere private record of the journey and what I saw and felt, expressly for my own especial benefit in afterlife.

A journey like this — two thousand miles across a trackless desert — over lofty mountains — across extended plains, and large rivers — surrounded on every side by savage Indians, with not a human habitation on the whole route, nor any means of obtaining subsistence, although there be hundreds and even thousands engaged in it, is nevertheless, a truly dangerous experiment! Coolly and deliberately, I have considered it — and, I have decided, — I will go! My all of property, of hope, and of prospects for the future, are staked in this enterprise — and trusting in the goodness and guidance of Divine Providence, I am

determined, if human exertion can avail me, to crown my
efforts with success — but never otherwise than by indus-
try and honesty."

∞∞∞∞∞∞

It's been more than 160 years since Dodge walked and rode across
a good part of western America, plenty of time for the world to over-
write and cover his tracks. He saw the country differently than we do.
It was a different place: much of it was still lands that belonged to
Native Americans.

Dodge found his way to Fond du Lac, Wisconsin from Ithaca, New
York: Leslie and I will pick up his trail in Wisconsin, flying from that
family gathering near Winnipeg to Chicago, Illinois, and O'Hare
Airport, where we find ourselves in a tide of people swimming through
the hallways. More than seven million passengers will pass through
this airport in an average October, dwarfing the flood of 1849 emigrants. O'Hare is a stew of different colours and dress, the melting pot
in action right there before our eyes.

The whole airport is filled with fragments of incomplete stories: a
couple standing stock-still in the middle of the terminal for no obvious reason, staring upwards, while their wheeled carry-on sits waiting
and the masses flow and break around them; a man in a hallway near
a men's washroom held lightly against the wall by two police officers,
one officer holding the man's arms almost gently as the other officer
empties rolls of money out of their prisoner's pockets onto the carpeted floor; someone behind the doors in the bathroom stalls arguing
loudly with himself. Families moving like small, self-contained islands,
everyone within arm's reach of one another.

We wind up at the end of one of the spokes of Terminal 2 and dug
through the suitcase for what we'll need at the other end: an American
highway atlas. I hadn't even thought about needing maps — Leslie
had bought the atlas in a Winnipeg bookstore a day or so before we

left. Also, taking up a big block of space, four bound volumes of immigrant trail guidebooks. Where the California Trail begins in Missouri, the guidebooks map every mile of the various routes immigrants took.

For now, the names are just words: the Applegate Trail, the Hudspeth Cutoff, the Lassen Trail. We study the routes out of the Green Bay airport for Fond du Lac, and think we've found our starting point. I deliberately didn't plan this trip in detail: like Dodge, I want us to find the end of each day as it comes, wherever it comes. No reservations, no plan beyond the actual route of the trail, as best we can reason it out, the only deadline a flight that's weeks away, out of Sacramento.

But all at once I'm regretting that decision. It's daunting: I feel that we've bitten off more than we can chew, with far too little in the way of planning and direction. Other people would have been better prepared. It's unlike me; I'm the kind of person who likes to be at airports for even the shortest of flights at least an hour early, for God's sake. This feels like parachuting stupidly into the unknown. Guidebooks, a last-minute atlas, and a sliver of a plan. What was I thinking?

Chapter 1

Wisconsin

The flight from Chicago to Green Bay is filled with a loosely connected pack of college football fans from LSU, Louisiana State University, ready for a game against the Badgers, thinking nothing of a two-day flip from the Southern U.S. and then back again. Unaware of the expanse of land they are crossing. They're clearly not thinking about the generations of people who have trudged along below them, but instead, about the way hotels are hiking their prices for the big game.

We edge ashore from the steady map-blue of Lake Michigan beneath us, and we're eating up the miles. Down below, it's all dairy land and square patches of fields, rivers and streams coiling in gentle meanders through the mostly flat land. Everything tamed into purchased plots, the trees controlled into fringes around cultivated land, the dots of towns connected by the criss-crossing straight string lines of roads.

The airport — Austin Straubel International — is long and beige, hard shoes loud against the floor, luggage wheels rattling in all the empty space. The rental car companies are all in a line, and the man at the Enterprise counter is waiting for us. Late middle age, a square, ruddy face atop shoulders that fight with his jacket and win, flaring the lapels outwards. It seems there's no one else from our flight — or any other flight — renting cars.

Leslie asks if he needs to see her licence too, so we can both drive the car.

"You married?" he asks. "Wisconsin's a joint property state. One of you signs, you both sign." That's all we wanted to know, but there's more, unbidden: "I found that out the hard way when my wife left. She had the credit cards; I got the bills." He looks at the screen: "Then I found it out again with the next one."

It's another kind of family story, the flip side of the familial coin.

I sign the forms and he slides the keys across the counter with my driver's licence. It's a $250 fee if you lose one of the car's keys, he says — but you can't lose one of the car's keys. You can only lose both of them, because they're bound together on a single wire loop sealed in rubberized plastic, an arranged marriage of keys, and as awkward in my pocket as two conjoined rolls of quarters.

The keys are for a cranberry red four-door Hyundai Sonata — we're taking it all the way to California and dropping it off. We start out by turning the wrong way leaving the airport, and we promptly get lost.

We'll learn we're not alone in that — Dodge spent plenty of time either lost or completely misled about how many miles he had left to travel to reach California. It does not bode well; we manage to get bemused directions at an Oneida reservation gas station. Then, we head south on Route 54, a road with a gentle uneven beat of dairy barns and farms and fields ticking by on both sides.

First official stop: supplies. We stop at the Shopko Hometown in Seymour, the "Home of the Hamburger." So many things are the "Home of . . .", so many that the word seems in danger of losing its meaning. Shopko is empty and echoing, a warehouse of a place that feels like it's open only for us. We buy toilet paper and crinkly silver emergency blankets, two small foam coolers with red drawstrings to hold their lids in place, and freezer packs to keep the coolers cold. (The drawstrings don't work, and every time we open the trunk, we have to reset the Styrofoam lids.) For the rest of the trip, we'll unload the coolers every night and shove the freezer packs into narrow, frost-encrusted freezers in a parade of hotel room bar fridges. Food and fruit, plenty of water. A bag of baby carrots that will slowly devolve into a wet orange paste before we finish the trip, the bag sunk in the pool of water that forms at the bottom of the cooler.

Leslie's buying emergency food, flat tins of tuna with crackers built right in. Sensible things. I'm distracted by the multitudes of jerky — beef and turkey, bison and elk, even bacon jerky. (I do not recommend bacon jerky — it is soggy cold strips in a bag, like take-away from a sad hotel buffet where the Sterno has gone out under the stainless-steel-lidded serving tray.)

When our purchases are lined up on the counter, a loud smash reverberates through the store. One of the employees has dropped something large and glass — it has to be one of the employees, because we're the only customers. It's like our own personal department store, as if it will close forever the moment we leave. It's the Saturday before Labour Day. The store echoes with the shards of glass settling.

The return to near silence seems to take a very long time. Someone swears quietly in the aisled distance.

Underneath the harsh glare and hum of a thousand fluorescent lights, we hand over a gaggle of American bills and lug our purchases to the car, nearly alone in the shadeless sun of an early September parking lot.

There's plenty of corn ranked along the sides of the roads, the pickup trucks muscling up tight behind you when you dare to follow the speed limit. SILVERADO is spelled out in all caps across the windshields and on the hood-mount bug deflectors.

Occasional formal towns, city halls, and main streets are bisected by state road intersections, some with traffic lights, others with as little as a lonely hanging, single red flashing light.

The pattern is clear: a sign warning that the speed limit's going to fall, then another as buildings start to rise on both sides of the road, then 30 mph and the very centre of towns. The home of the Vikings, the Cavaliers, the Mackville Nationals Truck and Tractor Pull. Sometimes you're on the main street, other times you cross it. But then the houses thin, going from brick three-storey formal homes to ranch houses, and finally, car and farm equipment dealerships. Then the speed jumps back up again to 55 and it's open road. For a while. Until the next small town.

Our Michelin road atlas covers the entire United States, and, depending on which direction you're going, you move from page to page in an arcane and confusing formula. One moment, Kansas — the next, Missouri, unless your route drives off the top of the page and into a completely different section of the atlas. Reach the bottom of page 25 driving along the Mississippi, and it's "Turn to page 36," where you come in through the top of the page. We have no GPS and only a limited data plan for emergencies on my cell phone.

We hit Black Creek and a corn-stooked farmer's market, turn left and head south on WI-47. There's something satisfying about that first map-directed turn, as if we've anchored ourselves to the page. The trip suddenly feels possible, the car cruising down now into the spine of the map and then up the curve of the page on the other side.

We get onto the I-41 between Mackville and Appleton. I feel like I should remember Mackville and its truck and tractor notoriety, but I don't. Yet each town is its own little collection of ordered lives, family successes and failures, every one with discrete economies, post offices, fixed in place on the map like a bug caught in amber. Each one with people who move, each also with people who never, ever will — if not delighted with their lot in life, at least having enough to outweigh taking chances.

Fond du Lac has a strange feeling of rot at its centre, even if there are still the sandstone and brick trappings of middle America's downtown core. The edges still seem to be prospering, the usual suspects from Pet City to Walmart to the new highway hotels springing up in cookie-cutter familiarity. But a lot of the rest of the place has no visible means of support.

The downtown cluster of buildings has faded. The away-from-the-highway malls too: the Home Depot is a shell, its signs pulled down but the corporate colours still obvious, the parking lot empty and drifted with yellow leaves.

In the parking lot of the Buffalo Wild Wings, I find a tiny zip-locked bag of pills on the ground — it's strangely exciting, especially after seeing so many police. (Did I mention? Police and their dark, combat-ready uniforms seem to be everywhere.) My small discovery was exciting, at least, until I look closely at my find and see that it's Prilosec and Gaviscon and Motrin. I've found the lost stash of an aged wing-lover coping with acid indigestion. I picture him patting frantically at his pockets, half a large-serving plate of 1,530-calorie Mango Habanero wings already down the hatch and no one else at the table understanding his sudden concern.

The Forest Mall is empty, the hallways to the bathrooms styled in early industrial terrifying, the empty storefronts hung with black fabric curtains as if in mourning. Most of the stores are service-based — hair salons, nail places. A bunker-like, former 1970s takeout place in the centre of a city block looks abandoned, and is plastered with election signs. At first I think it's telling that a closed restaurant is the only place where there are signs. Then I realize, walking by again, that it's currently the local Republican headquarters.

All along the I-41 are road signs for adult superstores and gun shops, and billboards announcing Hillary Clinton for Prison 2016. It's two months out from the U.S. presidential election.

There's no sign of the stagecoach routes, the corduroy of logs over patches of soft ground, the paths through forested land. The only mud is where the flags mark the gas lines and cable lines, or where someone's digging a shallow trench to hide some other piece of infrastructure.

There are roads and bridges and transport trucks, tires whirring on the grooved cement of the highway, and anything else seems ancient and far away.

We check into the Days Inn, our first overnight negotiation: the last room left and one of the most expensive we'll agree to on this trip. (We get good at negotiation: find a place, turn our phones on for just long enough to find out what web discounters can offer a room for, and walk that information in to the front desk.)

Later, we walk to Schreiner's Restaurant, which opened in 1938 — their website says Albert and Regina Schreiner borrowed money from her father after Albert lost his job at a factory during the Great Depression.

Like everything else, the restaurant has moved from Fond du Lac's North Main Street downtown to the edge of the highway, the regular evolution of towns in America now.

Portions are big, prices low — and there are family stories, like the way Albert Schreiner insisted all customers be addressed as Mr., Mrs., or Miss, even if they were regulars.

In the Fond du Lac Days Inn, the pool is full of an entire joyous Spanish-speaking extended family, but our room is dark and popcorn ceilinged, and old. There's dust gathering in the ceiling stucco. The indoor pool is right outside our room, and, if we wanted to swim, we're only a set of sliding patio doors away from the pool deck. You can hear the splashing before you even look, the hot tub's burble, kids' voices. Moving the curtain from the doors to look at the fun they are having is like being a peeping Tom.

A tired coffee maker, paper-wrapped soaps, the requisite battered and calcium-coated water-saver shower nozzle. I know that tomorrow morning, when I close the shower curtain and turn the taps on, at least one of the streams from the nozzle will travel in some unexpected direction, modified by hard-water scale. The desk clerk is Indian, and he does everything: he's there for night check-in, there again in the morning to restock the waffle machine with packaged batter and add yogurts to the ice bowl for the continental breakfast. He folds towels when he's not doing anything else. Not once do we pass the desk and he's not the one there.

Leslie goes out for a smoke, and two Hells Angels hold the front door of the hotel for her when she comes back in from the too-warm night. They're wearing long black leather coats with the Hells insignia. They're looking for a room. We've taken the last one. She rushes back to the room, giddy to tell me about the bikers, and I turn the deadbolt very, very quietly.

It's been a long day. I fall asleep to the sound of the kids still frolicking in the pool.

Next morning, near the foot of Lake Winnebago, the wavelets are limping ashore, the lake water full of browned plants, plastic bags, and other strips and gobbets of barely identifiable trash, but there are ducks and even a pair of loons, a cluster of muskie boats in a knot over what must be successful fishing ground. At the backwater boat launch, the surface is overlaid with green polka dots of algae and waterweed. The surface of the boat channel that parallels the funpark railway line — the narrowest of narrow-gauge lines for a tiny train — sports the same algal design.

There's a full-sized steam locomotive — Wisconsin Central 2714 — pointed away from the lake on a short length of full-sized track. It's 264,000 pounds of engine, built in 1914, and it logged two million miles on the rails, at one time running the 800-mile route from Fond du Lac to Winnipeg, marking the single-longest continuous trip of any steam locomotive in the United States. Winnipeg. It's hard to believe we woke up there just yesterday, the sheer coincidence of the train's former route like a message. The entire locomotive, gleaming in shiny black paint, is surrounded by a six-foot chain link fence, topped with three rusty strands of barbed wire.

Look at the impressive history. Don't touch.

A white concrete bridge spans both a fecund shipping canal and the railway tracks. The canal is clearly no longer operating, cattails fill in along the edges, and parts of the retaining wall crumble into the water at the ends of back yards of small, hunkered-down houses. An open field is being used as a dog park, owners throwing tennis balls to dogs that run and return, run and return. When a train barrels under the white-painted bridge, the dogs flee, tennis balls ignored. The train is a long line of double-stacked containers atop low-bed rail cars. It runs on and on, the wheels tapping at the rail joints, some wheels squealing as the train cars rock and clatter. There are scrap yards on both sides of the bridge.

At the Walmart in Fond du Lac, the cashiers are now required to hold $20 bills up to the light to look for a series of watermarks to make sure the bills aren't counterfeit. "It used to just be hundreds and fifties. Now, it's the twenties too," the clerk says.

Walmart can sell liquor in Wisconsin, crushing the family liquor business the way the Walton empire crushes everything else. One of those family stores, Gilmore's — "Fond du Lac's Oldest & Largest Liquor Store" and "The Low Price Leader" — is open seven days a week, 9:00 a.m. to midnight. The clerk is young and pierced, and sanguine: "Lots of liquor stores are going out of business," he says. He doesn't seem to hold a grudge, selling me a bottle of cheap scotch large enough to boast a built-in handle. "That's just business."

Maybe 20 percent of the downtown stores are closed. Tom's Military Arms & Gun Shop discount centre is still open on a side street, an oversized soldier in full combat gear out front. The sign pointing to the store has an assault rifle for an arrow. A few blocks away, Dutch's Trading Post advertises "Concealed Carry, Sept. 18, 11 a.m."

The box stores along the highway are busy, their parking lots full. There are more police cars pulling over more people than you can possibly believe. If you are Hispanic, wearing a sleeveless T-shirt and driving a wreck, you can expect to be pulled over and there will be a gleaming new police car pulling in right behind you, lights flashing. Especially if you're driving a pickup truck with rakes and mowers in the back.

It's like traffic violations are an immigration tax.

You learn quickly that there are "right" immigrant stories and "wrong" immigrant stories. Albert and Regina Schreiner are the right kind of immigrants. William Castle Dodge, making his way into and across the homeland of Indigenous Americans, is the right kind. My father's parents, fleeing the impending Russian revolution for a new life building a farm in Rhode Island, with their only child at Brown University in part through his time in military service, were the wrong kind at first, but then the right kind with the benefit of a son born on American soil. A Hispanic man in a lawn-care truck? Not the right kind. Not now. Not even if he's American-born or naturalized, not even if he's building the kind of bootstrap family business of self-made American legend.

The ground leaving Fond du Lac is yellow and brown grass, highway verges and flat fields, deer blinds in trees, and sometimes, deer decoys on the edge of the treeline, stuck in place and staring at a fixed point somewhere out ahead of them.

Dodge started his journey by leaving Fond du Lac too: he and some of his party left together by public stagecoach, at this point passengers more than adventurers. The rest of the group were to meet up in St. Louis to prepare and provision. Here's where Dodge began.

∞◇◇◇∞

March 21, 1849

We this day at ½ past 2 o'clock, P.M. left Fond du Lac in the stage on our way to California. Ebon N. Drury, Edwin R. Ferris, and myself. Roads bad, single team, progress slow, reached Waupun, distance 18 miles, at 9 ½ P.M.; took supper and proceeded. Rode all night in open wagon — weather cold — road bad. Reached Waushora at 2 ½ A.M. — Beaver Dam at 5 ½; took breakfast and proceeded to Columbus, where we arrived at 11 A.M. Reached Madison at 9 ½ P.M. of the 22nd. We stopped at the U.S. Hotel, but there being a ball there they were unable to give us any beds; which we — having rode all the previous day and night — thought to be a matter of some little importance;

and therefore we went to the Madison House. Before leaving in the morning, we visited the State House in company
with Mr. Driggs. It is a fine building of limestone, and from
the top of it we had a splendid view of the surrounding
country and lakes, of which there are four in a row.

∞∞∞∞∞

In Madison, things are different and busier. Walking to a food festival around the capitol building, we're bathed in marijuana smoke.
Perched on a hill, the legislature is head and shoulders above its
neighbours, on the site of the first capitol building. This is the third
generation of the legislative buildings — William Castle Dodge stood
(briefly) in the first, on a break from the stagecoach.

Madison was barely cut out of the woods then: today there's the
outdoor food festival in full swing; it teems with people, many drinking beer from plastic cups as they walk around and into the state
capitol building. There are no police here, no bulletproof vests, no
utility belts of weapons, no presence. No cars pulled over for licence
and registration checks.

Four big, noisy young men crowd a legislative men's room, filling
all the urinals.

When they push their way out of the building, they spin the revolv-
ing doors round and round, staying inside like oversized meaty kids,
and no one stops them. There's a band and too many people and too
much of everything, and all of it would be beyond comprehension in
1849. There are parents and children lying on their backs on the floor
in the capitol building, looking up at the elaborate rotunda. They're
talking about the view, just as William Dodge did at the old capitol in
1849. The ground has irrevocably changed, and yet is the same — not
just in topography, but in the commonality of constant shifting. Endless
stories of migration, of dislocation, of conquer. The towns and small
cities we pass now — towns that arose from overthrowing those who
last held the land — now find themselves overtaken and swept aside for
the new dominance of servicing the freeways. Even now, Amazon and

the other internet retailers loom, ready to change the American firmament again and force a new generation onto the road.

In nearby Sun Prairie, a stone's throw from the highway, the Cabela's outdoor equipment store is huge, and we put on hats, skulk between the aisles, trying various tools until we find a long-handled cutter, still in its packaging, and cut apart the car rental keys from their pocket-bulging knot. (Long before Cabela's, Sun Prairie was a popular stop for oxen teams on the old trail, nicknamed Traveller's Home.)

In a way, we're provisioning. I buy a hat for the desert sun we're expecting to face later, get some elk and bison pepperoni, and wonder at the variety of both outdoor gear and firearms. It's all about the extras: a man buying a scoped hunting rifle sees a carrying case, a cleaning kit, and picks them both up. You can buy lopping shears solely for cutting deer bones, a speed-loader for your revolver. In the discount room, buried in the back, you can get your daughter a pink Velcro-fastened ankle holster for her handgun, right next to the snakebite kits and the more outlandish of the trout flies that, at regular prices, couldn't even hook trout fishermen. At the checkout, rifles are going out the door in neat and anonymous triangular cardboard boxes. Scanning in barcodes, just like any other purchase. It's a process, at this point, about what we think we'll need, rather than what we actually need. It's an equation Dodge and his crew will make in St. Louis, preparing for a trip that they essentially know little about — nor did the other emigrants, depending on word of mouth when they chose supplies and equipment, often with no experience of the near-wilderness they were heading into. Overprovisioning, choosing equipment they'd later jettison — common mistakes that affected many of the emigrants.

Out in front of the store, under the overhang of the entrance, there's a charity barbeque selling hamburgers. They are big burgers, dripping fat so that the barbeques hiss and smoke like an old farm engine.

Food will finger its way into Dodge's diary constantly, part of what will become the calculus of survival: water, fuel, feed for the animals, and food for the emigrants themselves. It's easier for me: I had a four-cheese hamburger at Schreiner's in Fond du Lac, cradled in bread that was fried in butter, like a grilled cheese sandwich packed with meaty speed. I could die in Wisconsin. Easily. Well, maybe not easily, but early.

⬦⬦⬦⬦⬦

March 23, 1849

> We left Madison, where we bid Nobles farewell, at 8 A.M. with four horses to the wagon. During this forenoon's travel, we passed several Mounds in the shape of animals; and an old breastwork — buffalo rings — bluffs etc. At 2 P.M. we arrived at Blue Mounds — which place boasts of nothing more than a log house, good barn, and a fine dinner.

⬦⬦⬦⬦⬦

At the Blue Mounds turnoff on the I-80, we're right on Dodge's route, and we know it. We stop at Cave of the Mounds, a national historic site. We haven't cottoned on to the thrill of finding the exact points where Dodge stopped yet: soon, Leslie will start reading the diary out loud as we travel, and we'll find that we can apply his words to the things we see.

We find out that the cave tour will take too long, so we sift through the gift shop, the sand pile where kids can dig for staff-buried fossil treasures, the long, water-filled sluice line where you can take pre-loaded bags of sand and pan for pre-inserted semi-precious stones. It's easy summer work for college kids, either shepherding tourists through the cool temperatures of the underground cave tours or working the land around the rustic-styled park buildings, carving a farm's traditional market garden into the hillside.

As we're getting set to leave, just by chance, Leslie spots the story of Ebenezer Brigham.

On the hill above the cave site, they are restoring the red barn that used to belong to Brigham, one of the first settlers in the area, a farmer and landlord for guests along the stagecoach route south.

Brigham's farm, we realize, was Dodge's log cabin stagecoach stop.

We circle back along the road above the cave site, and corral an off-duty park worker, heading home with his lunch bowl in his hands, to fill in the blanks.

A huge red-ochre barn dates the farm to 1828, but only one of the original Brigham buildings is still standing — a patched and worn grey stable of weathered barn-board perched on a foundation of rectangular limestone blocks. It is the first time we can say with absolute certainty we're standing on the same ground as Dodge.

It's breathtaking and accidental. We stopped on a whim, Leslie spotting the farm information as the result of a simple washroom break.

It's strange to think of them, eating, sleeping, talking, while deep beneath them, hidden from sight — and from their knowledge — the vast underground caverns of Cave of the Mounds twist and turn, cathedralled rooms and gaps and chimneys and unexpected falls. The cave wasn't discovered until 1939. But it was there. They didn't know about the cave, and couldn't possibly imagine us, but here we are.

⊙⟩⟨⟩⟨⟩⟨⟩⟨⟨

March 23, 1849 (con't)

About noon it had begun to snow, and so continued all the afternoon, cold increasing. At dark we were at Dodgeville which is in the very heart of the lead mines. The streets and gardens are all dug up. From there we continued through the dark and mud to Mineral Point which we reached at 10 P.M.

⟨⟨⟩⟨⟩⟨⟩⟩⟩

Dodgeville and its lead mines are only a miner's shack now, the Dodge Cabin "open by appointment only" but with no numbers on the sign to call, so no way to set up an appointment. Look. Don't touch, because it's history. (It's named after a different Dodge than William Castle.)

Just before Dodgeville is Mediapolis, with the strange wonder of the Cast Stone Art company: a giant red-pink pig stands on a plinth among rows of stone animals, and a small car-trailer is laden with a massive eagle, wings outstretched, and five statues holding American flags, two of them reproductions of different sizes of the iconic image of marines raising the flag over Iwo Jima. There are many stories here — but not the one we're looking for.

Then we're in Mineral Point.

Dodge spent one night in Mineral Point. You drive downhill from the newest edge of town, dropping down into the old town and into a completely different time. The streets are tight and narrow, the buildings on both sides limestone and brick facades like a movie set of small-town America.

When we park, a bright-eyed and intense man with a veteran's hat asks me if I have a home computer, if I like pizza. I don't know what the safe answer is.

Why Mineral Point?

One offshoot of Dodge's trip was the box of rocks and mineral samples, collected along the way; for years, it lived in the basement of our family's house in Halifax, Nova Scotia, where I grew up. The why and the when of how those rocks had gotten to us died with my mother. The box itself was dark, stained wood with a fine, thin brass hasp and hinges, and was held together all along its edges by dovetail joints.

I had been fascinated with them as a child, opening the box like a treasure chest, unwrapping them, putting them back. (At least one, it turned out, was mildly radioactive.) Huge quartz crystals, a fat but cracked garnet the size of a man's fingertip caught in the grip of sandstone, volcanic glass, spear points and arrowheads. The box finally came apart, and the paper-wrapped rocks wound up with me. Some are scattered around our house now: others, the arrowheads and spear points, are more carefully stored. Cleaning up, going through the two empty sneaker boxes they lived in after their wooden home came apart, I found one last, forgotten chalky pink rock that had been overlooked when the box was emptied. On it, a faded white label, surrounded with red, with a handwritten notation in dark fountain pen ink: "Mineral Point." Then, what looks like "Buckley's Creek." The maps now show only Brewery Creek.

The topography is all rolling farms on low hills now, with rivers curling through the valleys. Silos like signal towers, calling each to each. The highways are cut straight through the limestone in rock cuts that look like the source of the stone for the oldest of the buildings. The highway signs say you are not allowed to stop, except in emergencies. This is stone that you are not allowed to touch, rough history that you can't press your face against and listen to for messages. I have the feeling that there are fossils right there next to us in their remnants and coils, tantalizingly out of reach, even when the shale beds press up under them and lift them, the shale pale blue under the stained limestone's toenail-fungus yellow. The limestone is shot left to right, and up and down, with straight cracks so that it looks as if you can simply prise out nearly square blocks and immediately set to building your own downtown.

∞∞∞∞∞

March 24, 1849

> After a good night's rest and entertainment at the Temperance House kept by Mr. Lathrop, we left at 8 A.M. and reached Platteville at 2 P.M. After a hurried dinner, we left there in a coach, but before getting out of the village, we were stuck in the mud, mud, mud! We were compelled to get out and walk about every half mile, & after changing horses at Hazel Green, another mining village, we proceeded, only however, to meet with a repetition of the same. Shortly after passing the State line into Illinois, the coach got set, and we were obliged to try several times before we could pry it out with rails! But by the driver going ahead with a light & our walking, we at last got through to Galena about 9 ½ P.M.

∞∞∞∞∞

We don't find Mr. Lathrop's Temperance House in Mineral Point, and no one's even heard of it, but we do find the Parley Eaton House from 1847, red brick and square with limestone lintels and windowsills, black full shutters, the front of the house evenly balanced with three windows on the second floor and two windows and a door on the first, the door below the window furthest to the left. The limestone window ledges are coming apart with age and weather. The building would, at least, have been standing when he passed. .

A big square building in the bottom of the valley in old Mineral Point is a hotel. The Walker House — their sign dates the construction as 1836. I email them later to see if they know where the Lathrop House might have been, but they don't. They add me to their mailing list unasked though, so every fall, I see the change of the seasons on their Mineral Point fall colours meter, hear a little more about how the storm window project is going. The emails are a connection every time they arrive, sending me back to Mineral Point, so I don't disconnect from the mailing list, even though I have no way to attend the special dinners or buy the sausage rolls. Once, the family that took on the hotel project wrote that they were planning to sell: I felt a sharp stab of regret for no legitimate reason except that in the search for shared history, they were a clear consistent thread, one that was long enough to stretch across the intervening years.

We travel south on Route 80 past a hand-painted Trump sign posed in front of a cornfield backdrop. The Platteville airport appears in the middle of nowhere, an asphalt runway bound by fields of corn silk, the runway lights more common than trees now.

In the 1840s, the stagecoach trails were barely wide enough for the coaches, the routes just gaps cut through now long-vanished woodlands. It's hard to look at the endless corn and try to reconcile that with the huge trees and impenetrable forest that would have been here in 1849. Leaving Platteville, there's barely a tree in sight, the open fields stretching away on both sides of us: on the horizon on the left, a windrow along two edges of a farm property, boxing it in; on the right, across the highway, a solitary line of single-file pines, planted to shield a long driveway. Other than that, it's wide open. From the air, what trees there are follow the shoulders of rivers, every scrap of useful landscape cut into the shapes of fields.

We head through Cuba City and Hazel Green, not stopping to change horses or to pick up "Wisconsin Cheese and Curds" at the Gasser TrueValue. The 80 turns into Wisconsin 11 and then back to 80 again, then we cross state lines and it's Illinois State Route 84 to Galena, Illinois, where Dodge said he boarded the *Anthony Wayne*, the only steamer available for days. The town is split in two: we drive along the newer edge coming in, past a funeral home with its own peculiar display graveyard of as-yet blank gravestones between it and the highway. "Your name here," I think.

Then, once we're past Galena Chrysler and the Stoney Creek Inn, the road bends down and left into the much older section of town.

Chapter 2

Along the Mississippi

<><><><><>

March 25, Sunday, 1849

Ebon and myself went to a Presbyterian and Ferris to an Episcopal Church but owing to the violent cold which I had taken by riding the first night, I was unable to remain. The weather was fine and the situation of the town, on the steep side hill, with its good supply of Churches, made it appear very nice indeed. Afternoon the steamer *Anthony Wayne* arrived from St. Louis and there being no probability of any other for several days, we left on her at 5 P.M., and reached the Mississippi, distant 7 miles, just at dark.

<><><><><>

T he Westminster Presbyterian Church is still standing, the construction date of 1846 high on the front under the peak of the roof, so it would have been brand new when Dodge visited. The centre of old Galena is clustered around the river, climbing up both sides of the valley now and even spreading across the high flat ground.

It takes us three tries to find the North Ferry Landing Road, the tiny side road that finally takes us first up, then plunging down to the Galena Boating Club, a gathering of finger wharves and flat-bottomed shallow river boats, only a left-hand turn away from the mighty Mississippi (which is all of that, when we cross it later on a massive bridge at twilight at Dubuque). We've ended up almost exactly on his route: Fond du Lac, Madison, Blue Mounds, Dodgeville, Mineral Point, Platteville, Galena.

The boating club has a clean, bright-blue Porta-potty perched on the berm next to the boat moorings. A sign reads "Members Only," but no one complains as we walk along beside the tied-up boats, the smoking barbeques, the pickups angling backwards toward the ramp to unload their boat trailers. Most of the boats are flat and rectangular with low trim lines and awnings stretching over many of their decks. They're recreational more than functional. Some are decked with artificial turf, others have plastic flowers standing along their railings as if they were floating yards. Under the surface of the water, some of the boats are festooned with long, trailing feathers of algae and waterweed — some of these homes-away-from-home clearly don't move much.

Men and women are standing around the edge of the water with glasses and beer cans in their hands, laughing and talking. The backdrop is a glassy river, and about 60 feet away, a long shoulder of trees that look to be big old elms against the darkening horizon. Huge willows trail long-stranded branchlets down almost to the water's surface. The Boating Club sits on a finger of water, a narrow channel that reaches out to the Mississippi. Small wavelets lap at the pier pilings, a gentle slapping you can hear in those few moments when all the other sounds stop.

There's a concrete ramp now at the spot where we're told the riverboats like the *Anthony Wayne* used to come in, dropping off supplies, picking up the product of the lead mines, and heading north to Dubuque or south to St. Louis.

The side-wheeler *Anthony Wayne* was built in 1844 and named after a Revolutionary War general who died, reportedly, of gout. Buried far from home, Wayne was disinterred 12 years later, his bones boiled free of flesh. His family had those bones carried to Radnor, Pennsylvania in a trunk to be reburied. A lot of hard, awful work to be sure that a loved one is finally home. And the steamer?

"Loss of the steamer *Anthony Wayne*: A telegraphic dispatch was received last night from Keokuk, stating that
the *Anthony Wayne*, from Galena to this city, was sunk
yesterday morning, at Wagoner's Dam, on the Lower
Rapids, four miles above Keokuk. Mr. Suss, by whom
it was received, has no further particulars. The *Anthony
Wayne* had a heavy cargo on board." *The St. Louis
Republic*, December 1st, 1851

The evening is loud and slow and happy, small dogs barking
around the crowd's feet, the midges coming out in clouds as the sun
runs through orange and purple to steady plum.

A small, buzz-cut ginger kid — maybe nine years old — squires
adults around in a faded red electric golf cart, and when he's dropped
them all, he drives too fast on the gravel parking lot, trying to pull
the back end of the cart into a skid, succeeding, but in the shortest
of swings. You get the feeling it won't be too many years until he's
doing the same with a clapped-out Ford pickup, his friends laughing
and hanging on for dear life in the box behind the cab.

There's another, even younger kid successfully talking his way
into the passenger seat of an old orange-and-white pickup, ready to
peel out of the parking lot for town. Heading for some big town?
No, just Galena, where the traffic slows to a crawl in the Labour Day
weekend evening because there's nothing to do but to see and be seen
passing the roadside mini-golf. Malt liquor's being drunk from the big
cans — you see them sprouting up empty in the ditches, as common
as mushrooms.

The Mississippi at twilight, the trees full of the songs of katydids,
the swamp on the other side of the berm bright electric green and stagnant and pregnant with the calling frogs. There's a black bull in the
meadow behind a split-rail fence, standing stock-still and watching the
road cut up and away through a narrow valley. A man in a sleeveless T-shirt is driving an aging pickup truck with an American flag
nailed to a one-by-two, affixed erect in the bed of his truck. He guns

the engine to make the truck jump forward, the flag stretching out to its full length. People on the boats point and yell and wave, then circle back into small knots of conversation.

The sky has taken over, the sunset full above the boating club like a movie playing at a massive drive-in. Towering dark clouds poke up over the horizon, promising imminent rain, rain that starts to fall, taking the temperature sharply down with it, when we're mere miles away from Galena.

Three states today, and the experience feels like middle America at its loudest and largest.

The Sunday before Labour Day.

∞∞∞∞∞

March 26, Monday, 1849
> On awakening in the morning, instead of being on our way down the river, we found ourselves at DuBuque in Iowa — 30 miles from Galena by water and 15 by land. It is a fine place, with a population of 3,500, with the buildings and walks entirely of brick. Nothing of importance this day and next morning.

∞∞∞∞∞

We follow Dodge's wrong-way travel, finding ourselves in Dubuque at nightfall instead of morning. We drive across the big grey metal span of the Julien Dubuque Bridge just as purple twilight shifts to black. A quick rain has come too, and the shiny streets and sharp reflections from the streetlights make it hard to find a hotel. We aren't making reservations: we don't know, one day to the next, where we'll end up, so the idea is to find a cheap hotel at the end of the day; if we can't, we're at least equipped to sleep in the car. Later, we'll segregate our choices still further, into the hotels and motels where you bring the luggage in, and the ones so dank and questionable that we leave the suitcases in the trunk.

Our first foray into darkened Dubuque finds only the riverside downtown; we end up back on the highway, taking an exit with a hotel sign, and follow a velvet-black road through a residential area, hope fading and sure that we're lost, until we find the Glenview Motel, its dated light-up sign offering "Budget Rates – Cable TV – Dial Phones – Free Local Calls." The owners live in an apartment directly behind the narrow check-in desk — we pay the $49 while listening to a television's chatter and a hum of quiet voices. Like in Fond du Lac, it's the new settlers, a South Asian family that's running all aspects of the small motel, from desk clerk to housekeeping. Two things are absolutely in common with Dodge's diary: people are migratory, and we all hold our lives together with the roadmap of family or personal stories. When Leslie and I tell anyone why we're on the road, they're both instantly interested and ready to respond with a similar element of their own story. Ancestors who built towns or fled the confines of them; relatives who later went back to see where they came from; people who built things from nothing. It seems so important to trace your place, to talk about how your branch connects to the family tree. The other constant? That it's the small "e" of economics — as small as a single nuclear family — that often drives that change.

The Glenview is cinderblock rooms with the door and window on one side, a struggling window-mount air conditioner, and a small bathroom where the failing shower stall ceiling indicates another bathroom directly above our own. The room has a cellblock feel.

It's a restless night after a long day on the road, the short panic of finding a place, the relentless drone of a cicada above the door outside. We've finished the day hungry and tired and out of sorts: after trying to find a place to eat and ending up in a maze of older suburban streets, four-way stops, and odd merges, we ask the woman at the desk in the motel for directions to anywhere where there might be food and are given directions to a McDonald's. Behind her, a curtain hides her family from sight, but releases an enticing smell of curry for dinner.

We manage to get lost on the way to the McDonald's, short-tempered with each other. Then, when we're back at the room unpacking our takeout, I think there is nothing sadder than cooling, limp French fries and the way diced lettuce surrenders so quickly to the heat of a hot beef patty.

When Leslie goes outside to smoke, she says the other smokers feel threatening — two men, one on either side of her, also smoking silently but staring. When she comes back into the room, a small cloud of moths that had been circling the outside light join us.

The next morning is brighter; pack the car, head out, and on Central Avenue in downtown Dubuque, we spy "Dottie's Café — Meals and Lunches." A neon "OPEN" sign blinks in the front window, but the old marquee on the front of the building is the real neon treasure: red, yellow, green, and faded dark blue, the yellow vertical column chevroned with descending triangles that aim for the front door, every letter of the sign picked out with neon tubes. It would be a wonder to see it lit up.

The diner has a sticky aluminum storm door and white sheer curtains in the front windows, battered booths, and a long counter with round red stools.

The building dates from 1861 and the toilet flush lever in the men's room is a cupboard handle, but the coffee comes by frequently and the corned beef hash is plentiful. It's a classic diner — red booths, eggs and rye toast, and it's clung to "American fries" on the menu instead of French fries, a hint that little's changed in the fare since the Gulf War.

The clientele, except for us, is clearly familiar, our waitress calling, "Oh no, they got in," each time anyone makes their way through the door. We've got the atlas open to plan the day's travel, and she regales us with stories of her parents, working at Dubuque's Hotel Julien in the days of mobster Al Capone, about night-time runs across the wide dark Mississippi at night for liquor. I realize everyone is waiting, just waiting, to fill you in on where they fit in the human firmament. (The Hotel Julien is still there, by the way, the last one of the four major hotels that Capone was rumoured to have owned still standing, and his purported ownership is part of the hotel's promotion. There's even a Capone Suite, $500 a night.)

We find William Dodge's brick walkways: they're also still there, occasionally peeking up through breaks in the asphalt.

We stay to watch the Labour Day parade, teen marching bands and semis hauling institutional floats, fancy cars from dealerships and too many antique tractors to count. The parade-watchers had arrived well in advance, setting up lawn chairs along both sides of the street, pointing and taking photographs when their kids march by. Police are everywhere: heavily armed, sunglassed, serious, as if prepared for a violent high school marching band revolt.

Some of the tractors carry signs explaining just how rare they are. A Teamsters' 18-wheeler advertises the power of the union. I wonder if the truck has any other, more pedestrian purpose, or whether it simply moves from parade to parade.

We walk to the river in the flat, unusual morning cool that the rain has brought, and we find our first casino — the other American gold rush. The Diamond Jo Casino, right on the waterfront. Outside, it's rail-yard industrial with the concrete swoops of overpass on-ramps, a glistening warehouse of a building surrounded by football fields of parking. Inside, it's the usual clatter and confusion. I'm convinced that the awkward routes from front door to bathroom to cashier in every casino are all designed to keep you moving through the place without ever having a clear exit — trying to keep you playing simply by confusing you enough to keep you from finding a straight-line way out.

It makes me wonder about escaping from a fire, especially because so many of the patrons are old and infirm, moving with chopped, hitched gaits or wheeled walkers from machine to machine, their players' club cards lanyarded around their necks or hanging from their wrists. The noise, the lights, the cigarette smoke cumulonimbus bearing down from the ceiling. There's money to be made here, lots of money, but not by the patrons. There are 23 casinos in the corporate stable that owns Diamond Jo, ranging from the Fremont in Las Vegas to California to the Louisiana bayou to the Par-A-Dice in Peoria. Capone would love it.

Dodge passed hidden gold he didn't know he was passing, at mines that would surface along the trail long after the 49ers were gone, buried beneath his feet, just like the caves at Blue Mounds. The new gold rush? We'll touch on or pass directly by casinos in cities as far-flung as St. Joseph's, Winnemucca, Las Vegas, Sparks, Wells, Rock Springs, and Jackpot. Our route will take us within 20 miles of scores more, where the big money isn't being made by those with the picks and shovels seeking their fortune, but much further up the corporate ladder. It's like the gold in more ways than one: the real money isn't made by miners, it's made by those who control the market for provisions and shovels.

∞∞∞∞∞

March 27, 1849

> We were at the upper rapids which we passed in safety
> & arrived at Rock Island, famous for the murder of
> Davenport on the 4th of July in '44 or '45. This too is a
> nice place of 2,500 inhabitants & on the opposite side of
> the river is Davenport numbering 2,000. At 11 A.M. we
> were in Bloomington, and at 5 ½ P.M. at Oquaka, a little
> place on the Illinois side; and in another hour we reached
> Burlington, a beautiful place in Iowa containing 2,500.
> We passed Nauvoo during the night.

∞∞∞∞∞

Like Dodge, we're only just learning the ropes of travel and diary-keeping, still sometimes caught in the notation.

Near Delmar, Iowa, there's a grass drive-in movie theatre set back into a hill, surrounded by cornfields, and its double feature is *Bad Moms* and *Sausage Party*. The speaker posts, out of place, poke up through the turf. Shortly after that, a dead coyote. Almost to the grass of the highway median when it ran out of luck, its lips pulled back now in a stiffened snarl. It joins all the other near-constant roadkill: the raccoons, the possums, the squirrels, the deer, and even a rounded and bloated young wild pig.

In Clinton, there's our first coal train. We're driving parallel to the tracks, keeping pace with the two linked engines, but then we jog right up and over a rail bridge, the train passing under the highway so we can see into car after car, each one filled with regular conical piles of shiny black coal.

In Camanche, the police are busy collecting highway fines with the sudden plunge of the speed limit, four police cars with drivers pulled over, blue and red lights, angry faces behind the wheel of each stopped car.

The population of Camanche is less than 4,500 — there's only 4.2 miles of U.S. 67 South running through the whole small city and, today, a ratio of one police cruiser for each mile of highway.

Near Folletts on Route 67 — the Great River Road — we're inching back toward the Mississippi when we come across a branch of the Wapsipinicon River in flood, the silty brown water high, almost up to the concrete bridge, crowding in on the sides of the road and flooding well back into the trees. A nearby cabin is on telephone-pole stilts like a wader with his pants rolled up, the house a good four feet above the ground. The air is heavy again, the trees huge and hanging and reaching over the building, giving it an ominous feel.

The ditch is full of empty tall boys and the occasional one-shot liquor bottle. Every now and then, an empty flask bottle. The air hot and wet and heavy, the hoppers and katydids whirring, and laid over the top of it all, the constant whap-whap-whap of steady gunfire from the Princeton Shooting Range. Pulled over, we realize we're almost exactly under a sign that says we can't park on the shoulder. We run back to the car, wait for the police to round the corner, sure they'll have a ticket at the ready. Further down the road, seven power trucks and their crews puzzle over the intricate problem of a split elm, barrel-thick, that has fallen into the wires, stretching four power lines tight beneath its weight. Trees are big here and seem to fall of their own accord and on their own timetable.

The day has blossomed again into damp heat, and sometimes we see the Mississippi, a massive expanse of water, complete with high-bridged tugs towing low-freeboard barges in both directions. At one point, where the river's running fast, an entire tree, standing on its personal small grassy island, trundles downstream past us, turning slowly around in the current. It's moving faster than we are in the car. Motorboats buck forwards, bows white with foam as they bite into the waves and current coming downstream toward them.

◇◇◇◇◇◇◇

March 28, 1849

> At sunrise we were at Quincy, which is decidedly the handsomest place we have seen. Capt. Rogers lives there — Mr. Wood the first settler there had already left for California. Arrived at Hannibal at noon, where Dr. Ruddock & Co. landed. They were from Southport. Saw large numbers of very strange craft — barges — flats — steamers with one — two — or even three rudders — also with wheels at the sides — in the centre — and on the stern!

◇◇◇◇◇◇◇

The towns whip by, each one different in its own way. At Le Claire, the storefronts all match, and antique shops are everywhere.

In Bettendorf, the old Alcoa plant is measured in football fields, not square feet, and even has its own trade school. Its terminal station, the fat transformers settled near the edge of the road, actually vibrates with the low hum of the huge voltage passing through the wires. In the plant, there are 2,600 workers for 400 acres of works. It's got a new corporate name, but the same rolled aluminum product. There's a power dam at Davenport, another at Keokuk where the *Anthony Wayne* sank, and bridges — new, old, and out of service — reach back and forth across the river in styles from arched to tensioned cable structures to standard highway concrete. What they have in common is that they are all long, connecting state to state across the broad river.

In Davenport, across from the Casey's General Store gas station, it's so hot that kids working on a nearly vacant lot with their father rest pressed up against the wheels of the family van, shielded from the sun. They're clearing the remains of an old building behind the bait shop, knocking over cinderblock walls, loading it all onto a small flatbed trailer with two little wheels that hardly look up to the task. The kids slump, wilted, until it's time to start loading the trailer with broken rock and sledgehammer scrap again. The sidewalls of the trailer's tires bulge — everything's on the edge of failure, the father pushing everyone in the family enterprise, "Come on, come on, we've got to get this done today." The heat is punishing.

It's time to fill the tire again — we've been losing air regularly in one tire, the low tire pressure light on the dashboard winking on, but it's not clear yet which one it is, so we try to square them all up when we stop for gas. Inside the store, the air conditioner is fighting hard. Gas station sandwiches, more jerky, iced tea for Leslie in a big green can. Switch drivers. The satellite radio is working right now — we will discover that it doesn't work after St. Louis, so we'll be left at the mercy of the static-y arrival and departure of local AM stations, angry FM talk radio, and occasional slices of religious stations offering hellfire for the unbelievers. It will be a fitting soundtrack.

Storefronts metronome by. Dodge knew nothing about what is now the regularity of the Pizza Hut and the Burger King, of the Commerce Bank and the Taco Bell. Of Denny's and Dominos, about the way they trip by like franchised mileage posts. We pass Nauvoo in the daylight.

At Keokuk, we swap Iowa for Illinois, crossing the Mississippi and making a plan to cross back at Quincy and shift into Missouri. The bridge at Keokuk feels like any long highway bridge, concrete-sided and featureless. But north of it stands the old Keokuk & Hamilton bridge, a double-decker railway and roadway steel bridge, the old road on top, rails below. A turntable section is left open for river traffic to transit through a lock. Only the lower rail section of the bridge is still

in service. It's built on the same piers as a bridge that stood in 1869 —
it makes you want to sit and wait for the train to come.

Quincy's bridge is another story: it is alarmingly modern, great
fat white suspension cables shooting down from towers until they
meet the concrete deck, while, just downstream, the girdered strength
of the old bridge seems both tantalizingly within reach and also a
more solid choice. Quincy is not, in fact, the handsomest place we've
seen: a solid little place, but the downtown bricked, industrial, and, in
several places, boarded up.

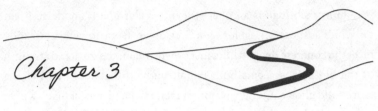

Chapter 3

St. Louis, Missouri

◇×◇×◇×◇×◇

March 29, 1849

This morning at 9 we were in the mouth of the Illinois
— & shortly after at the Missouri, whose muddy waters
refuse to mix. At 10 ½ we landed at St. Louis & put up
at the Virginia Hotel where we remained one day, and on
the 30th we commenced boarding at Miss Woodland's, at
$4.00 per week — up six pair of stairs & poor at that. We
remained there a week during which time we visited all
parts of the city. Among other things the Shot Tower —
Rotunda — water works — circus, a mere sham, churches,
Catholic Cathedral, Odd Fellows Hall, the Arsenal,
Sybyl's Cave & co. attracted our attention.

In this manner we waited more than two weeks for
the rest of our company, who were to meet us here from
Cincinnati by the first of April. As time progressed, the
days seemed more long and dull, and on the 12th of April
we sent a telegraph dispatch to the keepers of the Hotel at
Cincinnati to see if we could hear where they were.

He returned answer that they had left there on the
previous Tuesday for St. Louis. At the expiration of the
first week we changed our boarding house to Mrs. Post's
who was a distant relative of Ferris, and where we met

with much better fare. In the meantime, Ferris, who was sick of the job before he started, although his pride alone prevented him from saying so, continued to get "no better fast" & on the 13th of April, he fairly "backed out" & left for home on the Danube at 5 P.M. At this time the excitement which has seldom if ever had a parallel in this country, is raging with great fury; and every boat that arrives comes laden with the adventurers. The city is filled completely — every boarding house, both public and private is crowded to overflowing and the cry is "still they come." So great was the rush, that, having gone to the circus (a mere farce) to pass away the evening & not returning until our door was shut, I tried at nearly every tavern in St. Louis to find a bed but after walking the streets till past 2, I was compelled at last to spend the rest of the night in a chair at the Doniphan House! That was Monday, April 2.

⋈⋈⋈⋈⋈

We drive into St. Louis on a great concrete rope of highway. It might have taken Dodge an hour or more to get to St. Louis from the mouth of the Missouri, but it's a far cry from that now: the city and its environs spread almost as far north as the spot where Missouri joins Mississippi. We shoot right into the core of the city; Leslie's driving, more at home on the multi-lane highways than I am. But even with both of us trying to find our way, we end up in a tangle of brick neighbourhoods near an old brewery, using our precious store of cellular data to try and find where we went wrong. We pull over, ask a woman walking her dog how to get to the hotel. She flinches away from the car when we call out and looks around as if preparing an escape route. Her directions are good, even though we question them as they pull us through a concrete-and-vacant-lot wasteland under the arches of highway on and off ramps. By chance, an online reservation has put us into a massive and ridiculously cheap suite at the St. Louis City Center Hotel, only a short walk from the famous riverfront arch. Our room looks down at a transit rail terminus, at the long arc of Route 64 heading toward the setting sun.

We have 14-foot ceilings, a sitting room, a huge bathroom. It's too fancy a place for us to be bringing in our Styrofoam coolers, emptying out the melted ice, and cramming everything into the hotel fridge — we do it anyway. As usual, we ignore the unopened baby carrots.

Downtown St. Louis feels almost post-apocalyptic on Labour Day night. We're not used to the weight of the heat and humidity. The streets are empty, stores closed, and we forage for a restaurant that's open. Homeless people shift around us like zombies in the heat, some pushing shopping carts, one pushing a baby stroller filled with shoes. One man, muttering and gaunt as he crosses six lanes of empty street under the glare of streetlights, is wearing a priest's collar. There are long open green spaces in front of imposing buildings of great stone block walls — the former 22nd Judicial Court of Missouri, City Hall — and in under the trees, sleeping pads of flattened cardboard, worn soft-looking and marked with dents in the shape of the human body.

There's no traffic at all.

A flip-flop lays on a parking lot, poised flat and left as if someone had run right out of it, leaving it behind to mark the direction of travel.

We find a restaurant, the only one open, it seems, with tall, high-backed chairs — the difference between the temperature of the night, over 100 degrees and thick with humidity, and the cool of the inside is remarkable. You come through the door soaking and the sweat wicks away quickly. The inside of the front window of the restaurant is hot to the touch.

There's artisanal beer and artisanal food — pickled whole carrots with leafy fronds still attached, a sweep of charcuterie meats and specialty cheeses on a wooden board, Andouille sausage, steelhead trout, cold beer. Outside, a man wearing a ragged knit cap, incongruous in all that heat, stops beyond the front window, stares blankly inside at us for a moment and at the only other patrons — a man at the bar with two laughing young women next to him on barstools — and then moves quietly off into the night.

A huge sign runs down the outside of a building across the street, "FARM & HOME SAVINGS ASSN," except the "&" has fallen off. I'll soon realize that removing signs on buildings is more trouble than it's worth, so they stay on as the buildings pass from one iteration to the next. The ground floor of this building is empty, the windows taped over with brown craft paper that has started to peel away and fall down. It reminds me of the particular parochial ownership of those who live in just one place for their entire lives and offer you precise yet useless directions: "Then, you turn left at the corner where the grocery store used to be."

Our meal is excellent. The bathrooms are down a long hall and their décor is completely different from the rest of the restaurant: the front of the restaurant has towering ceilings, a great wall of glossy wooden shelving full of rows of liquor bottles and with a sliding wooden ladder for reaching the high shelves, and antique chain-drive ceiling fans. The bathroom suggests a mid-eighties singles bar, all black and white and silver and abrupt, as if you might come back out after washing your hands and hear Duran Duran. Restaurants, I learn, evolve with new owners and new themes: often their bathrooms, not a critical investment, stay stubbornly the same. Art and artifice.

Next door, a tiny bar is called, fittingly, the Tiny Bar, with seating for only a handful. The scattering of outdoor tables is wired together and locked. The bar is an homage to the smallest baseball player ever to play in the major leagues, Eddie Gaedel, who was three foot seven and wore the number 1/8 for the St. Louis Browns when he pinch-hit in the second game of a 1951 double header. Earlier, he'd popped out of a papier-mâché cake as part of a celebration of the American League's 50th anniversary. His strike zone must have been impossibly small. Not unexpectedly, he was walked with four straight balls and was replaced with a pinch runner.

The Tiny Bar opened in 2015, apparently with a tiny parade: a smart car, a very small dog, Thumbelina (the world's smallest horse),

and a one-piece brass band. A little internet research finds out that the
bar is hardly ever open. It's actually the lobby of a public relations and
digital marketing firm, and a bar for only a handful of hours a week.

◇◇◇◇◇◇◇

April 14, 1849

    A very bad cold day — nothing new except that I am quite
unwell. Dr. Post wrote home that he is not going — many
are giving it up for fear of scarcity of grass & suffering
among the emigrants.

    5 P.M. Drury who had gone down to the levee some-
time before, returned with B. Holcombe and A. W.
Ingalsbee, part of our company, whom we did not expect
till next day, but who arrived that forenoon about 10.
They had looked for us, but not finding us concluded we
had not come, and were about selling a part of the outfit.
Myself quite unwell — very bad cold etc.

◇◇◇◇◇◇

An explanation about Dodge and "The New York Company." Groups
of emigrants headed for California gold in 1849 regularly formed
"companies" to pool resources and buy equipment. The companies
could be quite formal, with written articles of association and strict
rules and bylaws about meetings to discuss their operations and even
the disposal of assets. Some, like The New York Company, were asso-
ciations of the like-minded or groups of friends — others had outside
investors eager to share in California's bounty by financing groups
of prospectors, but who were not willing to cross the country or put
in the hard work of actually prospecting. One thing the companies
all had in common? Few of the 49ers setting up their ventures were
aware of the planning, equipment, and food necessary to make the trip,
and internal strife over shortages, equipment failure, and other issues
meant most companies broke up or were formally dissolved out on
the trail, or shortly after their arrival in California. As he points out,

Dodge's company was close to foundering in St. Louis, with some members already preparing to sell off equipment, simply because they thought other company members had decided not to make the trip. The corporate bonds may have been formal, but it didn't mean they weren't fragile.

<><><><><>

April 15, Sunday, 1849
> This morning finds me worse, and I applied to Dr. Vastien,
> a homeopathic, boarding at the same house, who gave me
> a dose of his little pills and left me some more to be dis-
> solved in water and taken. The day passed away without
> any improvement — sore throat, headache, & chills.

<><><><>

Maybe it's because it's the last long weekend of the summer, but even on a working Tuesday, downtown St. Louis is mostly empty. The baseball stadium sits listless in the heat, parking lots clear, a major league baseball event from the weekend now past, leaving only metal crowd-control barricades holding back banks of red plastic beer cups, an empty black stage and backdrop. I think that it will be hard to find Dodge's footprints here. Everything is paved over with wide sidewalks and towering new office buildings. At first, it looks as if nothing in the long list of spots he's visited so far is even still standing. The Shot Tower, for example (where molten lead was poured through a screen and then fell through six storeys of air into water to form individually-gauged musket balls) is long gone, though its products — musket balls and small lead ingots stamped with the company name — still turn up in Nebraska, Wyoming, and Colorado on the westward trails.

Nothing is left until I reach the cathedral.

The old cathedral, down near the waterfront, has clear windows instead of stained glass, but it still feels the part with its banks of lit candles and when I come in and the door bangs behind me, a single black woman, tall and impossibly thin with iron-grey hair, turns to look at me sternly. She is the only person in the building and there is bright sun outside, angling in the tall windows and catching dust motes moving in the air.

It is one of the few buildings that remains from Dodge's era. Short days after he left St. Louis in 1849, the Great Fire of May 17 ripped through the downtown, leaving the court building and the old cathedral and not much else. The church — an imposing limestone cube with four tapered, round limestone columns on the front of the building — escaped another near miss when the iconic Gateway Arch was built. It was the only building on the grounds that wasn't torn down to build the great metal curve. The Rotunda of the Old Courthouse is also still standing and under its richly painted dome, there's a circle of displays that include the fire. The waterfront of 1849 is long gone, the shore of the river filled in so that the city reaches further out into the Mississippi.

Downtown St. Louis is a construction site, even under the arch. One of the workmen is wearing an orange shirt with "Bruce" written in script on his chest. He's carrying a cordless drill in one meaty hand — "Christ, Bruce," another worker says. "It looked like you were packing there for a second and I thought 'Whoa.'"

In front of the cathedral, tucked into a corner of the stairs, there is a pair of bright pink panties with blue trim, balled up, a small blue bow showing. A score of possible stories, but no clear explanation.

The foreshore of the river is the preserve of money — banks and tall buildings, the lodging-houses long gone. There are only replica riverboats now, offering tours on vessels that date back to the 1960s. Old enough, but hardly antique.

Dodge stayed three days short of a month in St. Louis, leaving on April 26. St. Louis was where much of Dodge's "company" formed up, bringing together and buying what its members thought would be their necessary supplies, getting mules and wagons. (Part of their gear, once the whole team was together, would be a 150-square-foot rubber tent, bought in New York for $40, the equivalent of $1,400 today.) The group began making their first short forays out of town and back again.

Three weeks after he left, all of Dodge's lodging places burned to the ground.

No word must have reached him on the trail, because he doesn't mention the fire, even in passing.

∞∞∞∞∞

April 18, 1849

Cold bad weather. Spent the morning helping to purchase outfit & a great time in the afternoon training the mules — Health improving.

April 21, 1849

Great time breaking our mules. Weather fine — afternoon took part of them out 6 miles on the road to St. Joseph. Coming back the wheel ran off & the team attempted to run away, but we finally stopped them without injury. Reached town at dark.

April 23

Telegraphed to Cincinatti for Wainwright and Chapman. Rainy day — not much done. Remained at the house. Fixed the whips &c.

April 24

Received answer that the boys had not been at Cincinnati, determined not to wait for them.

April 26.

Left St. Louis this morning at 10 — 4 mules at one wagon and 2 at the other — fine day and good time of it. Bogus, a fellow who with his brother we carry across, stole a dog on the levee & brought him to St. Charles, where his master reclaimed him. Reached St. Charles and crossed the steam ferry at 5 P.M. Staid at a splendid house 5 miles from there. Rolling land covered with scrubby oak brush — very fine rich soil and country — apple blossoms falling. Lots of slaves at the house here. Travelled 25 miles today.

◇◇◇◇◇◇

We leave St. Louis hungry.

We're on the edge of the highway, looking for gas and breakfast. We end up in a Denny's, in a window-side, red-leatherette banquet, and Leslie goes to buy a newspaper. Which may have been a mistake.

She reads in the *Post-Dispatch* that Phyllis Schlafly is dead. We're in Schlafly's hometown, where this is big news.

The first two paragraphs read, "Phyllis Schlafly, a political force who fought against the feminist causes and helped pave the way for today's thriving conservatism movement, died Monday (Sept. 5, 2016) at her home in Ladue.

"For decades she was a political icon, often a polarizing one, using her Eagle Forum — a Clayton-based national organization of volunteers she called her army — to rally against the Equal Rights Amendment and abortion. . . . Mrs. Schlafly fought feminists and three presidents to bring the Equal Rights Movement to a screeching halt. During the 1950s and '60s she helped build the anti-Communist movement in the United States."

That's far more charitable than Leslie's take.

Upraised newspapers all around us tremble when Leslie announces to the restaurant that Phyllis Schlafly was a cunt. "A fucking cunt," in fact. Strangers peek around newsprint at us.

St. Louis may be mourning its own, but Leslie's story is different, a sharp bend in her own personal road. To her, Phyllis Schlafly was responsible for a U-turn in modern women's rights in America, uniquely responsible for the defeat of the Equal Rights Amendment, responsible for statements like, "There are many cultural, societal, family, pregnancy, and practical reasons why women should not be drafted. Women have more important things to do, such as taking care of their babies and keeping their families together."

Leslie sees Schlafly as an example of someone who took the slowly opening door of opportunity for young women just like Leslie and slammed it firmly shut. Leslie was an American-born-and-raised teenager. When Schlafly defeated the Equal Rights Amendment, Leslie left for Canada at 18 and never moved back. Schlafly, Leslie says, stole her country.

Leslie opines, quite loudly I think, that she's glad that Schlafly is dead.

I believe, for a fleeting moment, that we might just get beaten up by a mob of old people in a St. Louis Denny's.

It strikes me that I don't have that anchor in place, in time, in a larger history. Leslie, like Dodge, had direction — and all of it is family history, baked into who she is. I've meandered, moving away from my family at 16, living a long train ride away for the next seven years and then even further. My brothers set similar tracks quickly out of the nest and onto the road — my parents were careful to tell us that they expected us out and on our own after university. Eventually, we scattered to the point that all of North America was between us, with me in contact through Dad's neat, round hand-written letters and Mom's more rushed ones, her cursive sloping more and more as she rushed to make her point. I have bundles of those letters in my office, postmarked from the Netherlands, the former Yugoslavia, Australia: my father was an oceanographer, often on the road. Opening and reading them now only serves to remind me how often they reached out and how often I failed to respond, full of my own world. And how my own world now feels particularly small.

Oh, and the St. Louis Denny's grits were apparently not very good.

On the highway, motorcycles blow by us, exhaust pipes blattering, their riders with beards and ponytails blowing back over their shoulders, occasional passengers clutched to their backs like oversized limpets.

A billboard says there have been 554 road deaths in Missouri so far this year, nine months in, and another billboard points out 60 percent of those involved people without seatbelts.

The motorcycle drivers and their passengers are 90 percent without helmets, many with bandanas tied over their heads. I've been to motorcycle accidents as a first responder. I would never want to see a helmetless one, especially not a high-speed, interstate one. I think that the world often suffers from a critical failure of imagination and can't take the time to try to conceive of the sheer collapse of all order that happens when your parents or your wife opens the door and finds a sombre police officer standing there.

∞⟩⟨∞⟩⟨∞

April 28, 1849

Started rather earlier this morning — weather fine with cool breeze — high rolling prairie all day — travelled 34 miles today. I drove a pair of wild mules — went well; put up at 5 P.M., 2 miles west of Dansville with Mr. Fulkerson. Many of the settlers are Germans & their women were planting corn all along. Roads fine but not much worked. Slaves at nearly every house — most of them appear contented and happy.

April 29, 1849

A company from Tennessee passed us as we were hitching up, with oxen and horses to ride. They encamped on the opposite side of the creek from the house where we staid. We had gone but a short distance before one of the mules in crossing a mud hole threw herself square in the mud and could not get up till we got him out of the harness.

Bogus rode a new one and got throwed. The country is good — high & rolling, some timber. Just after passing a little village 7 miles on, we came onto a beautiful prairie where we saw a large number of mules & a great many grouse, so tame as to be within good shooting distance. We travelled 30 miles and stopped with a private family on a fine large prairie. Two young men leave this house next day Sabbath, for Santa Fe. The evening before leaving St. Louis we went to the theatre & saw Dan Marble — poor show. Bogus got another dog of a farmer. The family here, Carew, are an ignorant set of people, as indeed are most of the lower class throughout Missouri. Holcombe, Ingalsbee "Bogus" alias Smith, and myself started with the teams & left Drury to wait for Chapman and Wainwright & then come up on a boat, with our Loading, or as they call it here — plunder. No wells in this part of the country — all use cistern water. The country is very thinly settled.

April 30, Sunday, 1849

With sorrow I record that we were compelled to travel this day — the place where we stopped not being a fit one to remain at, and we also getting rather late. Mostly large rolling prairies with occasional timber roads, rather rough, with some stumps. Travelled 22 miles and stopped at Mr. Palmer's, a very fine place. A great place for raising stock — large numbers of cattle and mules ranging at large on the prairie. The common class of settlers are far inferior in intelligence to northern people generally.

Started in good season this morning and soon a rain came up with a very strong wind most of the forenoon. Passed about a dozen ox teams en route for St. Joseph — five yoke to a wagon. Drove 25 miles to Huntsville (oh blame the hogs, how they shake the wagon!) before stopping, then took tea and proceeded 5 miles farther and put up at a house where they said they could accommodate us, but we found, after unhitching, that they had neither hay nor oats. This I write sitting in the wagon, by the light of the moon, with my book upon my knee. Travelled 32 miles today.

∞∞∞∞∞

On the outskirts of Salisbury, there's a strange little Subway restaurant plopped down in the middle of farmland, with fields and silos on both sides, its only real company a funeral home. A middle-aged man at the counter makes our turkey bacon clubs and pulls iced tea from the cooler. There are no other customers, no other staff, and I think the man behind the counter might be the franchise owner. There are clean bathrooms and a sense of unreality about the whole thing, as if it had been dropped from space. A business built on the hope that traffic would stop, that customers would come. The whole time we are there, we see not one other customer. Not one car passes.

It's unbearably, wiltingly hot: in the time it takes to make two sandwiches and pay for our order, the temperature in the car has gone from cool to baking.

Highway 24 parallels the railway, but the railway is higher up, so that the view from the driver's side is all high gravel berm, from the passenger side, alternately fallow fields and corn.

We pass something that becomes a regular sight along the highway: a vast collection of old cars, trucks, and utility vehicles — fire trucks and electrical boom trucks among them — lined up and slowly settling into rust and dust, tires either flat or flattening as the air pressure slips away, the company names on the doors painted over with matte spray paint, all past that point where asset crosses over to keepsake. Each vehicle has its own precise past, a history of roads travelled and different hands on steering wheels. They seem to convey how the world has changed for many Americans — and not for the better — creating the need to hold onto relics from better times. To hold onto what you have, lest a changing world reaches in to take it all away.

The drier the country gets, the more often we'll see vast dirt parking lots of old vehicles, inventories mouldering, too good to simply send to the crusher, too in need of work to actually be used. There's something both hopeful and depressing about them, these never-to-be-driven-again vehicles that the owner still sees some slight potential in. Many of these are workhorses at the end of their own trails, broken down, kept for last-chance parts or a shift in history that just isn't going to come.

◇◇◇◇◇◇

May 1, 1849

Proceeded on our way 7 miles through timber and the same distance over a fine level prairie. For a few miles before reaching Keytsville we found some very bad road — no bridges at all over the slews. The people here appear not to have any of the energy or enterprize of the Yankees, but are ignorant and destitute of any knowledge of what is going on around them. We are nearly 200 miles from St. Louis and we have not seen yet a single village of any importance, and those we have seen appear old — mostly dilapidated log buildings, and no appearance of life or business about them. We have seen no kind of manufactures or machinery at all. Saw a few large tobacco warehouses. Came 28 miles and stopped at Brunswick, a very pretty little place on the Missouri 297 miles from St. Louis by the river. A couple of boats passed up loaded with Californians. The spring is uncommonly backward, weather cool and vegetation not advanced. A fine piece of bottomland here.

◇◇◇◇◇◇

Keytesville is a blink of an eye, but still there is a traffic light on the unexpectedly one-lane girdered bridge across Mussel Fork. Our light turns green and we start across the stop line into the narrowing lead-up to the bridge, but the gravel hauler coming at us doesn't care about the light and charges through, taking up the whole road. Even after he's gone and we've survived to take our turn crossing the bridge deck, it feels like the bridge is still shaking from the weight and speed. Or maybe the shaking is just me.

I work in the news business. I know nothing makes a highway accident vanish from the local news cycle faster than when the news comes out that the victims are from out of town. Horrible deaths are important when you know the victims, when they're from your own town. People passing through? A mere blip of curiosity. They're not a missing thread in the community fabric: not a familiar sight at the fire department chili cook-off, not a long-time volunteer at the senior's home. The weave and weft of belonging is highlighted by its absence.

We wouldn't even rate a handmade grave marker by the side of the trail.

May 2, 1849

Rain last evening — damp and chilly this morning. Crossed the Grand River where it empties into the Missouri in an open ferry boat rowed by two negroes. We were till 10 A.M. crossing on account of the wind which drove us upstream. The landlord at Brunswick acted very ungentlemanly indeed with us. Grain and Hay very scarce from here. Corn before 25¢, is now 40 and no hay to be had. Travelled through bottom land most of the day — arrived at Carlton at 8 P.M. and put up at Mr. Stovall's, one mile beyond — travelled 25 miles. Lewis is quite unwell owing to having taken off his flannel & caught a severe cold.

We cross the Grand River with the Missouri out of sight to the south.

In Carrollton, KMZU promises two options: The Farm at 100.7 FM, or The Grenade at 101.3. The Grenade's slogan is "Blowing up the airwaves." The period in the number is a graphic drawing of a hand grenade.

Down the street, La Bella Motel's sign is a study in 1950s flying-wedge neon, the motel the typical park-straight-in-front-of-your-room.

The beer from the trunk is warm to the touch, so perhaps it will be the House of Stuart blended scotch instead, ten bucks for that plastic-handled 80-proof 1.75 litre bottle, a Scotch that once advertised itself as, "the Scotch for people who don't have to prove anything to anyone."

In the bottomlands after Brunswick and again after Carrollton, the ground is rich and heavy and stretches out flat along the river. The flood gauge measures up to four feet above the road, above the roof of the car, and the railway's straight line and gentle curves of gravel are the flatland's highest point. It would all be under water at once. Corn on both sides, brown and dry, irrigation pipes gaping like great mouths every few hundred yards. The corn is so high that there's the illusion that you're already under water; the surface, the tassel tops of corn silk.

You find towns in the distance by the slow appearance of treetops over the corn. Each rumpled cloudline of the crowns of big elms and oaks and big poplars slowly resolves itself into the two sides of Main Street, each town comfortably familiar in its grid layout and collection of necessities. Gas station, garage, hardware store, coffee shop/diner — it's Norman-Rockwell-comfortably-static and Stepford-Wives-unsettling all at the same time. You get the feeling that you could move right into the same feuds and concerns no matter where you chose to stop and put down roots, know that you would be considered an outsider in each place for exactly the same amount of time. I've lived in small towns like that, ones where the coffee shop has a table where the regulars all have their assigned seats. Where the daily routine is not only expected but is an essential part of life — where not showing up for coffee on time one morning makes you the subject of open public speculation.

In Brunswick, a storm-toppled tree has driven a great fat branch directly through the wood-shingled side of a white house. It looks like it happened some time ago, but the tree's still in place, as if no one had figured out how to deal with it. People walk by on the sidewalk without even looking now.

We take pictures.

All along the 24 West, Keytesville, Brunswick, Huntsville, the road follows a natural depression that's almost pleasing to the eye — if you were planning a trail, this is the route it would take. And it did.

It still makes sense, even when the land starts to rise and roll after Plattsburg and the first piece of the muddy Little Platte River appears.

Pecans. They grow pecans here.

∞∞∞∞∞

May 3, 1849

Lewis a little better — our route today lay across the finest bottom land I ever saw, the road running from 1 to 8 miles from the banks of the Missouri. Some of this land strange to say is yet government land, that foulest of our nation's stains — slavery — preventing the most enterprising of our people from living here. Had gone but a short distance when we came to a bad place where we had to cross a small river at the foot of a pond on the dam. Crackey, how the wind blew! It seemed as though creation had summoned all her powers for one mighty effort, and had drawn a sigh that was destined to take every hair from our heads! Travelled 30 miles and put up at Richmond, a mere shadow of a place on top of a hill. Continually passing companies with oxen, in one of which a man died the day before of the Cholera, which was at St. Louis when we were there, and is prevalent up the river.

May 4, 1849

Rained during the night and rains this morning, good and strong. Remained till noon and got some little things fixed up. Then hitched up and went 9 miles & put up at Elkhorn with a very clever fellow. Rained all afternoon. Had great sport with Lewis who thought he had the Cholera. Took in another fellow to ride to St. Joseph, who had started from Freeport, Ill., in company with two others with oxen, and their teams had given out. Met a man going back from St. Joseph who started from Michigan. Many are returning, fearing to proceed because so many have gone that they fear there will not be sufficient grass.

◇◇◇◇◇◇◇◇

Chapter 4

Omaha, Nebraska

Omaha is a sudden huge, grey concrete octopus of road overpasses. We come into the city from the worst, most industrial of angles, the horizon dark with thunderheads, the view construction-filled and almost post-apocalyptic as 29 turns into I-80. The light certainly doesn't help, nor does the rain.

The city is broken up into clearly delineated sections: expensive homes with swooping rooflines cut away suddenly to poorer neighbourhoods. One side of a thoroughfare is different turf than the houses on the other. Up near the Mutual of Omaha headquarters, a planned arts district makes up both sides of the street. Downtown, brick streets in the historic market, the market's edges clearly defined by the sudden decline that surrounds it.

We meet a former school principal working in an upscale wine and beer store — the store has expensive lighting, ferns, floor-to-ceiling windows, and a lunch place built in. He wonders why we're there, and when he finds out we're following the diary, he immediately tells us about going back to find his grandfather's roots in Croatia, about how delighted he was when villagers came up with small details they remembered without his prompting — about the fact his grandfather had three wives, that he was a wartime pilot. That they can show him the house where his family used to live. I know how satisfying putting a pin in exactly the right geographic spot can be. We're talking

the same language, but about completely different experiences —
at the same time, it feels like we're taking part in a necessary human
ritual. Affirming that we fit in specified places, before heading in different directions never to see each other again.

Our hotel is a university residence; guests are packed together in
neighbouring rooms to make it easier for the cleaning staff, but before
we've even unzipped our bags, we get moved to an empty floor after a
yelling match breaks out in the room next to us, a clown-car of a room
where we've watched five people, four of them children, stream in
through the door while we stand still fumbling with our keycard.

The empty floor feels haunted: there are fugitive footsteps, doors
opening and closing, late-night voices muttering at the end of the
tunnel-like halls.

Two big white cops arrest a small black man in the lobby. He protests in a long circular argument as the police move closer, their arms
crossed at first but their hands slowly, slowly shaking loose and moving toward their belts and handcuffs as the man gets more agitated.
He finally gets into a police car without being restrained. It's not clear
what the problem is. As they leave, you can feel the tension melt out
of the other people in the lobby, the desk clerk dropping his shoulders
with a sigh.

Leaving, the road south, Route 29, is alternately clear and humid
and then pounding with rain, big stacks of cloud heaving down water
that overwhelms the wipers. Then, just as fast, it's gone again, and the
pavement outside a highway rest area is like stepping into a steam bath,
the humidity rising off the drying asphalt like steam out of an iron.
Trucks are sweeping by on the four-lane, throwing up clouds of mist,
and in the distance, the sky is as dark as tarpaper in the sun. Off to the
east, there are great hummocked hills of sand and sandstone, all in a
line like the ridged spine of some huge and buried animal. It shows just
how pavement-flat the whole valley is, fields high with corn but still
vulnerable to flood at a moment's notice. We stop halfway between
Omaha and St. Joseph to get things out of the trunk. A little further
on, a car has swerved right down the shoulder, leaving twin wheel ruts

in the soil and a car-shaped divot out of the side of a field of yet more corn. Something ended here violently, and not long ago. Car parts dot the torn-up soil, as if someone has tried to grow an automobile from its leftover constituent pieces.

Not even 15 miles down the road, a gas station, forlorn at its own empty highway exit, has crime-scene washrooms, the area around the doorknob patterned with greasy handprints as clearly defined as if they had been outlined with fingerprint dust. There is blood on the floor, on the counter around the sink, on the mirror. The sliding lock on the door has all four of its mounting screws pulled out of the wall, the door kicked in. But outside, on the cracked and puddled asphalt, the sun has burst out and is hot on our faces, the humidity still rising as the rain jumps back up into the air.

We are, just now, back in Iowa and only a scant few miles from where the Platte River joins the Missouri. And the Platte was Dodge's route west.

∞∞∞∞∞∞

May 6, 1849

A very poor place to stop at indeed. Everything looked dirty & unfit to eat & not enough of it at that. It is decidedly the worst place we have stopped at — No hay or oats. Weather still cloudy. Raining hard about 11 — slacked up and we started for a "more genial clime" — where there was less of the soil to be seen. Hot & showery — travelled 18 miles & put up — passed large numbers of teams, camped, some having women and children. The crowd grows greater the nearer we get to St. Joseph — places where they have camped by the roadside look like barnyards. It is astonishing to see the rush. Many of the ox teams will never reach California — it is impossible — they must winter this side of the mountains. Rumours along the road are so contradictory that it is impossible to find out anything; and the manner in which the poor

emigrants are imposed upon by the settlers, buying grain
etc. is shameful. They represent corn as being worth $5
per bbl. up the river and thus compel them to buy of them,
at their own price, when, as they afterwards ascertained,
it could be had in the upper country for $1.25 and $1.50.
Double price for meals, lodging, etc. is often charged,
but they have not fooled us bad — we did not come 2000
miles to be sucked in by such a set of pukes.

May 8, 1849

Harnessed up one team & went back after corn — also
to a sawmill and got some boards for making boxes —
fine day. About 4 P.M. Holcombe returned and Chapman
with him. Wainwright and he arrived at St. Louis the day
after we left, and they with Drury had arrived in safety at
St. Joseph. Several cases of Cholera on their boat.

Hitched up immediately & proceeded to Platte River
8 miles, which we had to ford. The banks are steep and
muddy — the water side-deep to the teams, but we crossed
in perfect safety. There was a large company from Illinois
with horses, camped on the front bank — we went 2 miles
and put up with a nice family who say they begin to think
these Yankees are pretty fine people & better brought up
than most people here.

May 9, 1849

After partaking of a fine breakfast, we proceeded continually passing teams, some camped, and others coming
on. Arrived at St. Joseph about noon, and after waiting
some time for the pickets to fasten the mules, we went a
little out of the village by the side of the river and picketed
them, & then went to the Edgar House, where the boys
are stopping and after waiting a long time got what they
called a dinner — but if it was, it was the meanest that I

have seen for many a day. There were about three hundred teams here to cross now.

St. Joseph is quite a smart little place in ordinary times, and at present the streets are literally crammed. The merchants and dealers are set of churlish, bigoted cheats, and it is seldom that a man can be waited on when he stands with the money in his hands.

We came 8 miles this morning & 10 last evening, which makes the distance from St. Louis, by the route we came, 331 miles.

◇◇◇◇◇◇◇

Chapter 5

St. Joseph, Missouri

T he road down into St. Joseph is high-treed, the highway
travelling through sudden rolling hills — but the entry into
the city is a harsh one, with over-and-under bridges, a hard
industrial edge to a brick and sooty back-end of town. It doesn't sell
itself well, and that doesn't get better.

At least, not right away.

St. Joseph is at the western edge of the United States as it was in
the 1840s, and it was here that 500,000 would cross for the California
and Oregon trails. After this, there were no real towns or settlements.
Navigation consisted of following existing trails and hopefully clear
landmarks. The American government's presence in all that land was
the occasional fort, columns of travelling soldiers, and little else.

We go looking for Dodge's Edgar House. It's supposed to be on
Main Street, except there isn't one on the map. There's a painting of
Abe Lincoln getting a shave at the Edgar in 1859, people watching
the straight razor's progress across his cheek from both inside and
outside the room. It's far easier to find a postcard with that John
Falter painting than it is to find the current site of the Edgar. But we
keep looking.

The city did well by the emigrants; by 1890, it was apparently
the wealthiest city per capita in the U.S. Now, its median income of a

little more than $43,000 puts it 20 percent below the national median. The downtown near the river looks worn and down on its luck, with plenty of closed stores and tired buildings.

The population has fallen by some 30,000 since its apogee at 102,000 in 1900, and it's clearly not the central point of western travel that it once was. No longer a jumping-off point, its luster has faded. Healthcare and the school district are the biggest employers, though there is manufacturing too.

Look out from the back of the Radisson Hotel and you can see the Missouri River, as wide and fast as it ever was, the surface buckling and roiling with the current, and hints of the promising flatlands beyond. I learn that the room we were given by sheer chance looks straight out at the ferry crossing William Dodge would have used, taking the rope-and-pole ferry at the end of Francis Street.

In front of all of that now is the overlay of the busy rail line, the concrete curved overpass to the bridge across the river, and the square broad concrete pad of a fenced transformer station. The arms of the off ramps encircle and reach in toward the hotel on both sides. The West doesn't have to be won, it's right there within easy reach, and the cars and trains and trucks thrum by in steady rhythm all night. The hotel isn't perfect, but at least no one is dying of cholera. The pool feels cold, but only because September is in the 90s here this week.

St. Joseph was owned by a man who named many of its streets after his children. Joseph Robidoux did well by his investment but still managed to die a pauper.

There are heritage plaques aplenty throughout the town. Jesse James died here in 1882. The first railway to cross the Missouri crossed here in 1859. The Pony Express, wildly mythologized but in operation only from April 1860 to October 1861, had its eastern base here.

The sign for the Pony Express Motel, 1950s neon with a galloping rider and an arrow made up of scores of light bulbs, still exists. For those who chronicle signs, the horse has a "neon gallop in three positions" and still lights up at night.

The motel — 66 rooms on Route 169 — was torn down in 2007 for a fast-food franchise restaurant and the sign went up for sale on eBay before its owners were convinced to donate it to the Pony Express Museum and stables. A postcard for the flat, one-storey brick motel shows a ship's wheel mounted as a centrepiece in the Captain's Lounge, while the rooms shown have glossy wood-strip panelled walls, the ceilings wooden too — "TV, radio, phones all rooms, air cond. 24 hour service, banquet rooms, dancing weeknights. . . . Free coffee and papers."

The markers that we choose to keep are odd and eclectic ones.

Empty buildings dot the downtown core, all brick, windowless in a way that makes you feel like they are turning their back on you.

Mysteries inside too: every time we close or open the bathroom door in 517, there's a faint metallic rattle that makes me curious. I discover that the access trap in the bathroom wall to reach the pipes is unlatched. In that small cubby, there's a fat quart bottle of Barton vodka, its shoulders and cap heavily coated with dust, the bottle empty. There's no real way to tell how long it's been there. I saw a bottle just like it in an auto body parking lot in Fond du Lac, Wisconsin, only a few days earlier.

Making stories from the leftovers: was there a hotel handyman with a penchant for a few Barton straighteners to get him through the day? Hotel cleaners with back pain from lifting the huge heavy mattresses to remake the beds, looking for a quick shot to loosen stiff muscles? We leave the bottle but use a coin to turn the latch so that the rattle stops, and the bottle's safely hidden away until the next plumber needs to do some work.

Down on the waterfront, where the Edgar House used to be, there's a faded blue sign for the St. Jo's casino, a gold rush remarkably close, geographically, to the earlier one.

Deep-fried alligator appetizers at the St. Jo's Louisiana-themed restaurant: "Juicy, tender nuggets fried and served with cream-style gravy. We call this 'high-class' chicken." It's $8.99 for a plate of something indistinguishable from popcorn chicken, so the legacy of St. Jo's profiteering isn't dead yet.

◇◇◇◇◇◇

May 10, 1849

Holcombe & Wainwright went back 18 miles to get a pony. Ingalsbee and myself got up at 3 A.M. and drove the wagon down toward the ferry, where they were crowded in so as completely to fill up the road for rods! At noon we crossed. In the morning the steamboat *Mary*, on which our provisions were shipped arrived, having had 43 deaths by cholera on her trip up. Oh, what a day this has been — crowding — swearing — firing guns and pistols — it seems more like some gala day than like an ordinary business day. Wrote home, expecting it to be the last time till we reach California. I am weary, tired, and sick of this place. I long to be gone. How strange are the desires of the mind! Not content at home, living in ease and happiness — that ever craving appetite for wealth has led thousands to forsake home, friends, & every convenience and luxury of life for the toil and hardship with the attendant privations of a long & dangerous trip through a country inhabited by savages, & possessing but few even of the means for prosecuting it! 'Tis strange! Even <u>Women</u> & <u>children</u> by scores are now starting upon this perilous journey — even while I sit in the wagon writing this, in one of the hardest showers of thunder and rain I ever saw, I can look only a few rods from me & see several tents containing females and even children <u>not a year old</u>! 'Tis strange what a man will do for <u>gold</u> — how much of pleasure and happiness — aye of life even — is sacrificed for this one thing! Even I have left the dearest of friends & forsaken prospects which but few young men in my situation could enjoy — but it <u>is not for the</u>

love of gold that I do this — no, I have an object — two
fold — and one too which every manly & noble impulse
of my nature would prompt me to strive to fulfill. I am the
only son of poor and honest parents — to try and make
their old age comfortable and happy shall ever be one of
the first objects of all my actions.

⋄⟨⋄⟩⋄⟩⟨⋄⟩

Reading between the lines across a span of 160 years is never easy, but
I find it hardest when Dodge occasionally waxes woeful and poetic.
When he waxes pragmatic, I have absolutely no trouble believing his
words. A cross by the trail, a tent holding emigrants dead of cholera?
Absolutely. But when his goals become lofty, the notes ring hollow to
me. Maybe I forget he's a 22-year-old filled with trepidation about the
size of the new adventure he's undertaking, looking for reasons to jus-
tify what comes next. After all, Dodge and his "New York Company"
are finally on the edge of the real wild west part of the journey, and
they suddenly can't seem to fully commit to it, heading away from St.
Joseph and then just as quickly coming back, over and over. They're
not alone: others are also taking part in what was called "shakedown
trips," testing gear and getting used to their animals.

So, while Dodge cloaks his expedition in a sort of principled
and maybe necessary selflessness, we head, more mundanely, to the
Robidoux Row Museum. Ivana Calhoun is the executive director.

Joseph Robidoux came south from Quebec and reportedly spoke
12 native languages. The museum is in Robidoux Row, a collection of
apartments built in the period between 1840 and 1850 — some emigrants stayed there, but the original purpose was to offer temporary
homes for those buying downtown building lots from Robidoux. Four
of the units are now the museum, at least one still boasting the original
wide-board floors.

Calhoun is everything: sole employee, tour guide, chief booster.

She's collected a lot of material. Each room in the space is themed,
the museum detailed yet scattered: local farming inventions, a failing

and torn burgundy silk chair Robidoux brought from Louisiana for his wife, bread bowls and mixing spoons and silver spoons and bottles and furniture and cast-iron stoves. A miscellany museum, with everything from taxidermied beaver to pictures that may — or may not — have been historic St. Joseph.

The kind of place where Robidoux's bedroom has been carefully recreated with period furniture, except that only one piece actually belonged to the fur trader. A wardrobe might have come from the family; the spittoon belonged to his son. It has the feeling of a place that's never been able to turn down a donation or fail to find it a place among the permanent displays.

We buy postcards and try to get more information about the Edgar, which we simply haven't been able to find.

Turns out the Edgar Hotel is still standing — at least in part. When we find it, the spot that was supposed to sport St. Jo's first three-storey building is, instead, a one-storey Carpet Masters Mill Outlet, the dumpster next door piled with curling mounds of used and dirty broadloom. Across the street, there's a WireCo WorldGroup products plant, but you can see why the hotel was there, just yards away from the edge of the river, ready to offer lodging to those waiting to cross the Missouri and head west.

We cross the railway tracks and under the double-stacked and dingy highway ramps to reach the river's edge.

The distance across the Missouri is nearly narrow enough to throw a rock to the other side. At the concrete lookoff where the ferry crossing once was, there's a pair of jean shorts hanging over the railing, abandoned. The water is brown and slowmoving, the mud banks exposed. All in all, though, it doesn't look like it would be expensive to cross. It's a hiccup of trundling water — it looks like a mere impediment, but it's hiding its strength. This is the same river, after all, that capriciously ate the city's Levee and Water streets with nothing more than high water and a change in current.

This is where we see our first trail marker, down by the river where the ferry had once been, the official start of one leg of the California

Trail. The markers will become a welcome sight. When we find one, we know we're exactly on the route west, seeing a version of the topography Dodge saw.

When William Dodge crossed the river, he became a traveller effectively outside his established country.

Later, driving, we cross the river on the Pony Express bridge, Route 39, heading west.

We're up and over the river into Kansas. No toll, no ferry, just open road. Turn back to St. Joseph? We already know our South Korean wagon and its 185 horses of power well.

We don't even look back.

⟨∞∞∞∞∞⟩

May 11, 1849

Commenced camping out. I cooked our breakfast — the first meal of our journey! Weather warm — spent the morning in fixing the wagons and loading our provisions. Don't get along very fast — After noon I brought over the tent poles, but not having sufficient rope we were unable to raise it. Hard thunderstorm, so we cannot do much — The rain pours down in torrents, and the thunder breaks peal after peal overhead, while I am writing this.

May 12, 1849

There was a fire in town last night — a warehouse with a little powder in it — loss about $8000.

Hitched up and took part of the loading out about 8 miles and camped — A most awful road indeed — nothing but trees and mud holes without any bottoms! Set up the tent — an india rubber one 12 by 13 feet which Wainwright brought in N.Y. for $40 & got out the stove & I cooked our first meal on it — to us, then, it tasted delicious. Fred Smith & myself remained while the rest went back. We had no matches and there was no house nearer

than St. Joseph — what could we do — ah, I found it —
I made a fire with a pistol & we had a fine time of it that
night — nothing at all troubled us, except we awoke once
and found one of the mules loose. This has been a fine day.

May 13, Sunday, 1849

I awoke early, & not being able to raise a fire, sent Fred
to a tent a little way off for some. When he got there he
found one of them dead with the Cholera, in a tent a little
to the left was another death. Got breakfast, washed up
etc., & afternoon all the boys but Drury came out with
the rest of the stuff. I cooked them a fine dinner, bacon,
pork & beans, coffee, apple sauce, etc., which was far
better and cleaner than any meal we got in St. Joseph.
Holcombe, Chapman, & Wainwright went back to town
on horseback, Ingalsbee and they all having bought them
a horse each — Ingalsbee foundered his the first night
after he got him, through the negligence of the hostler.
I sent back my trunk and sold it for $3 to make our loads
lighter. It is now 11 P.M.

Near Washington, Kansas, the land suddenly starts to change from
ordered crops to grassland. But it's a short mirage. Pass through
Kansas and back again into Nebraska and the flat is hard to comprehend after the dips and whorls of the states we've passed through.
There are no corners: until you change routes, there are no curves, no
bends around any features. The tumble of Wisconsin brooks heading
downhill is gone and the hills went with them. Now, it is corn.

On the 81 North, we're passed by the fuselage of an airplane, all
silver, cruising by on a trailer behind a pickup, friction straps pulled
tight and shivering in the slipstream.

The 81 North has almost nothing to see but vast fields of corn tops,
the roof lines of buildings, the distant bulge of the very tops of the

trees. The sky is big, the horizon is a forever away. There is a big rig behind us, full in the mirror, red front, silver pipes, and the overhanging stainless-steel visors make the truck look angry. He gains only inches on us with every mile — but there are so many miles.

Out of the blue — or more to the point, out of the corn — a train appears. A very old train, another steam engine and its coal car. I'm driving, Leslie's sleeping, and I don't want to stop the car or turn around. It will only wake her up, and I'm not sure that I'll see anything more than I already do anyway.

Both are weeping rust. A flatbed and a yellow-orange, partially boarded up passenger car sit behind them. No tracks anywhere, no sign of how it became massive Nebraska yard art.

But you can follow anything with a serial number. And because everything seems to have its followers, all surviving steam engines in Nebraska are recorded, some 25 or so, and this one's no different. I look it up later. The engine is a former Grand Trunk Western Railway switching engine, built in the 1920s. After the Grand Trunk was finished with it, it made its way to the Northwestern Steel and Wire scrapyard in Illinois. After that, GTW 8074 was one of 12 engines donated to the Illinois Railway Museum. It was later sold to its current Geneva, Nebraska, owner — there's no clear reason why it's here, miles away from any railway tracks. Its own small binder of history and we flash by it in an instant, the corn closing in again shortly afterwards, broken only by occasional bands of shrub trees around creeks.

There's a kind of birdwatcher who travels to try and fill in the species on their lists that they haven't seen yet: they are (somewhat derogatorily) called twitchers. I wonder what the people who bird-dog old trains are called — because every steam engine's got at least one photograph online, and a lot of them have many.

I've learned there are California Trail twitchers, too, people who map and photograph and add to the guidebooks for every inch of the trail we're now trying to follow. It's like a family made out of a kinship of interests: the family of steam locomotive watchers, the family of California Trail enthusiasts. For us, all of the trail enthusiasts' work is a help, especially when Dodge is confusing; the landmark towns are behind us, and there's hardly anything but sheer geography to divine from. The guidebooks we've bought and carried all this way come into their own. They head step-by-step westward, their work so thorough you can't help but feel like an amateur. Drive two miles down this road, open a yellow bar gate, drive 1.3 more miles to a spring — it's almost microscopic analysis of thousands of miles of trails. The focus is almost too small, like directions that include counting the number of footsteps from your refrigerator to the back door.

><<><><><

May 18, 1849

Got under way again this morning in pretty good season & soon came to another crossing of Wolf Creek where a few of the <u>Sacs and Foxes</u> wanted toll for crossing. We gave them a few shillings and proceeded. Saw an Indian burying ground, & close by, a few huts. Arrived at the "Station" where the Indian Agent lives, about noon — ½ mile from there is the Missionary Station, where there is a fine school containing 15 female and 21 male Indian children. Passed 30 teams and camped where there was water but no wood — a large company with oxen camped close by; and a little way off is a place where some company has been camped, & two days before had buried a man, who, from the quantity of clothing left there, we presumed died of the small pox. This day has been full of interesting incidents. About 3 P.M., Wainwright & Ingalsbee rode off a little way & laying down for a moment, soon fell asleep. When they awoke two hours afterward both of their horses were gone. We did not know where they were till just at dusk, Ingalsbee came up on foot nearly tired out, & told us that he left Wainwright sitting on his saddle by the side of the road about 8 miles back! H. took his mare, & Bogus with one of the mules, started back in search of their horses. Just after dusk Wainwright came into camp having backed his saddle till he met Holcombe, when Bogus took it. In coming into camp he passed through another encampment, & having frightened one of their mules, he came near being shot, they supposing him to be some suspicious character.

May 19, 1849

Rather foul weather this morning. Took breakfast and went to fixing some little things intending to wait till Burt and Bogus returned. About 10 A.M. they came in with the horses, which they found in the possession of the Indians where we crossed Wolf Creek, a short distance beyond the Station, who had them hidden in the woods & refused to give any information concerning them until they were paid. He gave them $3 and they brought up the horses from their hiding place in the woods. They rode nearly all night, having lost their way on the bare plains, amid the howling of the wolves, of which there appeared to be great numbers. We did not travel any before noon on account of the rain. At 1 P.M. we started, and travelled nearly all the afternoon without meeting any signs of wood & water, except a few mud holes. We began to think our chances of finding a good place for camping rather slim, when toward night we came upon a very pretty little stream — narrow but deep — with a little timber. On the bank was a newly made grave, with a board at its head on which were the letters M. W. It was a beautiful camping ground, but the grass having been fed off, we filled our water cask, took some wood, and went back a short distance from the stream to camp.

The I-80 is terrifying — you can see nothing but the flow of the traffic or else you'll be wearing it. Flatbeds with great coils of metal and long metal bars, every type and colour of semi that's ever hit the road. Four-lane divided highway, paved shoulder with a rumble strip, but the road with grass right up to the edge of the left-hand lane. Pull out too far when you're passing, and you're carving up lawn. We're heading west again after 81's ruler-straight jag to the north, making the top side of a triangle toward Fort Kearney while Dodge had taken the long side that follows the bottomlands of the Little Blue River. But there's no way to stay with the Little Blue, because no road goes that way.

When he reaches the Platte near what's now Grand Island, we're close again.

We cross the river, wide and shallow and sandy, before we reach Grand Island. We're ahead of him now, crossing the flatlands on roads that overlay Kansas and Nebraska in what looks, from the helicopter eye of the map, like something close to a perfect grid. It doesn't match well with Dodge's route through river valleys, his trail following watercourses that the roads now simply bridge and cross.

<hr />

May 20, 1849

In accordance with the desire of most of the company, particularly Drury and myself, we laid over today. The morning was spent by most of us in washing up and changing clothes, after which the two Smiths went to try for some fish, leaving the rest of us to take care of the camp, sleep etc., which time I improved by writing this & reading a few choice books that I had with me. A small shower of rain at noon, with a very strong wind, which has not abated for the last 24 hours, in the least. It was my watch again the forepart of last night & if ever there was a time for <u>thought</u>, it was then. To take one's gun and blanket & go off from the tent among the mules, when it was so dark you can't see one of them two rods off — without

knowing anything of who or what is near you, is not quite
as pleasant as a good bed at home! Still there is an interest
— a wild excitement in this kind of life, which can never
be found amid the tame scenes of fashionable life — and
more than all else is the sublime grandeur of these plains
or prairies. Turn our eyes whichever way we will, and
nothing but one boundless vast and extended plain meets
our view! Not a human habitation; not a hill, nor forest,
nor valley, nor mountain stream — not even a single living animal is anywhere to be seen! Save here and there
a little clump of stunted oaks, and in the far off distance
the white covers of some emigrant's wagon looking like
a distant sail, not a speck breaks the even horizon! How
truly grand is the sight! Gentle swells of the prairie with
its carpet of unspotted green, extending on every appearance, is one of the grandest sights I ever saw! No language
can describe it — no painting can resemble it. It seems as
though vastness, grandeur, and sublimity had here combined to exhibit some of Nature's works in their best and
grandest light. When persons talk of there being teams
sufficient to reach across these plains, it is evident they
have no more correct idea of their extent than they have
of Heaven! Rainy, storming all day.

⬦⬦⬦⬦⬦⬦

We've crossed the Platte River eight or nine times. It spreads out like
a fan through the flat bottomlands. On the map, from above, the fan
looks like the back of a great and old hand, tributaries and courses
spread out like myriad veins and capillaries.

⬦⬦⬦⬦⬦⬦

May 22, 1849
Hitched up in good season & started again. On the riverbank we saw another new grave. A little farther on we

75

came across a party of four men with one wagon, who had their whole team — two ponies, two horses, & two mules — all stolen by the Indians the night before! Two of them about 8 P.M., while the men were at supper rode in among their stock, & frightened them so they broke loose and then followed them off. In addition to this their fore axle was broken. At some time game must have been very plenty here, as we saw a great many Elk horns, some of them of enormous size — three or four inches in diameter — lying scattered along the road. We got along finely & passed 16 ox teams. At night we camped near a small stream where the extensive swell of the prairie, more flat than heretofore, appeared bounded by a kind of ledge which reached around to the right out of sight. Saw two more graves here. Weather becoming warm and fine. Saw mosquitoes here for the first time.

◇◇◇◇◇◇◇◇

The Fort Kearny state historical site is empty. We are 18 minutes late arriving, and it's closed up tight, its low brown buildings surrounded by broad swathes of neatly trimmed grass. Dodge is approaching the same place, though he was there long enough ago that he still mostly uses the fort's original name, Fort Childs.

The state historical site has split-rail fences, and, if that's not bound-in enough, fields of corn march right up to the roads on all sides. There are mourning doves calling from the cornfields, swallows shooting out from under the eaves. There are no lights in the men's room, and the tall standing urinals — like the ones I can remember from grade school — are full of crickets who came seeking water and now can't escape the slick of wet enamel. A crab apple tree drops tiny apples all around us, as if it alone has been waiting all day for our arrival.

There's a light, misty rain falling, the scrim of it caught in the cottonwoods, and though the parking lot is empty, the windless warm air adds to the feeling of waiting for something. Leslie smokes a cigarette.

76

The tiny crab apples patter down on the car's roof, roll awkwardly, their stems interfering, until they line up in a straight rank all along the windshield wipers.

∞∞∞∞∞

May 23, 1849

The past night cold — very cold winds nearly all the time since we started, from the N. & N.E. Appearance of rain this morning. Started before 7 and went about 3 miles when we came to a beautiful stream of water which was very difficult to cross; the bank was very steep and the road narrow, but as usual, so far, we crossed without an accident. The banks of this stream were lined with cotton-wood and other trees with luxuriant foliage, and on the bank near where we crossed was one of the most delight-ful situations I ever saw. The ground descended from a point near the road on each side, & the trees were low and shady, and covered with bits of paper stuck up by compa-nies with the time of their crossing and their condition, for the information of those of their friends who were behind. Just after crossing the stream, a little to the right of the road, was the grave of one of the St. Louis Company. The roads are fine & smooth & the feed pretty good, though eaten close at the best camping grounds. The timber of which we have seen none scarcely is becoming more plenty along the streams, another of which we crossed at 3 P.M. Here we passed 7 ox teams camped & a little far-ther on 14 mule teams. We camped at a pretty good place — plenty of wood and water. Today, we met an ox team returning to the creek with a man very sick.

May 24, 1849

Started in good season & proceeded a short distance when we met a small company who was starting back — having had enough of the expedition. We passed 3 teams, part of the Milwaukee Company, and near the road we saw another grave which appeared to have been made by one of the earliest companies — beside this we saw one other today. Stopped at noon, where we met another company with one wagon-ox team returning. The mail carrier passed while here & reported that several teams and persons have been destroyed by the Indians — not very pleasant news, but we are bound to go ahead for all that. Weather cold, windy, & rainy. Fine camp with nice water.

◇◇◇◇◇◇

Chapter 6

Kearny (or Kearney), Nebraska

Kearney is the sandhill crane capital of the world. It takes me a few minutes to process that claim to fame. Everything needs its own particular bookmark, it seems.

The town's name is the result of constant misspelling. The town was named after Col. Stephen W. Kearny (later a Major-General), who had started building an outpost in 1846 in a different location to protect the emigrant travellers near the mouth of Table Creek. Unfortunately, the post wasn't on any of the trail routes. After moving to the location on Grand Island, the soldier charged with the construction, Lieut. Daniel Woodbury, named the new outpost Fort Childs after his father-in-law who had achieved some distinction in the Mexican–American War. The army ordered the name changed back to Kearny, but the town ended up being called Kearney because it was misspelled so often by the mail service.

Why point all this out? It's all about what's in a name — the arbitrary nature of simply arriving and deciding what everything would be called, as if by arriving, they'd invented the place, and all other names, any other history, has simply been retired.

Some pieces of history get the star treatment — on I-80 just before Kearney, we pass under the Great Platte River Road Archway, 1,500 tonnes and, originally, $60 million of Disney-designed museum and monument. It claims to have Nebraska's longest escalator and showcases the region's history, a history that arbitrarily starts with the Lewis and Clark Expedition and the first expansion of the settlers across the Great Plains. It went bankrupt in 2013 — in part, many believed, because the facility didn't have its own off-ramp from the highway. It does now, after $20 million in public investment.

It's hard to believe a facility designed to commemorate a pathway to the West didn't recognize the need to have a pathway of its own.

The arch has since reopened; as the *Kearney Hub* newspaper wrote at the time, "The mission of The Archway is to memorialize the history of the Great Platte River Road and to provide educational facilities, programs, and materials that will demonstrate the route's significance in the continuing development of the American West." The mission statement seems to have forgotten that there was little more than a footnote's mention of thousands of years of Native American habitation of this land. Fifteen different Native Peoples of the Great Plains may have called Nebraska home, but you have to go looking for that kind of information. It isn't offered up easily.

In its history section, the city of Kearney begins with the settlers: Nebraska may be an Otoe word, meaning "flat water," but Kearney's all about the conqueror.

Fittingly, the arch in the misspelled city also has a misidentified mascot, Archie the Buffalo.

Buffalo are actually bison; the word came to North America when English explorers saw the beast, using the name already used to identify species like water buffalo even though bison already had a name.

We make all kinds of things — from family lore to the official historical record — into what we want them to be. Into what we want to see and how we want to see it. And how we want to be seen. And Leslie and I are doing it too, changing viewpoints, looking at the horizon slightly differently. With every day, every mile.

∞◇∞◇∞

May 25, 1849
Last night we had one of the most tremendous storms that

I ever saw — the wind blew a perfect hurricane — the rain fell in torrents — while peal after peal & flash after flash continued in succession for more than two hours. I expected that there would be not a mule or wagon left by morning, but thanks to a protecting Providence, when the morning dawned, we found everything in safety.

The mules turned their heels to the storm, while the horses laid flat down with their noses close to the ground — it was terrible indeed. After travelling a few miles we came to the Big Blue River, a stream several rods wide & just up to the wagon beds. Our first team crossed in safety, but the second became tangled from careless driving & for some time the leaders were in imminent danger of being drowned. Ingalsbee jumped in to wade, but got into a deep hole, from which with a little difficulty he swam out. After 4 or 5 of us having been in the water up to our waists for near half an hour we got them out safely. We continued on until quite late, having passed five more graves today.

Right off the highway in Kearney, we poke through the Stage Coach Gift Shop, the front facade like a movie-set saloon, a fixture on the edge of town since 1973.

"Where are you from?" and "Why are you here?" are standard introductions in any place that deals with transient visitors. The gift shop is no different, with the owner, Gary Glandon, at the counter talking about Canada and telling us he's never been to Newfoundland. The store's dripping with Westernalia, though it's also the kind of place that sells everything from mineral samples to mugs emblazoned with every name the manufacturer can think of, to scores of T-shirts with wolves on their fronts.

Mostly though, it's jewellery: Native American and turquoise jewellery, along with everything from Native American pottery to moccasins. I read recently that sales of traditionally made Native American jewellery and clothing are dropping off, as prospective buyers are afraid of being accused of cultural appropriation. It's the law of unintended consequences. Scented soap and bath salts, Himalayan rock salt lamps, and rock candy on sticks don't seem to be suffering the same fate.

Glandon doesn't relish what the 49ers experienced: "They said it was really a lot harder — the big storms rolling in on the prairies and everything."

Dodge had different views of wolves and Native Americans, clearly — and the romance of the western adventure? It's far more romantic now, far less sheer toil, than when he was crossing the prairie. Dodge tallies graves like a kind of gruesome milepost — deaths by misadventure, by typhoid and cholera and other diseases, by disputes and thefts and attack and weakness due to failing food supplies. His was a granular look at a far greater number of emigrant deaths. And the deaths didn't end when the trail did either — accidents and cholera stalked the goldfields as well. Worth noting though? Some estimates set the number of Indigenous deaths as a result of the gold rush at as high as 120,000, easily eclipsing the 49er deaths, which number in the thousands.

<><><><><>

May 27, Sunday, 1849

Last night a man from Racine Co., Wis., who had been out nearly to Fort Childs, from which we are now distant about 100 miles, and was returned on account of having lost part of their oxen by a stampede, remained with us till morning, by whom we wrote back. He reports the road as being completely filled with teams for 20 miles ahead. This morning Maj. Cross with a small escort passed us on his way to take charge of the troops which are 30 or 40 miles ahead destined to form new military posts & to assist the emigrants. All the teams in sight are moving.

We laid by till noon, then moved on to find water — came
to a good little stream in 2 ½ miles, watered up, and went
on. Very difficult finding good grass, it has been so fed off.
Here we came to a few miles, 3 or 4, of wet prairie. The
road — aside from this & the want of bridges, is as fine as
I ever saw. All well except that I have a bad cold.

<><><><><>

There's an 11- or 12-year-old girl across from us in the Mexican food
restaurant, while her brother — maybe four years old — gets yelled
at for misbehaving. She has a thousand-yard stare that absolutely can't
be broken, staring straight past us and out into the Kearney twilight
as if she has the ability to tune the world around her out completely.

The yelling finally culminates with the woman who appears to be
his grandmother turning the boy's chair around so he faces away from
their table, his back to the family and his own plate while almost everyone else eats. The squeal of the chair legs is harsh on the beige-glazed
terracotta tiles. The air goes out of our side of the restaurant, the windows dark with the late evening, so looking out only throws your own
guilty face right back at you.

The boy kicks his feet limply, toes frustratedly battering the air. He
doesn't speak, but tears pop from the corners of his eyes and run down
his face. He's got a cast on his left arm, white and dirty-edged, that no
one has signed. Everyone is eating mechanically now, rice and beans
going into mouths like coal into unforgiving furnaces. Everyone eating, that is, except the girl. Her hands are in her lap, her fork set next
to her plate. She's looking out toward the highway exit ramp, her eyes
unfocused, as if imagining getting away to anywhere but here.

Nothing quite like a family night out.

The restaurant must have once been something else, but I can't
put my finger on exactly what: the wooden captains' chairs and heavy
tables have the feeling of a franchise forced into a chain's design mould.
Orange wall paint and unnecessarily ornate archways are built into the
unforgiving rectangular confines of a strip mall slot. This bathroom's a

leftover, just like St. Louis was, black paint everywhere and bright fixtures, adding "bar" to "franchise restaurant" in this location's lengthy and rotating resume.

The wait staff and kitchen rattle along busy and loud, the easy handoff between them the mark of people who know the job, and each other, well. More familial, in fact, than the family next to us. I've worked in places like this and been absolutely broken-hearted to leave. Do some of us do that to fill a gap? To address a human need that we haven't even fully articulated to ourselves? My family never felt like it was lacking anything; was the lacking somehow in me?

The boy's chair eventually gets turned back to face the table, but he's left with only a few minutes to eat. All of the adults are finished and want to leave. They watch the boy's every bite. Now they are the ones who aren't speaking. The girl is still every bit of a thousand miles away.

◇◇◇◇◇◇◇

May 28, 1849

The weather has become fine again. It was my watch last night in the after part, and I am writing this sitting on a wagon & my book on my knee, just as "Old Sol" is pushing his golden face above the horizon, while every other soul is asleep! Just as I had finished the sentence . . . I looked up & 75 or 80 rods ahead, where some other company had formerly camped, I saw standing a huge wolf! Springing from the wagon I seized my rifle and hastened down a swail hard by, in hopes to get a shot — but he was too quick for me, and was soon out of sight at a brisk trot. Looking around about every rod to see if he was pursued.

This morning we took a late start, in order to give the teams a good time to feed. We had gone but a few miles, when we came up with a Co. from Missouri. Camped by a little stream, airing their flour and provisions. From them we learned that the Indians, as we supposed, had

stolen 80 head of oxen two nights before from a neighbouring camp — and that about 40 miles in advance,
the Camanches were up on the route, plundering all that
came in their way. Soon after passing them we saw three
antelopes — the first game yet except plovers and a few
prairie hens. A little farther on we started up another wolf,
which, after a smart chase by Ingalsbee on his horse, we
left. The weather has become warm and fine, and today
seems more as I had imagined our trip would than any
since starting. We camped at a fine place on the bank of
the Little Blue, which is from 6 to 10 yards wide — deep
and rapid — & resembles the water of the Mississippi.
Nearby was camped 3 U.S. soldiers, one of whom was
sick, and all of them started next morning to overtake the
advance troops. Did not get a very early start — hindered
by butchering an ox, which had given out & been left on
the plains by emigrants, for his hide to make picket ropes
for the mules. During the day we killed another, which
supplied us plentifully with ropes. We saw several lying
dead by the road having been completely worn out.

We find no game yet except occasionally a far-off deer
— a few small ducks, with plenty of plovers — none of
which we kill. By the roadside we have today seen several
buffalo skulls — the first indication of their ever having
been in this section.

The soil has become sandy and more broken. We
travelled till noon along the bank of the Little Blue, then
took a cut across the hills & struck it again toward night
when we met four loads of buffalo robes from the Rocky
Mountains — 22 days out from Fort Laramie. The course
of the river may be seen by the row of trees which everywhere lines its borders. Its banks are deeply indented in
the soil and its current swift. Poor feed & just ahead of us
is camped about 100 teams of oxen and mules.

May 31, 1849

Took a very early start again to keep ahead of the crowd.
Roads bad — weather cold and stormy. Passed a camp
toward night where a woman had just died — she had
eaten heartily the previous night of what they supposed to
be mushrooms. A drove of antelope came past at noon but
we could not get a shot — they looked beautiful indeed.
Met another team returning, besides large numbers of
deserters from the Army, a day's march in advance of us.
Camped early with good feed — no wood or water — a
deserter came into camp & we gave him something to eat
and lodging! In coming this far we have passed through
first the Iowas — next the Sacs & Foxes, the Kicapoos,
and now we are in the Ter'y of the Pawnees — none of
whom we have seen they having gone to the Platte River,
where they are now at war with the Sioux.

May of 1849 was particularly cold and wet: records kept at Fort Kearny
indicated an unusual 11 inches of rain fell that month, with thunder-
storms and hail three inches in diameter. The emigrant trail was soft
and muddy, the mosquitoes thick, forage for the animals late in coming.

It's a different world for us, the creature comforts comparatively
obvious.

Still, I feel like we're driving on the new emigrant trail — the
Kearney motel we're in, the Western Inn South, is the third one we've
been at that's managed by people from India, on land that was taken
from a people that were mistakenly called Indians because explorers thought they'd reached the backside of a completely different
continent.

It's a bit of a brain twister. Even more of a brain twister? That
people who were themselves immigrants to "the new world" are now
so opposed to, well, immigrants. William Castle Dodge's family came

from England; my father's family, from the Ukraine, making their way through Ellis Island shortly before the Russian revolution, my grand-father's name uniquely and phonetically transcribed from Ukrainian by an immigration official so that backwards lineage is difficult, if not impossible. Dad was a big kid, but grew up a "squarehead," the child of Eastern European parents, in a predominantly Italian neighbour-hood in Woonsocket, Rhode Island — and was relentlessly picked on because of his family origins. My mother told me her father didn't have time for immigrants, though his three sons-in-law at one point were a Wangersky, a Radomski, and a Gagliardi. Yet every single per-son except Indigenous North Americans is an immigrant, all of us moving from the old world to the new.

There must be a point when where we are magically becomes the place where we're from. How deep do those roots have to set? Not belonging takes a toll, even if you're not willing to admit it. Being classed as an outsider builds a wall.

I lived in the tightly knit province of Newfoundland and Labrador for 35 years but was still identified as a "come-from-away," clearly rec-ognized as being not from the province, most often because of my last name. Often, it was more curiosity than malice. For Newfoundland and Labradorians, the question "Who are you from?" is about estab-lishing who your parents are and fitting you into your spot in the relatively small provincial firmament. But not being "from" an accept-able place does cut.

Two months after I moved to a new job in Saskatchewan, a columnist at one of my papers asked if I was part of the big family — which big family? The Ukrainian diaspora. As he wrote in an email, "Brother! I might — just might — be able to overlook that you're in management. My father's family is from Galacia and my mom was born east of Gdansk." And I can't explain why that strange, tangential belonging felt so very good.

Since I moved, not one single person has heard my name and said, "You're not from here." For 35 years, I could hear it on any given day.

Outside the front of the Western Inn South, a woman sits in a white plastic patio chair. She's brilliantly colourful in a yellow sari, like an exotic bird against the western beiges and sedges, the asphalt greys and the stucco.

I ask her about rates for the night and she motions to the lobby door, then summons a man with better English to the desk.

The Western Inn is a bit of a relic. There's a metal fixture on the door that, when you twist a knob to the left, makes a sign outside the door read "Maid Request." Twist to the right, and the window reads "Do Not Disturb." It's a PRI-VA-CEE Art Deco A-100, made by Pride Barco Lock Co., the sort of vintage device that crops up on eBay for ridiculous prices and finds its way into movies as a device to make period pieces look right. The bathroom door is splintered, the surface veneer peeling off in great triangles that look for all the world like wooden flames: the door from the room to the parking lot has been kicked in, the frame repaired with both nails and lashings of plastic wood. Police? Thieves? An angry boyfriend or ex-husband looking for proof of infidelity? I've never been angry enough to kick in a hotel room door.

Lots of questions, few answers.

Breakfast is free, but it's juice and cereal and coffee, all on a narrow stretch of counter built into the hall next to the front desk. None of it seems appetizing.

Meanwhile, there's a crew of pavement sealing guys in town for roadwork, staying a few doors down the row of motel units from us.

The pavement sealing guys are going to fill cracks in the parking lot, along with the cracks between the pavement squares and along the side of the motel. The boss says he doesn't see why anyone would have the spaces between the pavement stones filled, but he's game to do it anyway: "Free rent for the next three days, you can't beat that." The barter system in full force, flying beneath the taxman's radar. A bit of a wild west tradition right there.

An empty restaurant next door is being gutted down to the metal studs so it can be rebuilt and reopened as yet another restaurant. A dumpster is full of shiny twisted metal that's been hauled out and thrown away, all of it on top of a base layer of broken sheets of Gyprock. Family restaurants must churn through the families that own and run them as easily as they churn through buildings, trashing hopes and dreams along the way. Dumpsterloads of perfectly good building materials, just thrown away. All before the next hopeful family arrives at the door, following their own trail of dreams, to start the process all over again.

◇◇◇◇◇◇◇

June 1, 1849

Continually meeting teams returning. Reports of 7,500 teams ahead with poor prospects of getting through. Provisions etc. being thrown away to lighten their loads. Cold stormy weather — very disagreeable indeed, & no wood to make campfires. Roads bad from frequent rains — started at 6, & at 9 the hills skirting the bottom lands of the Platte began to loom up & at 10 ½ we were at the bottom along which we kept all the afternoon within a mile or so of the river, though the water cannot be seen from the road. There is no wood on the side (south) of the river, but plenty of short grass. Along the bank the grass is all worn off by the great number who have camped there. Saw one grave. Two on the riverbank here. We are now within a few miles of Fort Childs. Just as we passed a small stream the 30th, we saw lots of prickly pears. Antelope are becoming numerous & this evening for the first time one of the emigrants saw a buffalo — he was being hunted by the Indians, a beautiful evening.

◇◇◇◇◇◇◇

Starlings flock into the corn next to Fort Kearny the next morning, swarming down and, at the last moment, kiting up to shed their forward momentum before dropping completely out of sight among the dry stalks. It's quiet at the reconstructed historical site, the air almost motionless, on the edge of light rain.

By the time Dodge reached the fort in June, 1849, Lt. Woodbury wrote that 4,000 wagons had already passed that year alone. How tightly condensed the timeframe was. By 1875, the fort had been torn down and only the cottonwoods and some of the groundworks were left. Everything has been rebuilt. It doesn't look that way, the low buildings full of everything from Mormon handcarts to the kind of short wagons that the 1849 emigrants used to carry their supplies.

The last original cottonwood was 150 years old when it finally toppled in 1998. It's been lying where it fell, rotting, alongside and overlapping the asphalt path that runs down one side of the parade ground.

"I don't know why they don't clean that up," a woman says to her teenaged son as they walk up the quadrangle of newer, younger cottonwoods. They seem surprised that I'm taking pictures of what's essentially a giant rotting log.

The big tree is breaking down: gnarled and barkless, its girth dwarfs the newer trees, a carcass like a whale beached and rotting. By now, the rain is steady, the drops still very fine and beading up on the blades of grass. They coalesce and then drip from the cottonwood leaves, a fat, cold surprise down the back of your neck.

I won't discover until later that the decaying parts of that tree are the only real remaining feature of 1849's Fort Kearny.

◇◇◇◇◇◇◇

June 2, 1849

Fine morning — started late and drove up to the fort & camped near Dr. White's Co. Opposite us is the Boston Co., selling off their outfit at ¼ cost preparing to pack. A good deal of consternation exists on account of the number going — half of whom it is said by the guides, can never get through the mountains. Many are throwing away their bacon and provisions — good wagons are sold for $10! Rifles for $1.50 etc. The commissary informs us that there are 6,500 teams and 30,000 persons. We let some of the bacon to be carried at the halves & our little wagon we let a man take who agrees to pay us for it if he is able when he gets there or to give us half of what he can sell it for. He is from Wisconsin — family with him. The valley of the Platte, where we first strike it, is fine in appearance. Some time before reaching it the row of sand hills that shuts in the bottom land of the river from the rolling land of the prairie raises in sight & in the distance looks beautiful — the bottom is about 3 miles wide, level with sandy soil. On this side of the river there is not a stick of timber, but on the other side there is a narrow belt of trees. Ft. Kearney, formerly Ft. Childs is on the S. bank of the river opposite Grand Island, on a strip of land 60 miles in length & 20 wide, which the government has purchased of the Indians, and is composed of a number of turf houses, an enclosure surrounded with a ditch, and one frame house just erected; the garrison is small.

❧

Inside the reception centre at Fort Kearny, we get corralled into watching a short video on the region's history: it's a dark room with hard chairs, seating for about 30 people, but we're the only ones there. It plays in a cycle, all day long. I'm fidgeting, chasing lost change that's fallen from my pocket when I pull out my phone. Beside me, I can feel Leslie starting to get agitated. The video is supposed to be an 18-minute highlight of the historic site, but each passing minute is making Leslie angrier.

When it finally ends, and the lights brighten the room with a soft yellow glow, Leslie turns to me and says, "Where's the story of the people who were already here?" The movie has erased the people who lived here before the white settlers, has turned them into just another imminent danger along a trail of glory. Not unlike Dodge did in his own words, when he was setting out.

I don't have an answer.

"I'm going to ask," Leslie says.

She has a "tell," the kind of thing that poker players watch for to get hints about the hands their opponents might be holding. When she's spoiling for a fight, when she's going into an argument she intends to win no matter how nasty it gets, she tilts her head back just slightly so that she's literally leading with her chin. Ready to hit; ready to get hit. You can see it every time if you know her well enough to look for it.

She passes me in the narrow aisle between the rows of chairs. Her eyes are flashing — and her chin is well out there now. As she heads purposefully for the reception desk, I step outside into the misty rain, making my way into the buildings filled with haphazard remnants of what the settlers likely couldn't carry any longer and were getting ready to throw away. I linger by a Mormon handcart, a short, two-wheeled wagon that allowed an individual settler to haul heavy goods without horse or mule.

The Mormon carts hauled every possession its owner carried. Leslie and I have so many possessions that I have an urge to explain what things might be important after we're gone, and I start a letter to the kids. It's more haphazard than I might have expected, flitting from thing to thing as I let my memory travel around the property.

A note to our kids:

It occurs to me that we will eventually be gone, and you will be left to sort everything out. This is a message, a map maybe, about some of the things in the house, and what you're supposed to do with them. Or at least about some of the history they have.

The bird skull on the wall in the room by the back door is from a gannet.

Holly Hogan told me that, and she's a birder, so it's probably right. She told me about the eggshell, mostly intact, near the window too

— gull, one side pecked open by a predator and cleaned out — and I've found lots more of those since and brought some of them home.

But that's not the point.

The point is that, if you're reading this, you're trying to figure it all out. What's important. What isn't. And you won't figure it out — I wish you could, but it's not likely to happen. There's just too much information that you don't have — too many things that you and I both will wish you would have asked about, but always thought we would have time for later.

My mother scuba-dived in salt lakes in Washington, doing research. I found that out years after she was gone. We cleaned out my parents' house to sell it after she died, hurrying, with no one left to tell us what anything meant. We knew the importance of some things: Mom's knives from L.L. Bean, Dad's stainless steel Italian coffee maker (the stovetop one we called The Volcano for the sound it made), but so many things suddenly lacked any explanation. Things left in places that showed they had some importance. But why were they? "Where" is much easier. "Why?" becomes ever so much harder when there's no one left to ask.

So this is an incomplete list. I'll add to it now and then if things strike me.

Wondering about the bits of bricks that are scattered everywhere? Good question. They're all different sizes, rounded by the ocean. We started collecting them, I'm not sure why, but I would keep them — there's a comfort in things that endure the harshest situations. But you don't have to. The gin bottle with the slim hips and the wide shoulders? It's just a nice bottle that someone gave me once for doing them a favour. The gin was worth much more than the favour. The marine compass on the same shelf, like the bottle, has lost all of its alcohol, but it will still find north if you hold it flat. I bought it for Leslie, so she'd always know the way.

There's a miniature cupboard on the wall in the dining room. It's got all kinds of tiny pewter objects: teapots and spoons and even samovars. It was Leslie's mother's — we've had it for years, but

93

I think we might have accidentally vacuumed up a spoon or two. They're missing, anyway, even though we cut open the bag in the vacuum cleaner and searched through dust and dirt like thorough detectives working a murder case.

Keep the picture of the canola field and the aspen or poplar trees. It was a wedding present from the artist, and it's important. Leslie's history is all piled up in there, it's like a kind of *Reader's Digest* version. It's Margaret and Ian's farm.

On the shelf nearby is a silver cigarette case with a monogram — that's from Leslie's family. And there's a folded photocopy of a poem about fireweed, right near the wall. It is Leslie's mantra, she says it out loud every year when the fireweed is high and purple in the yard.

The huge, toothed clamshell in the bathroom. Keep that. You'll never see another. Mom found it diving, 50 or 60 years ago at least. But don't take it across any borders: it's like ivory now, an endangered species, and if you were to take it anywhere, they'd seize it. Mom brought it into the country in 1965 — things were easier then, even for giant clams. Nothing you can do with it now to change the state of the world, or even protect the species, but don't get caught.

The lobster-claw cigarette lighter was bought for Leslie's brother Doug. We couldn't figure out how to get it through air travel in our carry-on. There's an assembly of car parts that's a bottle opener that Cait's husband Clay made. A crystal vinegar decanter with a glass plug — that came from Spain. The cream-coloured coffee grinder with the red spots originally belonged to my parents. When I was in grade school, it woke me up every morning, the sound of Dad grinding coffee beans from the Java Blend. You wouldn't know the Java Blend — it was a wholesale coffee shop in Halifax — it specialized in making huge bags of coffee for ship's crews to take on voyages. Dad convinced them to sell coffee in small bags. They tolerated his requests, didn't realize how far ahead of his time he was, that he was already looking for gourmet coffee in 1972. So, keep the coffee grinder. There are only four screws holding it to the wall. But they are long screws, the black wide-thread Gyprock screws that bite. It takes more torque than you think to grind coffee.

The dark wood umbrella stand/coat rack/mirror in the front hall? Don't let anyone get that off you cheap. The big bow-topped travel chest in the upstairs hall? When we bought that at a yard sale, the owner was going into a care home and we bargained the price down, not knowing that we'd find a Polaroid of a small blonde girl in the bottom of the trunk. We've always wondered who she was. No one to ask.

We got the wooden spirit level on the same day, and the two-handed crosscut saw in the hall as well. My grandmother Anna Kozak Wangersky's picture is on top of the CD player — she looks haunted. My father took that picture. It is the only one of her that I know of that exists. If you keep it, she exists for a little longer too. She died in Florida, years ago, speaking urgent dementia-driven Ukrainian to the uncomprehending night nurses. My grandfather died not long afterwards, leaving bags and rolls of American coins in the closets, in the crawlspace, the attic, rolled in paper sleeves and wrapped in yellowing masking tape. Some of those coins are in my office, in the white-coloured coin purse with the brass zipper. They've been mixed in with some of the coins collected by Mom's relatives: somewhere along the way, one of the oldest ones, a silver dollar worn almost perfectly flat, disappeared. I think I know who took it, and when, but there's no point in saying. Perhaps they thought I'd never notice. But that's exactly the thing: the archivist always knows the archive best, can put his finger on the file, knows all the related material. Until the archivist is gone.

(That coin pouch? There's a well-worn half-dollar in there that dates almost back to Dodge's trip — 1859 — and a big American penny from 1855. I can almost imagine the coins travelling somehow between Dodge and Konstanty Wangersky, through chains of hands and pockets. I love looking at worn coins, trying to imagine their travels.)

◇◇◇◇◇◇

June 3, Sunday, 1849
Having agreed the night before to reduce our baggage
Sun. to 100 pounds each, and throw away the surplus, we
borrowed a pair of steelyards & commenced the work, as
we were compelled to move on 12 miles to overtake the
men who had agreed to take part of our load.

But little sickness, though a man died nearby last
night. Holcombe threw away a fine trunk valise — Bogus
a trunk & Low sold a fine trunk that cost $25, for 2 ½. Had
for supper some antelope killed by our friend — best meat
I ever saw — Weather is splendid.

June 4, 1849
Rather dubious times — put all our load into the two
wagons and put six mules on each — started about 1/2
past 10 & continued along the bottom of the Platte, coming close to the bank of the stream for the first time this
afternoon — stream rapid — full of islands & sand bars
& looks like the Missouri. Along here the road is lined
with teams — more than 100 in sight, some moving and
others camped. Government train of 250 wagons & 500
riflemen, mostly mounted, is a short distance ahead,
moving slowly for 400 head of cattle behind to overtake
them. This afternoon we killed a small rattlesnake, the
first we have seen. Drury kept the rattles. Saw thistles
for nearly the only time yet. Fine grass but no wood.
Met 6 teams loaded with furs, owned by a man who has
lived 18 years in the mountains & who does not give us
much encouragement. All that can are throwing away
their wagons and packing. This morning we met three
teams returning — they lost 3 men within a few days —
cholera or dysentery.

◇◇◇◇◇◇

There is more, I write, of what to do with the stuff. What to sell — or like Dodge, throw away as surplus.

I asked my dad to bring me back the Russian pins in the wooden box on the mantle when he went to Moscow long before the Wall fell, during the Cold War. There were six on the card originally, but now there are only five. The five that remain have never left the backing paper; the sixth was on one of my jackets when it was stolen. This is all background, and I don't know how much of it is necessary.

There are boxes all over the house, and all of the boxes have things in them: pocketknives, rocks, handfuls of stamps, fishing lures. There's an oxidized gold-coloured "Mr. Champ" spoon lure with a single hook instead of a treble: it's caught more mackerel off the finger pier in Brooklin, Maine, than you can possibly count. It's heavy, casts well. Dad took the treble hook off because it was tearing up mackerel that were too small to keep. He would stand on the pier out in front of the yacht club, the only one fishing other than me, and up above us, the summering set from Washington, D.C., would watch us like we were the most curious middle-class specimens. They didn't clean their own fish, ever. We cleaned it, scaled it, cooked it, ate it. Oh, and Dad's fish knife, the Russell knife with the leaf-shaped blade, is in my blue knapsack, hanging on a nail in the furnace room.

In one of the open slots in my writing desk — left-hand side, halfway up — there's a bundle of letters from my parents tied with white string. If you want to hear their voices, you can read a few. They were good at that, writing as if they were speaking, so you can hear a little of their voices, even if you won't hear them talking quite the way I do.

The tools are tools: they are all useful. If I were going to keep only a few, I'd pick the brown wood-handled screwdriver, the drop-forged tack hammer, the counter-punch with the crosshatches ground into the metal all around the shaft — they were my mother's. She knew what she was doing. Things like the big monkey wrench are pretty much for show, but every now and then, they are the perfect tools for one job. I have two of the blue Lee Valley cat's paws. If you ever need to replace clapboard, they are the most necessary tools in the world. With a cat's paw and a hammer, you can have a rotten clapboard off the house in minutes, barely marking up the row above it.

Don't be distracted by all the stuff in the shed. A lot of it isn't anything to do with us. I don't know whose dog collar is hanging on a nail over the workbench, or where the girly calendars came from. The punches and awls were ours, and the sheep skull, of course, from the time I found the spread-out cushion of wool and the whole skeleton as if a sheep had exploded on Small Point. The bolts and nuts and railway spikes from the 1915 railway spur? Those we found, and you guys ran some of them through the grinder until they shone, though I don't expect you to remember that. The blue enameled cup on the nail? Your guess is as good as mine. But good friends bought us the rubber raft in there, and even though it's hopeless to try and steer, you should keep it.

There's chapter and verse I could tell you about the canoe and the kayak, but I hope you already know about that.

Axes and axe heads: they all have a story. The axe near the woodpile is the one most often in my hands, the right weight. There are two axe heads, one closer to a hatchet, that were part of the package deal for the brass coalscuttle. There's another one, much older, that came from the ocean in Broad Cove. The big splitting axe and the one in the front shed where the head is loose on the shaft are more for show than anything else. The splitting axe is too heavy, and the plastic handle is unwieldy: when you have something with a twisted grain, like tamarack, it can be great, but for everything else, it's too much work for too little return.

The scattered metal along the back of the workbench, all blades and ice picks, are the things you guys made on the bench grinder during that period when we could hardly keep a screwdriver that wasn't on the way to being converted into a shank. They may feel familiar in your hands, though I learn more and more that memories from childhood distill down into more of a sense of wellbeing — or not — than anything else.

I'm going to throw out the length of heavy pipe we used as a fireworks launcher until a white star from the Glitter Sky Octopus came out the bottom of the pipe in a wavering arc and landed on the soft skin of the crook of my left elbow, where it stuck and burned a spectacular blackened hole, and Iz made me lie about it. Your rock hammers and safety glasses are in the utility room in town, and there are a pair of matching sheath knives there as well, Scandinavian with wooden handles, that belonged to my brother Charles and me. Mine has the bent guard — it has left scars on both my hands, left thumb and right forefinger. Raquel's rubber octopus-tentacle finger puppets, from one of many birthday dinners, are in the green cupboard in the dining room. She may want them. I smile every time I see them. I'm making two stools — eventually — from the base of the dead maple that was the post for our clothesline on Quidi Vidi Road, the one that the merlin landed on one winter to spectacularly pull apart a starling and eat it; dry rot took out the core of the tree, but the remains are intriguing, so you may find them as well if the experiment works.

The chainsaw I wrecked by accidentally running it on pure gas is a decoy, sitting in plain sight in its fading orange plastic case in case someone decides to steal it; the newer one actually works, it's tucked out of sight under the workbench. The white bow saw with the left-hand bend in its metal handle arc? My go-to wood saw for more than 30 years, on its fourth blade as I write this. It's a bit of a wild card, moving too quickly when a blade is new and sharp and just out of its cardboard hardware store sleeve, so watch yourself. It's slightly longer than my parents' orange one was, a go-to also, but I have no idea where it ended up. Charles would know.

The lobster pot with no lid is good for, well, lobster, and the biggest frying pan can always serve as a lid. The little table in the living room in Adam's Cove is one of Leslie's treasures, and should never be left behind: the side table in the living room in town, the one with the teak criss-crossed top, was made from the floor grate of a whale boat that belonged to one of Dad's grad students. It was the only remaining piece after the boat sank at its mooring. My parents shipped it all the way to Victoria, B.C. when they moved out there. I prised out the putty over the brass screw heads, knocked it down flat with the legs jack-knifed inside, and mailed it all the way back to St. John's. Twice across the country? Clearly worth keeping.

Context is everything, and I don't have enough time to get this all down.

One example: Mom and Dad had a bolt-action shotgun, a 12-gauge with a three-shot magazine. They kept it hidden in Dad's darkroom in the Halifax house, but even as a child, I knew where it was, and I used to take it out and sight down the barrel, fascinated by the ball that served as a sight at its tip. (I once heard Dad lie to a police officer about not having a gun in the house after a neighbour's kid shot BBs through the drugstore window across from our house.) They'd gotten it in Florida when they were living there, worried about crime, and when Mom, hugely pregnant with Charles, had someone try to break in while she was home alone, she'd fired it, blowing a bird-shot-spread hole through the screen door. Mom kept it, had it tucked up under her bed in Victoria for burglars there. Once, as an adult, when I found shotgun shells in a hall closet with the hats, I told her I'd found her ammo. "No, Russ," she told me with a smile. "You found some of my ammo."

If you had only the gun, all you'd know about is the physical bare bones of it: 12 gauge, Remington, not particularly well cared for, illegal magazine, provenance unknown. When we cleared the house in Victoria, one of my brothers, George, I think, handed it over to the police.

The doorstop between the kitchen and the dining room in the Cove house is a drill bit for a highway dynamite rig — you might not remember, we found it on a vacation in a road cut in Swift Current. The stamp books? Most were Dad's, some were mine. Probably

mostly common finds, but there are some gems. Especially the numbered blocks of American stamps, the first-day issues, and all of the
mint Canadian stamps that Dad bought for years, untouched, still in
their fragile cellophane sleeves.

All, I hope, necessary information.

Or you can just get the dumpster in, set it down in the driveway
and start emptying the house, the way my brothers and I did when
Mom died. After Dad was also gone.

I shudder at the thought now.

I shudder at the thought, and also don't know what else we were
supposed to do.

There is no guidebook, except for the things you might already
know. And maybe that's what is really important anyway. I'll add
more when I think of it. It's like a road map or a diary. You can read it,
ignore it, and still just go your own way.

Dad

<<<>>>>>

June 5, 1849
Started in pretty good season and made a fine day's travel.
Passed about 30 teams — Myself quite unwell today,
Holcombe lost his dog Venus. Saw ground puppies for
the first time. They are about the size of a rabbit — of a
reddish color & their head resembles that of a bulldog —
they live in communities, like the beaver, & the entrance
to their houses underground is by a perpendicular descent
— they are quite saucy little fellows and will stand and
bark at you with their heads protruding from their sub-
terranean mansion until you approach quite near them.
Fine warm weather & feed good — camped at 5 and commenced unloading our bacon — of which together with
the boxes, we threw away about 300 lbs. Almost everyone

is lightening their loads as much as possible — retaining
nothing but barely enough provisions & necessary articles to carry them through.

∞◇◇◇◇◇∞

It turns out there wasn't much of a fight to be had about the Indigenous
Peoples absent in the Fort Kearny video.

Inside her waist-high ramparts of shelving and countertop, the
site interpreter was ready when Leslie asked where materials on
the Indigenous history were.

"I'm so glad you asked," she said, and by the time I was back
inside, Leslie has an armload of reading material. It defuses this battle,
but not the war: the further we go, the larger the public historical footprint of the settlers, and the correspondingly smaller any explanation
of sites significant to Native Americans. Signs that mark the settlers'
achievements are large and treated with deference. Later, we'll see the
very few signs commemorating important Indigenous sites marred
with graffiti and shot through with high-caliber ammunition. It's
abundantly clear that the victors get to write the winning history and
don't care to share the limelight.

What did the Sioux think of my great-great-grandfather?

They probably didn't think he was anything close to the sort of
hero he loosely casts himself as. I'm sure they would have written the
entire narrative differently — probably closer in tone to the words you
hear muttered now, as people try to hold onto the security of their own
small personal forts and lives from the new emigrant trails that flow
into America. I read the histories of Sitting Bull that Leslie's bought,
reports of the Indian Wars and the repeated failures of treaties on the
western plains, as the expanding American states offer up treaty lands
in negotiations, and then take them back when unexpected wealth is
found on them. I think about how Americans overran these lands,
brave settlers all, and are now firmly hunkered down and uncommonly
afraid that they're about to be overrun themselves.

June 6, 1849

The government train which camped just ahead of us, we passed as they were hitching up & they in turn passed us when we stopped at noon. Several of the officers have their families with them, in nice covered carriages. Poor fellows! Theirs is not an enviable position — sent off here far away from every comfort and luxury — and that for five years & may be more. Capt. Jones with whom we conversed appears to be a fine fellow and has his lady with him. Many of the recruits are young fellows who had no idea of the hardships they were to endure & are deserting at every opportunity. We saw some of the poor fellows — mere lads — who had been retaken, and were compelled to go on foot under guard. At noon we had a most tremendous thunderstorm & had rain at morning. As yet we are on the S. side of the Platte — most of the time from ½ a mile to a mile from it, with a good smooth road. The sand hills on our left grow more broken and mountainous.

June 7, 1849

Fine morning — Kept in company with the riflemen and Officer's families. Saw two buffaloes. Did not get a shot at them. One of the Buffalo was shot, first by Washington — brother to Mr. Cox — and afterwards Killed by one of Dr. White's Co., with a revolver. The Dr. with us got a piece of the meat & gave us some for supper.

Koppikus with Wash. & another went out to hunt & being separated, the other man saw a couple of Indians whom at first he mistook for white men, but soon found his mistake, for having come within about 60 yards they both fired at him at once, which he escaped by dropping on the ground — one ball cutting a hole through his hat!

He immediately fired — shooting the foremost through
the breast, the same ball knocking the other one down,
who jumped up and commenced loading. He succeeded
in loading & snapped at him three times before he got
his loaded — when he fired and shot the Indian through
the head killing him instantly, when he returned to the
wagons! Rather exciting times. Washington returned at
sundown — but brought no tidings of Koppikus. Just
at dark we saw an object which we could not make out at
the foot of the bluffs, and taking our rifles five of us went
over and found it to be a man belonging to the next camp
ahead, & who had been chasing six buffalo & lost track
of his company. About 9 Koppikus came in, having been
in pursuit of buffalo & had seen nothing of the Indians.
We are much troubled here with mosquitoes at evening &
even more during the day by a very small fly — a kind of
gnat or flea, which is constantly on our faces and in our
eyes. (Buffalo gnats).

It is a sharp and important juxtaposition: in one sentence, Dodge is
discussing the casual hunting of bison. The next, an equally casual
description of the deaths of two Native Americans — "Rather exciting
times" — and then a shift sideways into the ordinary torment of mosquitoes. It all goes by so quickly, so offhandedly, that it almost escapes
notice. The devil is, most assuredly, in the details.

There's also a detail in Dodge's diary that will become important
as the diary progresses. Dr. Thomas J. White, who Dodge mentions
in the diary only as "Dr. White" — and often just as "the Dr." —
will become a regular travelling companion of Dodge's, cropping
up regularly in Dodge's diary as he does in several other emigrant
diaries. White was from St. Louis and was heading with his family
and three slaves to trade in California — he ended up in Sacramento.
He joined the cavalry Dodge mentions after the unit's two doctors

developed cholera. Dodge and White will encounter each other regularly until Dodge heads toward the Black Rock Desert in Nevada,
leaving the doctor with the slower-moving Pioneer Line wagon train
near the Humboldt River.

◇◇◇◇◇◇

June 8, 1849

Hard thunderstorm again during the night. Fred shot at a
wolf which came close up to the camp among the mules
while he was on watch, but he did not hit him. Started as
usual & soon met a company of 7 or 8 men returning in
search of their Co., who went out hunting the previous
morning & had not returned — feared the Indians had
killed them. This morning, our dog Tiger, after we had
started, returned to where we were camped, & we have
not seen him since. Holcombe, Drury, Ferris, Chapman,
& Wainwright with Hawkins went out early in the morning to hunt buffalo. Holcombe & Wainwright stopped at
noon & after fastening their horses went to a little thicket
in the shade — where they had been but a few moments
when they heard their horses snort & looking out they
could see nothing of them. Ascending a hill, they saw
a man leading them off. They put on after him & succeeded in getting them — he pretending that the horses
were running away & he stopped them — though it was
evident that he meant to steal them having cut the strap
that fastened them & driven them where they would not
have gone of themselves — they came into camp about
6 having chased one buffalo, but got none. The rest who
were on foot did not fare quite so well — after parting
with them, they discovered 5 horsemen whom they took
for Indians ascending the hill where they were — they
holloaed and motioned to them not to advance, but they
paying no attention continued on, until Chapman Raised

his rifle, when they stopped very suddenly & for the first time the boys discovered they were white men. The Wagon Master & 4 others of the army — the boys were badly frightened — they expected to be killed, but determined to sell their lives dearly, each man was prepared to fight to the last. When the party came up they had a merry time over it indeed.

We passed a party of Texans who had just lost their Capt. & two of their men by cholera — we pass about one grave per day now. We found good feed and a fine running stream about a mile from the road near the river, besides any quantity of the most blood-thirsty mosquitoes that I ever saw — they tormented me so that it was impossible for me to sleep. It was my watch during the after part of the night & together with fighting mosquitoes & the serenading of a large pack of wolves, which dared not venture quite within shot, I passed a most interesting night (over the left)! The bottom is from one to five miles wide — & the bluffs are about the same, & the road runs from ¼ to 3 miles from the river. The whole bottom has the appearance of having formerly been covered with water, & the sides of the sand bluffs are furrowed as though they were once washed by the river, which is nothing but a broad stream of islands covered with bushes, and of sand bars. Whenever it rains the sand and earth from the bluffs tumbles down & washes into the river, thus making that constantly muddy and full of sand — and it is this probably more than any other tributary which gives the Missouri its dirty hue. The continued wear upon the sides of the bluffs has cut deep ravines, which sides nearly perpendicular, often from 20 to 100 ft. high, which run far back into the hills; frequently terminating in an abrupt precipice crowned with beautiful little cedars. This contrasts finely with the monotonous level of the bottom on the one hand & prairie on the other,

& reminds me more of the picturesque scenery of N.Y. than anything I have seen.

◇◇◇◇◇◇◇

Dodge had been shedding possessions: we're washing ours at a Kearney laundromat. Everyone's helpful: the owner has filled a washer with tokens to test the timer, and he lets us use it for free.

He's got advice about buying tokens, and one of the other patrons tells us the dryers run hot, so it will probably only take a dollar to dry our wash. That same patron is only washing blankets but finds someone else's clothes in with hers when she empties the washer. The laundromat is clean and bright, there are desks to work at and free Wi-Fi. There are televisions, one turned on with only a slight television murmur, nothing like the in-your-face, in-your-ears clatter of the music that seems always present in chain restaurants. The remote controls are chained in place so that they can't disappear, security cameras everywhere.

There's a cricket chirping loudly behind the gaming and vending machines, one of them a vintage *Gilligan's Island* pinball machine. Three balls for 50 cents, and an orange pixelated screen throws up the message "Say NO to drugs" in rotation with a badly rendered version of Gilligan's face and trademark hat. Both *Gilligan's Island* and the Reagan-era drugs slogan are a kind of cultural anchor: you fit into it if you recognize them. I want to play, but I don't want to disturb the quiet of the washers working and the dryers spinning. There's a well-thumbed Bible on a table next to the big square vending machine that lowers a claw to let you try to fish for small stuffed animals. A handful of tattered, torn, and well-read entertainment magazines.

I meet a man who has been in Kearney for seven days, travelling nonstop from Cuba through Florida to here. A small man, dark and wiry, and very polite — but, at first, cautious — as if concerned about what he's revealing, and to whom. He speaks only Spanish; I have just enough that we can communicate with broken sentences and gestures. The more we talk, the more he smiles. Grey T-shirt, cigarette, "ciao," he says, and waves when I leave. I see his pregnant wife sitting in the battered burgundy van in the heat of the sun, her feet hanging out the open door. It's got a cracked windshield, no licence plates and an "In Transit" paper registration in the front window. "In Transit" — isn't that what we all are? Their own battered carriage, heading west. There's that undercurrent again, that in every society, there's always some new group in motion, heading for better things, greener pastures that are, right now, only imagined. Economic necessity doing what the harsh truth of economic necessity always does: breaking the bonds of family, the land of opportunity trumping the extended family unit.

I wonder: what's different about this round of immigrants, heading into a new land and looking to reach their own dreams? What's wrong with the owners of the New West in Kearney or the Glenview, in Dubuque, wanting that? Why isn't their narrative also a narrative of heroes coming to a new land? Why are they invaders instead, taking over and wanting to "change our way of life?"

I guess, like always, it depends on who's telling the story.

I think you sometimes get to a point in life where you can't change horses anymore, when you don't really have new options. Having stopped moving and settled safely into your house and your job and your life, you know — even if you never consciously think it — that it's almost impossible to move to something new. You don't even think about the luck of it — the luck of even being born there in the first place, of not being forced to move to live. Maybe you begin to believe it's your right, or worse, that most awful of words, birthright.

In my work as a newspaper columnist, I hear about birthrights all the time, from people who will never, ever stop to think about what they are actually saying: that they believe a particular set of rights is conferred on them simply from the fact that they happened — completely by chance — to have been born in one place, rather than in another. That human rights, and the ability to wield them, are akin to a lottery win.

Age doesn't bring wisdom to that particular debate. Opinions harden, like arteries. And there's a reason for that.

Even if you suddenly wanted to, a day comes when it slowly dawns on you that no one really wants you anyway: you're so old that they look right by you. Eventually, experience isn't an asset anymore; it's grown large enough to have become a particular kind of millstone. Not surprising, then, that some retirees try to flip that on its head and become cases of near-constant motion.

But if you do decide to stop, get set in amber so you can't move for financial reasons, anyone who threatens your equilibrium is dangerous. They threaten you.

The low tire pressure light has come on again, as it does every day.

On the way out of Kearney, we stop at a tire shop where they finally tell us which tire is the low one. They suggest dropping the rental back for a new one, but this is hard to do when the rental pickup was so many states ago. Stopping for gas now means stopping for air as well: the two tasks dovetail well, the tire lasting about as long as a full tank's drive. It dovetails in a different way as well. When you think about it, it's one thing to be running out of gas. It's something else again to be running out of air.

∞∞∞∞∞∞

June 9, 1849

Travelled as usual about 20 miles and camped within sight of the ford — several trains on both sides & many more crossing. Holcombe bought 5 head of fat cattle of an emigrant who wished to return & drove them up to camp where we kept them until morning, when a soldier came up & informed us that they had been stolen from the army & relieved us of further trouble by driving them off! Poor feed — no wood, but a good running stream. Nothing unusual except that my previous opinion in regard to the villainy of a certain person was but too sadly confirmed by his abusive conduct toward me.

June 10, 1849

For once it has not stormed during the night. This Sun. morning we were most agreeably surprised by the discovery of about 300 buffalo feeding on the opposite side of the river. Chapman, Fred, Ingalsbee, & 2 or 3 from the other wagons, crossed over and having wounded several, drove ½ a dozen across to this side where one of them was killed by a couple of horsemen from another train. Seeing them come I mounted and rode down to see the sport, but much to my disappointment I could not reach them on account of the swampy stream that intervened, & before I could return around it, they had it finished, whereupon I rode back to camp, thus having lost a scene which of all I was most anxious to witness.

At noon we had a fine repast of milk and corn cake & for tea, warm biscuit with hot buffalo meat did not relish badly. Many of the emigrants have cows which they drive in the yoke for their milk. It is a fine plan — furnishes them with new milk and butter — than which nothing relishes better or is more healthy. The cows stand it to travel full as well as the oxen & though many fear that using their milk will cause sickness, yet we have not heard of any cases. Besides, when the weather is warm, bacon is not only very unpalatable, but in my opinion very unhealthy.

From the Fort to here, we have travelled in company with a Dr. Hardensteen, a German by birth, but now from Kentucky. He is a physician and a man of some talents. He was a student of the celebrated Baron Humboldt, who travelled so extensively in the south and west. The Dr. has been across to Panama, thence down the isthmus & through nearly all the S.A. states. In his train are 3, in addition to whom we have 6 men, 2 women, & 2 children with ox teams from Beetown, Grant Co., Wisconsin. The principal whose name is Cox is the man who has our little wagon. There are 18 of us in all. We lay over today.

Oh such sport & excitement as there was when the boys came lugging in the buffalo meat! None of them ever was close to one before, or had shot at one, & you may readily imagine how they were interested and excited by the chase! We are rather late for the buffalo, most of them having crossed the river and gone north.

Scarcely had I finished the above sentence, when there ensued one of the most exciting scenes that I ever witnessed. I sat in the tent writing, when of a sudden one of the boys cried out, "Buffalo, buffalo!" — I rushed out, and sure enough, there they were, two or three hundred of them bounding and splashing through the river a mile below us. No sooner had they touched the shore than pell mell after them came a party of horsemen, who happened to be coming along the road, turning them up the river and directly past our camp. Those who had horses mounted in "hot haste" & every man seizing his rifle, we too are soon joined in the exciting chase! None but those who have witnessed it can imagine how grand and exciting was the scene, as those grim-visaged monsters came tearing & snorting along at a rate that made the very ground tremble beneath them, with mane and tail erect — eyeballs rolling, with nose close to the ground, their mouths open and tongues protruding! I rode Low's mare — a spirited animal only four years old and poorly trained — having never seen a buffalo but once before, & then at some distance. I had to watch her so close to keep her from unhorsing me that I had a poor chance to fire. I got one shot however but without much execution though Field of our train, when standing near me and but a few rods from the tent, fired and brought down a

fine cow. Another man also rode over and caught a calf.
I rode close upon them for half a mile, the mare apparently liking the sport as much as any of us. The dragoons who were coming behind us also killed five of those we drove across the river in the morning. The best way to hunt them is on horseback, with horse pistols, as they are far more convenient, when close by, than a gun. Another drove was seen below us, just after, but having had plenty of excitement for one day we did not go after them — thus has passed this day — and that a Sabbath too! How very strange!

Cozad is an important point on the road west, but an arbitrary and invented one. It's where the 100th meridian cuts through the continent, north to south (or south to north) through the United States, a mark considered the exact dividing line between the East and the West.

It's a rectangular town, a grid set down and imposed without consideration for the ground it overlays. The invisible mapping line is the one proud boast, the heart and soul, of an otherwise unremarkable flatland town. Huge concrete silos stand in rows between the highway and the railway tracks.

There is little to generate excitement here — Dodge's bison herds are long gone, replaced by untroubled black-backed range cattle working their way head-down across prairie grass. We're north of the Platte and see parts of the river — it's flat here, so the river meanders, breaks apart, encircling and flooding marshy patches.

We travel the Lincoln Highway, paralleling the I-80 but smaller and slower, and we pass under the huge overhead highway sign marking the meridian.

We cut onto North Meridian Avenue when we see a diner, but it's closed, a hand-written sign in the window saying, "You learn that there are people you can trust, and people you can't. Thanks very much to the ones you can't. We're closed."

The sign looks like it has been in the window for a long time. The letters are faded from the bright afternoon sunlight on the eastern side of the 100th meridian. Across the street, the storefronts on the western side of the line stare back, impassive.

Then, another Great Plains small town, North Platte, the sky big and bright and open, the town pressed down by its weight.

At the centre of town, the Hotel Pawnee is massive and square and imposing — and also closed. It's eight storeys of Georgian Revival brick, 143 rooms, built in 1929 and firmly ensconced on the National Register of Historic Places, but closed for years after operating as an assisted living facility. Pigeons cluster on every foothold, the ground coated with their droppings. At a downtown family shoe store, surrounded by closed stores, Leslie buys shoes she can slip in and out of quickly from a capable young man, barely a teenager but with a salesman's patter already set deep in his vocabulary.

Stores and restaurants along the main drag are closed as well, the streets caught in the bright stare of early afternoon September. The streets are wide, but the towns are atonal and depressing. As seems to be the case everywhere, all the life and motion is close along the throbbing artery of the interstate, not enough other business in town to carry the weight. The Platte River splits just before North Platte, and we, like Dodge, will eventually follow the north branch toward Wyoming while the South Platte wends its way towards Colorado. We see miles and miles of steers behind barbed wire, mostly black and obvious as dots on plains, hillsides and dips, standing blankly. We do not see a bison. Not one.

<hr>

June 11, 1849

Did not get a very early start — nor did we cross here as we had expected — this is what is called the 5 mile ford — being five miles above the junction of the two streams or forks, of the Platte — a branch running near the bluffs on each side. We kept up on the left side of the river, which here makes a bend around to the left, and is narrower — the bluffs on the opposite side coming close down, & on this side terminating in high rolling prairie, the hills nearly all of sand. Low is unwell, & my cold which I took near the beginning of the trip continues to grow worse, and almost renders me unable to walk. Last night we had a tremendous thunderstorm again — during which the Government horses broke loose & many of them escaped. The Boston Co., which was camped three miles in our rear, had 12 of their 26 pack mules stolen from them by the Indians who first cut their larriettes and then ran their horses past them, when the mules followed. Four emigrants went out hunting today & in a little hollow they came upon the stolen mules and some horses guarded by 8 or 10 Indians whom they charged, & took all the animals but one horse belonging to Gov. on which one of them was mounted. Camped early, poor water & no wood. Along the road are many holes dug in the sand from 3 to 8 ft. for water to settle in — but it is generally thought that using the water from these and the slough holes is the cause of much of the sickness with which the emigrants are troubled. None is equal to the river water unless it be some running stream, of which there are very few. The river water is good, but very roiley and full of sand — let it stand over night & settle & it becomes very fine.

June 12, 1849

Started as usual and proceeded 2 or 3 miles when 5 buffalo were seen crossing from the other side, being driven by 2 horsemen. We did not want them and therefore did not stop the team but a Co. from Missouri of about 100 men close behind us killed them all. They wounded them while in the river, when the buffalo came directly at them & were all shot down. Overtook the Gov. train which passed us on the Sabbath with Dr. White's Co. & a large number of emigrants camped close to the left bank of the river, where some teams have formerly forded. On the opposite shore are encamped 1500 Sioux warriors, just returning from a successful engagement with the Pawnees — their tents are of buffalo skins of which they have a plenty, and their ponies are fine. They are anxious to trade their ponies for large horses and their robes for blankets — they also have several mules, which have probably been stolen by them or the Pawnees from emigrants. They cannot speak any English at all — will not take money for anything — apparently know nothing about it, & are very friendly. They are fine, strong, healthy-looking people & and many of them are richly dressed, in Indian style.

When they first came over to see the Gov. train, they evidently expected some very fine present from the U.S., but not receiving anything but provisions, they appeared quite offended & indignantly threw them away before the Officer's faces!

∞∞∞∞∞

The terrain changes subtly: grassland one moment, and then we are surrounded by the first sand bluffs we've seen. We have to stop.

We're out of the car, the sand and dust clouding up around our feet and ankles. We startle a jackrabbit — the first of a countless number — and it springs away after allowing us to get surprisingly close. They bound away, and you jump backwards at the sound. They wait until the last moment to move, and after a while, you realize that there must be many, many more that you haven't seen, rabbits willing to take their chances and hope that you change direction and pass them, unknowing.

There's flat-lobed cactus with long spines, small-balled cactus with fuzzy spines, the sword grass and the sage. The Sandhills are a

very different place, rising on both sides of the Platte rivers like gla-
cial-bulldozed sandbox remnants.

Deep chasms with open sand breaks, the dry air, and the plants
so different. There's corn in the valleys, and I stop on a dusty side
road to look at the mazed irrigation system that waters the corn —
trenches full of water, closed-in places with heavy wooden gates that
have huge spinning wheel-cranks to lift and lower them. The sand
and dust create an ambient noise I'm not used to. If there's nothing
actively making a sound, your ears make up something that's almost
a hiss.

The road is soft with the dust; tire marks are perfect reproductions,
right down to reflecting any cuts or mars in the rubber, any rocks
caught in the treads. It is like flour, and while there's almost no wind,
if you crouch down next to the tire marks, you can see how they will
fade: the sharp edges soften right there in front of you.

It's clear that someone has been to the irrigation gates today. The
marks of two pairs of shoes, two different strides, and a span of an
axle that shows a vehicle equipped with two different types of tire.
I can't tell if the gates were moved or simply checked. The sound
of the water pushing out from under the bottom of the half-opened
gate is both familiar and different; already, water seems almost out
of place.

Union Pacific trains are rumbling by with coal one way and empty
coal cars the other, and there are long trains of wheat or corn hopper
cars. It's hard to imagine now, but the Sandhills must be the way much
of the land used to be, inhospitable and holding onto its own space
adamantly. No roads, no rail, virtually no path. No easy connection to
water, whether miles away, or hundreds of feet underground. The only
real human features, the criss-cross of roads and near-endless miles of
fencing.

One thing that hasn't changed: it's hard to escape the feeling of not
being alone in that big empty — the feeling that there are always eyes
on you, even if it's only the fan-tailed hawk wheeling and kiting high
up in the thermals above us.

As we pass through Ogallala — cattle trucks and open farmland — and then head north on Highway 26, the land rises steadily and the trees, except for occasional scruffs of alder, vanish. It's open range, sometimes with rock poking up through but more often with tears in the turf that reveal long pockets of sand gouged by the wind. It's steadily upwards, the speed limit rising by five miles an hour as the view opens up. What we can't see from the car windows, could only see later, shot from the air (even in satellite images), is how much of the land is covered with parallel till-marks. Any place that anyone's driven off-road, there is sand in the open ruts, pale yellow to white.

The emigrant trail is out there, too, in any place it hasn't been ploughed under, the traffic of tens of thousands of people creating a change still visible in the vegetation along its route.

The biggest difference from Dodge's time is the reservoir system. They have flooded the valleys that Dodge passed through, creating vast lakes for irrigation or hydroelectric power or both. But we can begin to see what becomes more obvious as we head further west into drier land: that the emigrant trail followed a path along river bottoms, then from pass to pass in high land, and finally, a soft zigzag from water source to water source. There would have been long stretches with no reliable water supply. The reservoirs haven't just filled in parts of the trail — they would have changed its course if they had existed then.

Lake McConaughy in Nebraska is one of them.

The reservoir is a Depression-era construction, a 22-mile-long lake that makes a good chunk of Nebraska's agriculture possible. In all, 32,500 square miles of ground drain directly to this point, filling the space behind a huge earthen dam with water up to 140 feet deep.

We realize how high we've climbed when a canyon opens up in the sandy rock to the right of us, and the reservoir is splayed out in blue along the near horizon, the hills, maybe even just high plains, behind it a soft blue-beige line against the sky.

It was river bottom flatlands when Dodge was here; he would have followed those flatlands, had he actually managed to ford the North Platte earlier. He hadn't.

✧✧✧✧✧✧✧

June 13, 1849

Great question about crossing the river here this morning. We should have crossed at the other ford 40 miles below — but many seeing the Gov. train pass on, followed, supposing of course they would choose the best. The reason for their passing, as we afterwards ascertained, was that when they passed the lower ford the Guide lay drunk in the wagon, & after he found they had passed he would not return. Gov. train passed on to another ford 8 miles above, but some having been there said it was not as good as this, and therefore the emigrants determined to cross here. The river is near ¾ of a mile wide, & from 1 to 3 feet deep — the bed entirely of quicksand. We could not go straight across on account of holes in the stream but were compelled to make a circuit downstream. It will not do to stop for any time while in the river, as the wagons will immediately settle in the sand so as to render them immovable. It looked really strange to see men crossing and recrossing on foot, on horse, on mules & oxen — some leading and others driving their teams; and all hallooing and shouting at the top of their voices, while the bank on either side was lined with persons looking on and trading with the natives. It seemed like a gala day — By one o'clock nearly all had crossed when the Indians struck tents and marched off over the bluffs, and we started on up the river until we came to a good camping ground where we halted for the night. No wood except a few small brush.

✧✧✧✧✧✧✧

Chapter 7

Lewellen, Nebraska

On Windlass Hill, outside Lewellen, Nebraska, there are distinct downhill ruts from the 1840s trail wagons that have grown into their own remarkable jagged downhill canyon, the plant life crushed and torn 160 years ago and the sand still coming apart beneath the trail and sliding downhill every time there's rain. The thousands of wagon wheels broke the plant cover and erosion did the rest, the angle of slope clearly more than the soil's safe angle of repose. The hill got its name from the cables that slowed the wagons' descent from the plateau into the lusher valley.

There's a bull yelling/lowing/grunting/calling from a nearby gap, owning the valley. I can hear him clearly, recognize the direction the sound's coming from, but it still takes me time to pinpoint his black standing shape against the prairie grass. The bull runs downhill, silenced, when a rancher's truck approaches.

Windlass Hill Park is empty, with signs warning us to keep off the grass because of rattlesnakes, but we only hear sounds like rattles, only see a small dun brown lizard who likes the warm dark paint of the bridge under his belly. Northerners like Dodge, we are unused to rattlesnakes. All around us, there are clicks and buzzes and sibilant hisses, all of them most likely made by insects, but we stay religiously on the asphalt path, alert for any reptilian threat. Later, I'll read that emergency medical care for rattlesnake bites can cost over US $150,000, a brutal sum if you're not carrying insurance. For Dodge, the rattle-snake danger was far worse — a bite would almost certainly be fatal.

At the top of the bluff, I could see the long line of the old trail clearly for the first time, running out toward the horizon, the change in the colour of the vegetation obvious as the track winds its way across the plateau, heading back towards the fork of the Platte. Here, inside the historic state park, there's a sign that remains, a dent that's visible on satellite pictures. Almost exactly on the park's borders, the parallel lines of cultivator tracks — in neat-boxed rectangles or whorls like massive fingerprints when seen from above — eat away any trace that remains on their side of the line.

There have been trail markers, standing sticks all the way back to the first one at St. Joseph, to tell you you're on the trail. But here — it's indistinct at first, but as my eyes adjust, there's a clear path of different vegetation — the trail is a slight bowl now, filled in with plants that are redder than their surroundings, leaving a reddish curve just wider than a wagon's axle, heading away.

The drop here was steep for carts without brakes, but it was the only way down, the only way forward. Limestone cliff faces and crags, small cedars, knee-high plants and grasses competing for sunlight and water. Yellow fistfuls of blooms atop succulent stalks. More lobed cacti with red, ripening fruit. Columns of green capped with evenly spaced flowers, each flower a bristled bunch of purple threads. Riotous bushes that look like collections of small sunflowers — they're a hardy one, that one, they've dogged us in roadside ditches all the way from Wisconsin. The prairie seems almost homogenously sedge-coloured until you get up close, and then you imagine that you could spend days cataloguing all the different plants and their blooms in a space just three feet square.

Desert plants: their thorns fill the bottoms of your sneakers, rub off on the mats in the car, small knobs of cacti you can't even see until you find their gripping remains. Some have spines so small they go unnoticed until you try to pull them from your socks or pants, your fingers finding sharp furred points that draw blood and keep hurting long after you think you've gotten them all out.

Looking from the top, it's a rolling mat of sedge hills and dales, folds and dips and curves and shoulders, with the wind rushing for the horizon always. The sweet smells of mountain sage and cedar. It's been a steep climb that you feel in your calves and hamstrings.

No wonder the wagons fell like stones down the precipice and sometimes broke apart as they descended. (The official Nebraska government website points out, "Travellers did not call the hill 'Windlass Hill' in those days; rather, it was called 'the steep hill' or 'the perpendicular hill.'" Dodge refers to it as "a very steep and difficult hill to descend.")

Not much romance to their trip, but an unbelievable amount of work. After the dry of the high prairie, the folds and wrinkles of the valley ahead sprout with ash and poplar, the trees' leaves a brighter, more hopeful green than the sage.

A green that's a clear sign of water.

∞∞∞∞∞

June 14, 1849

Travelled about 4 miles and came to where the Gov. trains were crossing — this is not as good as the lower ford — they lost a couple of mules and some of the emigrants came near losing their teams & and their lives. Here the road turns square off to the right and leads over the high rolling prairie to the north fork of the Platte, up which we would have followed had we crossed at the first- or 5-mile ford, where we ought to. There is neither wood nor a particle of water except 2 or 3 mudholes all the way across — the distance is said to be 24 miles, though, & seemed less than that to us. When within sight of the river the bluffs begin to descend very abruptly, & there is one very steep and difficult hill to descend, when we came out into Ash Hollow — so called from a few ash trees growing along the valley. The hillsides are very rough and broken

& composed usually of limestone rock, along the brink of which grow a few stunted cedars, while the valley is filled with wild roses and bushes. A short distance after descending into the hollow, we came to a spring of beautiful clear water, almost the only one we have seen since the second day after leaving St. Joseph. It is close by the road, on the right-hand side. The hollow is strewn with the carcasses & bones of buffalo. Fred & myself went up among the rocks to get some wood & I sat down on a flat rock while waiting for him to cut off a cedar root. Scarcely, however, had I leaned my head on my hand when chir-r-r-r, within 3 feet of me sang out a large Rattle Snake! It may be that I didn't <u>vamoose</u> from there, but I <u>reckon</u> I did! Before I could recover sufficiently to kill it, it had crawled out of reach into the rocks. We drove out and camped on the riverbank, where we had the pleasure of being very closely attended by as blood-thirsty a set of mosquitoes as ever bled man, which swarmed about us in legions. It rains as often as every night.

◇◇◇◇◇◇◇◇

Ash Hollow, the first spring on the trail for a hundred miles, is in a state park now, separate and a few miles from Windlass Hill.

The park is closed for the season when we get there, so we are the only ones who wind our way up the battered road and park on the high ground near the interpretation centre. It's on the hill overlooking the spring because the Ash Hollow Cave entrance is part of the park buildings, a cave used by humans as long as 6,000 years ago — yet one of the most frequent complaints posted on message boards is that the trail ruts are actually on the Windlass Hill, not at Ash Hollow, and that visitors have to go back to see them.

History's an odd thing: people so often only want to examine the parts they can see themselves in. So much of the focus is inwards — and I'm no different.

We're alone on the downhill paths to the spring, checking for snakes, and there's still no one else when we reach the edge of the spring's pool. The limestone cliffs on the way down erupt in granular points and vees, managing to look both permanent and fragile.

Looking down the long, manicured grass toward the spring in the direction the emigrants came, the ash trees on one side, the limestone bluffs on the other, the spring itself is a rare dot of blue, reflecting the sky.

When you get right up on top of it, the water is slightly greenish-blue and silty, barely larger than a backyard swimming pool, and while the emigrants thought it sweet, a sign warns the water's not drinkable now. Minnows dart away when you approach. The water source doesn't rush out of the ground as much as it seeps in fast at the top edge, so it comes into the pool roiling up aquatic dust-devils of silt. The spring sits surrounded by a broad field of mown grass, more like a summer picnic park than anything else. If you knew nothing about its history, it would be a handy day park, picnic tables under the trees, the small pond of the spring almost unremarkable.

Above the spring, pitted limestone cliffs loom, many with holes that look like they should be full of watching animals, snakes, and birds. Looking down at the pond in the direction the emigrants would have when they arrived, the gap in the trees and the surface of the water is almost magical.

The ash trees alongside the spring are massive and magnificent, their leaves turning in the wind so they are half dark green and half silver with reflected sunlight, and the sound of them whispering together is like a balm.

The park is, it turns out, better empty, even if you have to walk a mile to find an unlocked outhouse.

◇⟩⟨◇⟩⟨◇⟩

June 15, 1849
Our road this morning lies along the riverbank at the
foot of the bluffs & is over wet heavy sand — very little

grass — bottom narrow. Found a paper sticking in the road signed by some of a small advance party from Gov. trains stating that one of their party — an Officer — had become insane and run off among the bluffs! Several emigrants, among whom was one of our party, saw the poor fellow a little distance off from the road among the rocks. He had on no coat, hat, or shoes, & appeared to be in great trouble about his family. They gave him some food which he ate but could not be prevailed upon to leave the bluffs. About 2 miles below where we camped last night were a party of squaws and Indians, most of the former of whom belonged to several white men who lived among them. We only saw one of the men — he was from Missouri — had been with them 13 years — The rest had gone to the States to sell their furs. Neat contrivance for carrying their young — pole lashed to each side of a pony, extending out behind where there is braided in a willow basket, with a top to protect it from the sun and storm! Among other curious things along the river, we see lots of Jack O'lanterns, which if persons are not careful, they will mistake for tent lights & be led into some confounded slough hole! Travelling today is extremely hard — over loose sand all the way, which with every gust of wind fills our mouths, ears & eyes, & renders it very disagreeable indeed. We passed Castle Bluff & many others resembling castles, towers, fortifications, etc. The bottom is very narrow, no wood, & feed short, with mosquitoes without number or mercy! At this place the Co. agreed to divide & dissolve when we should reach Ft. Laramie, distant 90 miles.

∽∘⋉∘⋊∘⋉∘∽

The river, broad and flat, passes behind Lewellen's back. The town is small, a couple of hundred people at most. The main street that runs perpendicular to the highway is overbroad, with room on both sides for nose-in parking and three lanes left beside, as if built for grander things. There's a huge flagpole with the American flag right spang in the middle of Main Street: the whole street runs for just two and a half blocks or so, ending at the post office.

Several businesses, including a restaurant and a motel, have geese in their name. There's a huge snow goose migration in the spring. Camouflage and hunting gear are a constant theme: search the internet for images of "geese" and "Lewellen," and you get camo-clad hunters with long rows of dead geese laid out in front of them.

We head for the Gander Inn Motel and Breakfast, one of the only options in town. You check in at a small alcove behind what seems like a bank teller's screen and sliding window. There's an old black dial phone in case no one's in the office. We find ourselves in a two-bedroom suite, twin lawn chairs out front. The standard motel design that we're getting used to: cinderblock walls on three sides with all the windows and the door on the remaining one.

Back up Main Street, the dining room in the Blind Goose Bar and Restaurant is at the back, beyond the pool table alcove and a short jink to the right. There's a fresh-faced 4-H girl at the cash and waitressing; the place has a family-run, family-farming feel, the other diners plaid- and denim-shirted, ball caps next to them on the square wooden tables. The arcade game near the front door lets you hunt geese or ducks without getting cold and wet.

"White or brown gravy?" That's the question I'm asked when I order the chicken-fried steak. Dodge is eating bison, fresh-killed in front of him, while our fare is a little more well travelled. I have discovered that I love chicken-fried steak — Leslie thinks it's a great way to hide the taste of meat that's almost spoiled. She is not a fan, but she puts a fork in my mashed potatoes and brown gravy anyway.

We had planned to stay late, move from the dining area to the bar and soak up bar talk; local or national politics, whatever issues might be open for discussion. It's a small group of customers for a Friday night, and we're the only outsiders.

Two pool tables, no one playing, and the shortage of customers is because there are two memorial services this weekend as well as a high school football game.

Two booths are full of one family — a family that includes the wait staff.

The talk is about politics, alright, but it's family politics: the ins and outs of parents and divorce and how harvest time throws a wrench into the ordered schedules of custody and access, divorced dads on the road with combine crews, working long days and nights, moms fed up with their own long days.

"It's harvest, Jack's not home. But she's happy — she's with granny."

I see a strange kind of tequila, ask to try it. I'm quickly told it's the cheapest, the "well tequila" used for mixed drinks, but I'm in too deep and order it straight anyway.

We play a game of pool, badly, blame the warped and curved cues. No one says anything to us directly, but there's an overwhelming feeling that they'd like us to leave. They're making small talk, waiting to have a full-scale discussion in private. The children are eating sundaes they're not supposed to have, but the grandfather — a young-looking grandfather — rules here. He commands chocolate sauce and sprinkles.

The childrens' parents are not pleased, but it's obvious that everyone has their own long-established place in the hierarchy, their own fit in the family puzzle.

We're out the door earlier than we'd like, shoved by the feeling of strained and formal hospitality.

Trains howl mournfully down the valley, their horns followed by the deep thrum of their engines.

On the way from the Blind Goose to the motel, I see the Cuban couple's van parked out front — the same van from more than a hundred miles earlier outside the laundromat in Kearney. I'm sure it's the same van, same cracked windshield, same "In Transit" Nebraska registration. The family's nowhere to be seen, and I wonder if Lewellen is their end point or just another stopover. New help for the Goose, maybe? They've been travelling progressively west and north: at this rate, if they keep going, their emigrant trail could well end in Northern Oregon or Washington State.

The next morning, I·go back looking for it, but the van is gone, as if it had never been. Lewellen is as empty as a western town in the movies, waiting for a gunfight to break out. All that's missing is an occasional wind-driven tumbleweed.

∞∞∞∞∞

June 17, Sunday, 1849

After passing a night the torments of which could not have been surpassed by the Inquisition, we were awakened by the cry of the watch, that "the mules are gone!" Tearing off the handkerchief which I had tied over my face to prevent swallowing the largest of the Mosquitoes, I rushed out, & just caught a glimpse of them galloping off at the top of their speed — led by an ugly bitch of a mare belonging to one Menden from St. Louis, who had been travelling with us for several days past! The horses although hoppled were gone too, thus leaving us no means of pursuit except on foot — but being hoppled they could not run far, & having overtaken them, we soon caught up with and stopped the mules after running about 3 miles. Soon after the whole Gov. train, which we passed at the ford, came up and passed us, as we did not travel, & were followed by Dr.'s White's and Brown's Co.'s from St. Louis besides an immense number of ox teams. A great deal of excitement exists among the emigrants about getting through. Many — nearly all who have mules — intend to pack from Ft. Laramie. Col. Loring, the commanding officer of the troop, came up to camp and conversed with us some time· about the route etc. He is quite a gentleman and lost one of

his arms — the left — at Chapultepec — he thinks we
will be obliged to pack from the spur beyond the Pass.
During the afternoon a meeting was held at which it was
agreed that Wainwright Drury & myself might have a
choice in the passengers whereupon we took Lewis and
Holcombe; Chapman & Ingalsbee took Frederick. We
gave them $40 for a choice of mules, and the provisions
were equally divided — the tent we cut into two parts,
and all the small articles which could not be divided were
bid for. We gave them 10 dollars for their share of the
spring wagon, & they gave us $1.75 for our share of a
$6.00 note taken for bread sold to the Dr.

◇◇◇◇◇◇◇

Late at night, I walk to the high school at the edge of Lewellen listening to barking dogs and an unfamiliar, constant birdcall that
sounds for all the world like ripping paper. I wait there in case there
are trains, the wind now cold on my arms. I can hear truck tires whirring on the pavement, the sound of passing night-lit semis. I wish for
simpler answers and listen in case I hear them. I am invisible in the
dark, watching the occasional cars and trucks turning, their headlights flashing across my legs, but clearly no one sees me. And why
shouldn't I wait for trains and piss on the rail ballast and look up at
cold hard stars and fade into everyone's background? I'll be home
soon enough, I thought, but now, up high in Lewellen, all I can think
of are the same two sentences, "Send me trains, send me trains bright
wheeled ground shaking brighter eyed lights of everything erasing
trains. Let the gates swing down, the diesels roar, the red lights flash,
the full of it; send me trains."

But there are only cars and soon I will have to leave my level crossing, unlevel perch. I see light on the horizon but that is not enough to
keep me in the cooling air.

I'm at the end of the streetlights and must turn back.

(Send me trains.)

A car noses onto Main Street, drives as far as the flagpole in the middle of the street, does two full loop-the-loops around the pole, and heads back to the highway, disappearing into the dark.

I find Leslie hoarse at the motel end of Main Street, hoarse from yelling my name under her breath because she came outside to find me gone from my tilted, two-legged lawn-chair perch, an empty beer bottle left standing sentinel. And when she did come out, a big black dog ran up to her and barked, then ran in the direction of the river, stopping every few yards and staring at her over its shoulder as if she was supposed to follow. As if I had fallen in the river and the night-fool dog was trying to take her to rescue me or to at least find my body out there in the wandering sandy fingers of the Platte, somewhere in the soft sand-pit bogs and steadies.

She had followed the dog for a while, then doubled back and resisted its second visit, its insistence, but she was weakening. There's almost no sound in the town and I've just been kneeling on the rail ballast, my hand against the cold steel of the track, trying to see if I can at least feel the hoped-for train I can't yet see or hear.

She's both relieved to see me and legitimately angry about my disappearance. It's like suffering from the flu: fever followed by chills followed by fever again, and she can't decide which is the right and fair temperature to be.

We sleep with our backs to each other, each on our own side of the vast acreage of bed. Late, late in the Lewellen dark, I hear a coal train's horn, distant laughing.

⬦⬦⬦⬦⬦⬦

June 18, 1849
We remained there until Monday afternoon to complete our division, then moved on about 12 miles and camped in company with our former companions who passed us that morning. We finished our business here, divided the fund on hand, & disposed of Churchill by giving up to him his $75 note and paying back to him ⅔ of the $50 which he

had paid in. Wainwright then took him for his note and money, & we let him travel with us to Ft. Laramie.

At this place we found splendid grass but no wood or water except the river, which is a mile off.

∞⋄⋄⋄⋄∞

The motel owner cooks the breakfasts. He pours us juice, brings plates of fruit in the small motel dining room — you can see right into the kitchen. It looks more like a house than a motel. Lewellen is dwindling, he says, to even fewer than I expected: "There are maybe 50 people here."

There is only one other couple in the dining room, but they are more cheerful, so the proprietor turns his big-smiling eager attention to them.

They are from California and have a map open on the table, planning their travels for the day.

"He has maps for everywhere we've been," the woman says to us brightly. They keep records of everywhere they've travelled, every road taken, making careful notes on what they see, marking locations, both places they've visited and others they've simply passed through. I don't have the heart to tell them it's a record that will end up being intelligible only to them. Or that, like many of the things that are personally important, their carefully kept logs will end up being meaningless to anyone else and will likely be discarded once they themselves are gone.

They ask us where we're from.

"I don't have a map for Newfoundland," the man says pensively. "I'd have to get one."

Leslie is vibrating, wanting more coffee, her cup empty, her irritation growing. I'm almost ready to go and get it myself by the time it arrives, and we step backwards from the brink.

In the morning, the town is big sky, flat-faced small buildings, and a rooster calling. We have to mail a letter — the post office is open from 8:30 to 10:00 a.m., two and a half Saturday-morning hours.

A boy and a girl have climbed the scaffolding against the side of the white house where the rooster is, their voices singsong and bright. It's quiet enough that, all at once, the nearby rails are singing, a high-pitch sharp whine like something metallic being stretched to its breaking point.

When the train passes, you can feel the ground heave under your feet, see the concrete ties pumping with the weight of the passing cars. Every other car has a thumping weight to it, as if the wheels have flat spots and the whole weight of the car is pounding down for an instant of the turning wheel. The wheels shine like liquid metal, like mercury.

There are bones on the tracks behind the Lewellen grain elevators — what looks like a dog and also a possum, their fur and hides like torn blankets, the bones white and bare, eye sockets empty. At another spot, the railway roadkill is a full-sized male turkey, stone dead, tail feather fan-spread, one wrinkly clawed foot separate and away.

There is a mourning dove strolling on the lawn in front of our motel room, different birds calling across the flatland valley, the air cool and the sky a washed blue. There is an aluminum pontoon boat on a trailer hitched to a red four-by-four pickup. The big lake here is apparently muskie heaven as well as a pit stop on the goose and duck migration route.

Two mourning doves on the lawn now.

We leave Lewellen looking for some sign of a different piece of local history. Sometimes incorrectly called the Battle of Ash Hollow, sometimes called the Battle of Blue Water Creek, it's more properly called Harney's Massacre: 86 Lakota were killed, 70 women and children captured in the 1855 battle — a battle to keep the Oregon Trail open and the massacre that signalled the start of the Indian Wars. Five hundred U.S. army soldiers with superior long-range rifles forced the Lakota towards mounted soldiers who attacked them from behind. From Lieutenant G.K. Warren's journal: "The sight on top of the hill was heart-rendering, wounded women and children crying and moaning, horribly mangled by bullets . . . I found another girl about 12 years old laying with her head down in a ravine, and apparently dead.

Observing her breath, I had a man take her in his arms. She was shot through both feet."

Warren also wrote that he "was disgusted with the tales of valor afterwards told on the field, for their [sic] were but few who killed anything but a flying foe."

We find a sign marking the massacre on the side of the road just past Blue Water Creek, backed on to a harvested cornfield. The railway is directly behind the sign, coal scattered in the ballast stones on both sides of the rails. The sign is oddly dedicated to a park superintendent at Ash Hollow. On one of the sideposts that hold up the marker, there is a sweetgrass or tobacco bundle, wrapped tight with criss-crossing fibrous twine.

There is no way to tell how long it's been there or who placed it.

But it's a poignant sign that there are different versions of the story, just the same. Still immersed in reading material from Fort Kearny, Leslie reads that the women and girls captured at the massacre were passed around among the soldiers.

A coal train roars by, oblivious.

◇◇◇◇◇◇◇

June 19, 1849
Our road lies along the narrow bottom, parallel to & some distance from the river & is quite good, except the dry sand which is blown by the wind in drifts all along. In many places the sod has become broken, & the wind & rain together has worn the bluff completely down, cutting deep gullies, and heaping up the sand like snow drifts. This Morning we passed Church Rock, a solitary rock rising abruptly, & much resembling a church from which it takes its name. The weather has become very warm. Toward night, we arrived at Chimney Rock, which is a most singular appearing rock indeed. The base rises in a circular form until it reaches about half its height, when there rises from the center of this base a large column, which towers

to the height of 160 Ft. It is of a quadrangular shape &
10 or 15 ft. wide at the top. This like the adjoining rocks
& bluffs is composed of light coloured sand rock, interspersed with thin layers of various kinds of rocks. A short
distance to the left under the foot of the abrupt bluff in
a ravine is a fine spring of cold water. Beyond the chimney the bluffs have the appearance of being large castles
of various shapes & sizes. Churchill took Low's mare to
catch a stray horse & did not return at dark — Lewis went
after him with the Dr.'s mule. Feed short, no water, wood,
or chips near the river — a few small cedars in the bluffs.

◇◇◇◇◇◇◇

Court and Jail Rock are huge, standing alone on the flat prairie. A pan-
oramic photograph makes them seem like islands, unattached to any
continent. We detour south to see them — their lure is irresistible, the
only high ground for miles.

You can get right up to them, unlike many of the other bluffs and
buttes; just ascend a wandering, curving road of white dust, its surface hatched with deep, eroded cuts from sudden rain. Leave the car
and climb on white sandstone. When you are up high enough on its
rounded whiteness, you realize the wind gets pulled up and over them
like a jet stream, full in your face. The curves are fluid, the kinds of
shapes you associate with erosion by water — but there is no sign of
water here, wind and sand the only possible explanation. It's impossible to comprehend how long that must have taken, the two buttes
standing and being sculpted smooth for millennia while the ground
around them wore away.

There is no way to pretend that your feet are the first ones there,
no matter how hard it is to find your way to difficult viewpoints: up
close, there's spent ammunition, broken glass, plastic bottle tops, and
even graffiti, some carved, some spray-painted.

A tiny sunning Western hognose — maybe six inches long — plays
rattlesnake with me there, shaking its black-button tail and coiling as if it

133

is going to strike. I had thought it dead at first, then saw its black tongue flicking. It postured as if it was a rattler poised to bite, and I scrambled away quickly. It does a good and frightening job, in among the sage and dust — I back off, photos only, and from a yard away at that.

The wind has drilled holes and gaps through the stone, and here, up high, there is much more than there is at ground level. Here, you can understand the eagles and hawks kiting without moving their wings. You can see to the horizon in all directions, the fields and the drylands stretching out, the occasional huge crop circles of the irrigation rigs clear, green and obvious.

We come down through the dust and small gravel slowly, slowly, watching our feet.

The car must be visible for miles, the sun winking off the roof and the windshield as the huge columnar clouds transit slowly over us. Before we leave, we watch two pickup trucks take turns winding up the narrow road, one red, one dark green. We come down from our climb to find them waiting. The drivers ask if we're alright, and we think they must be used to lost, stuck, and broken-down drivers and climbers.

There are no prohibitions, yet at least, at Court and Jail.

Not like nearby Chimney Rock, which has become just another opportunity to shoot your own long-distance postcard. The closest you can get is the deck behind the visitor's centre, a spot framed neatly so that you can photograph the rock from the exact same vantage point as everyone else has for the last hundred or more years.

It's not the same rock Dodge described, soaring 160 feet overhead — it's more eroded now, though still remarkable, and you have to squint hard to try and imagine how singularly stunning it would have been if you'd come upon it by chance, standing rigid and alone. You don't have to try hard at all to imagine why its original name was Elk Penis.

∽∽∽∽∽∽

June 20, 1849
Leaving Chimney Rock we were soon in sight of Scotts Bluffs, which we reached about 2 o'clock. These bluffs

are among the most magnificent sights I ever beheld —
a short distance off, they have the exact appearance of a
vast collection of palaces, towers, turrets, forts, & monu-
ments, & present a most imposing aspect. The road turns
off from the river to the left at the foot of the bluffs & five
miles on is a good spring in one of the handsomest little vallies I ever saw, completely surrounded by the bluffs
except where the road enters it. At the foot of the bluffs on
the right of the road is some very deep ravines, up one of
which is the spring. We took our mules across the ravine
to feed, & on going over to watch them, at night, I lost my
path in the ravine, not knowing exactly where they were,
and till 10 o'clock had a most interesting time indeed
climbing ascents and descending precipices, at the risk of
breaking my neck, where in the daytime it would have
been impossible for me to have gone. A Frenchman by the
name of Rubadeau has a trading post here & a squaw for
a wife — he has been here 15 years.

◇◇◇◇◇◇◇◇

The Rubadeau that Dodge referred to was Joseph E. Robidoux, the
oldest son of Joseph Robidoux, the man whose fortune was built with
St. Joseph as a crossing-point over the Missouri.

We pass the Monument Mall; it's dwarfed by the hunched bulk of
Scotts Bluff. The city is 15,000 people or so, tucked in under the hill and
completely overwhelmed by the looming mountain behind it. We double back to try and get a clear view of the bluff — to try and see what
for Dodge was such a magnificent sight — but there's no way to avoid
seeing it with the big cube of a Walmart standing proud at its base.

For us, it's a slight shift of highway, then the city and bluff are
gone, as much a blip on the flatlands as the other buttes are.

Stock trucks and coal trains run endlessly, the stock trucks filled
with beef cattle or curious-nosed hogs, their snouts pressed out through
the vent holes.

◇◇◇◇◇◇◇

June 21, 1849

Started in good season & left Dr. White's Co. behind us. Towards noon we came to a small deep muddy stream with steep banks and bad crossing: ¼ of a mile farther we crossed Horse Creek where we camped for noon. The road here lies over a sandy bottom & in the afternoon over sand hills to the river, where we found good feed on the bottom, no water except the river & a hole not fit for use — No timber or chips. The weather has become very warm for a few days' past, & we find that those who do not let their teams rest at noon are falling behind & their mules are giving out. Teams have been travelling on the opposite side of the river ever since we struck it at Ash Hollow. A couple of days since we passed a woman with two ox teams, who has lost her husband, & her 3 sons, who are all the help she has except a little girl, lie sick in the wagons. We are now travelling in company with a Mr. Ewing, a friend of the Dr.'s who also is an old trader on the Santa Fe route.

June 22, 1849

Started early — road dusty, sandy & weather warm, very. Large companies of ox teams are strung along the route. Stopped at 10 A.M. after travelling 12 miles, on the banks of the river, where for the first time we found a few dead trees. Feed poor — plenty of driftwood on the shore. A man who has some molasses is selling it for $5.00 per gallon! A couple of men with an ox team passed us on their return — they had been 150 miles beyond the Ft. and said they came back because they could find no grass — they said they passed on their return 3500 teams. Leaving them we travelled on over sandy bottom and hills, arriving at the Ft. at sundown. There is no feed of any account within

several miles except that occupied by the Gov. trains,
which is fine.

Through the agency of Dr. White, who has accepted
the appt. of Surgeon & is travelling with them, we obtained
a chance to camp with them.

∞∞∞∞∞

The town of Fort Laramie is oil tank farms and 230 people. The
National Historic Site of the fort — when you get there — is broad
and grassy and spread out across the prairie. It's hard to think that it
was only one rough brick building when William Dodge was there,
but you can find that building, still standing, and see the ford where
the carts crossed. In September, the river itself is nothing more than a
shallow riffle and an easy wade over the gravel.

The shed skin of a three-foot-long snake, as big around as my
wrist, rolls lazily past, driven by the light evening wind. After we
see it, we're watching our feet in the grass again, even though the
only thing that rises at our footsteps are clouds of small white flut-
tering moths.

The sun is already angling down, the site preparing to close, most
of the re-enacted history finished up for the day. When we stand and
look across the river from the fort, there's a solitary standing tepee,
white canvas against the yellow grasslands. No explanation for it, no
idea if it is part of the recreated fort or not.

Other visitors meander, guidebooks in hand, but most are heading
for their cars. I'm struck by the similarity in age of many of the visitors: early fifties to late sixties, as if there is a time when a connection
to history suddenly becomes personally important.

Is this all an aging person's conceit, something for people with
enough money and time to go and look at what came before, as if seeking the fugitive concept of worth in ancestors because we can't find
that sort of worth in our own lives? And is that part of why I'm here?
There's not an easy answer. It's hard to say that you're looking for
something when the feeling you're trying to address is more an absence.

137

But I remember my father, around the age I am now, taking a sideline trip from a Russian scientific convention to try and find the site of his father's village in what is now Belarus. And I remember his extreme disappointment, the tremor in his voice, when he told me that all he could find was vast open acres of collectivized wheat farm where the town had once stood. No people. No buildings. Even the graveyard stripped of its markers and converted to farmland during a Stalin-era push for food production. I remember he took off his glasses and rubbed tired red eyes.

The trail, broken.

I have a copy of a different handwritten diary that came to me after, and in a way because of, my father's death, a coming to the part of America that Dodge was leaving behind.

&cooloooo;

June 23, 1849

This morning finds matters in rather dubious shape. Burt has an offer as Wagon Master which he will probably accept, having sold his two mules to W. for $100 each. We talk of packing, but don't know what to do. Spent the forenoon trying to dispose of our wagons & to find a place for Lewis, we being unable to carry him if compelled to pack. Provisions and wagons are being thrown away to lighten the loads, and all who can are preparing to pack. The villain I. who has been the cause of all our difficulties proposed to Drury that we should carry their passenger Fred, threatening if we did not, to seize our property to pay a debt we owe them, but which was expressly understood not to be due until we could make it after reaching California. We refused, determined to protect ourselves by force if necessary, in which determination we were seconded by Dr. White & all who knew the circumstances. Men are leaving heavy wagons, & buying lighter ones at from 3 to 50 dollars. They sold their wagon for a horse & gave $30 to boot — we sold ours for $35, and the little wagon for $25. Low bought Pat & Del of Burt for $200. An offer being made me by a young man in Dr. White's Co. by the name of Dickerson to put my two mules with his two before a very nice carriage of his & travel with him, I accepted it while Low & Ebon, not being able to purchase a light wagon to suit them, determined to pack. I gave them $25 to relieve me of my share of the responsibility of carrying Lewis, and Low bought two ponies intending to carry him and Churchill. Great difficulty exists between the members of companies that are dividing, & also between passengers & those who undertook to carry them through — the latter being hardly able to get themselves through & the others swearing roundly that they are not to be left there! Quarrels are frequent, but the public opinion of the body of intelligent emigrants has prevented any resort to force.

<><><><><>

Dodge wasn't the only member of my extended family who was willing to travel great distances to find a better life. The other handwritten diary that has ended up with me was written by George Wangersky, my father's uncle, and, I think, my younger brother's namesake.

It came to me after a distant cousin tried to reach my father about an ill family member and found my father's obituary instead. Tracking me down, he sent me his grandfather's 32-page diary, titled "My Russian and American Life." It talks about life in the small hamlet of Starynky — several generations living in a small wooden cabin, farming and even dealing with packs of wolves. "A whole bunch of wolves came after us, at each side, in front, and in back. There must have been more than ten of them. The men were shooting all the time, but they had only single barrel guns. Each of them could only shoot one time, then he would have to load his gun. It took about two minutes to load the gun . . ."

Dad's father, Konstanty, his brother's diary says, was handed over to an uncle as a servant "with an agreement that (he) would receive about sixteen rubles a year and he may do what he wished with the money."

Like Dodge, George pulled up stakes in his early twenties — to head to America. The first part of the diary: "In 1913 in February, my father said to me, 'How would you like to go to America?' I said I would like very much to go because everybody said you can make money very quick and very easy." (Konstanty had finished his indentured servitude and was already in America by then.)

After borrowing 200 rubles, George's father sent him on his way west with another, more experienced traveller: "On February 23 we packed our luggage, In fact, I didn't have a suitcase. I had a white bag, and inside I had one dry cheese, two kolbase, and a half a loaf of bread." He threaded through European borders on foot, by horse carriage, and on trains, both passenger and freight, before leaving Hamburg on a crowded ship: "As we came to the big ship, it was evening time. The ship was lighted with so many lights, I thought it must be very beautiful inside. But when I got on, it wasn't. The beds were on three stories. I took the middle one.

"Every day we went to the kitchen to get our food. The food was very poor. Mostly two unpeeled potatoes and one salted herring. . . . Everyone had one blanket, but the blanket was kind of dirty and had plenty of lice. They were fat, too. Very often when I was in my bed, the lice would fall on me from the bed above me. Even when it was dark, you could hear them when they landed on you.

"On March 6, we came to New York Harbour. Everyone was saying we were going to land soon, so we changed our underwear. Then we threw the old ones overboard into the water."

∞∞∞∞∞∞

June 25, 1849
I packed up with Dickerson & left about 10 A.M. The Co. were talking of dividing & did not until afterwards. Gov.

train had gone 2 hours before. All our harness, tools etc. we were obliged to leave, which with the loss on the wagons amounted to near $200.00! When coming from the east to the Ft., as you first strike the river, a mile below the Ft., is a ford — & over to the right at the junction of the Platte and Laramie branch, stands the ruin of Ft. John. Near it is a small ferry, where teams which come from Council Bluffs, on the north side of the Platte, cross. There are two fords just opposite the fort, which is nothing but a small block house made of burned bricks belonging to the American Fur Co. & used as a trading establishment. They have established a P.O. on their own hook, by which letters can be sent to the States every fourth week, by prepaying 10¢. Most of the teams have taken the mountain road to our left — we took the river road on account of grass. The country is sandy and barren with a little grass, & plenty of cedar on the hills often growing out of a fissure in the solid rock. We encamped with the rear of the Gov. train just before crossing a small stream of good water.

⋄⋄⋄⋄⋄⋄⋄

The one building from the Fort Laramie of 1849 that is still standing is the Sutler's Store — a blockhouse and former trading post of adobe and stone. We can't get inside, but you can peer through the windows at the wide plank floors, the space dim from small, high windows. Little is original though: research shows that even the floors were torn out before the store came back into park service hands, either to harvest the wood or to search for coins that had migrated down through cracks between the floorboards.

Drawings of the fort from 1849 show a much more extensive square fort with high walls, apparently adobe over logs. There's dispute about the condition of the fort in 1849, when it was purchased from private hands to serve as a U.S. Army post. Now though, it's a broad and quiet quadrangle, filled with explanatory signage.

The one thing that Fort Laramie has in spades is the feeling of a complete lack of meaningful activity. Once a crucial anchor of the Oregon and California Trails, this is now the definition of a backwater. The town, the bend of the river around the fort grounds, and the fort itself are still enough for it to seem as if time has stopped: there isn't even any wind in the trees along the river. An emigrant hub has become a nearly silent shrine.

I think that is the biggest disconnect about historic sites: you may be able to see the historic footprint of a place, it may have been scrupulously rebuilt and historically accurate in every structural detail, but there is no noise or bustle. It's as if we believed people in our past lived at a whisper, and maybe in black and white too. Visiting, we set the tone of our voices the same way, low and reverential, hardly above a murmur.

<hr />

June 26, 1849
Started early and passed Gov. train before they started, —
passed several ox teams, overtook and stopped with some
mule teams at 11 A.M. on the bank of fine clear stream of
good water with a pebbly bottom and plenty of fine grass.
At 2 P.M. Gov. train came up & camped for night, the
guide stating that there was no grass or water for 12 or 15
miles, which induced us to remain till morning, especially
as we had good feed. Frequent showers during the afternoon — myself and Dickerson both ailing. The face of the
country is entirely changed — it is sandy and barren —
very little grass, the ground being covered with artemisia
or wild Sage. It is broken and mountainous and presents
some picturesque scenes.

June 27, 1849
Started ahead of Gov. train & crossing the creek before
mentioned, we inclined to the right, travelling N.W. across

a rich bottom of clay and sand, after ascending a few gentle ascents of sand hills, toward the river, which we struck at noon. A little to the left & nearly in front, but several miles off rose Laramie Peak, towering majestically above the surrounding hills, with its head lost among the clouds with which at that time the sky was filled. This peak may be seen from Scotts Bluffs, a distance of 40 miles from Ft. Laramie & from which the mountain is at least 60 miles distant.

Note: On Laramie Peak was a little snow and some ice — it could be seen by the naked eye though not near so plainly as with a glass.

Camped with Gov. train in a hollow to the left of the road — but little grass, plenty of wood and a fine clear stream of water — weather cool and showery — extremely so.

Chapter 8

Heading for Independence Rock

The road through Guernsey to the Register Cliff is the first one we've taken that sports regular cattle grates on the pavement and fences that come right up onto the gravel shoulders. They've become common with the open rangeland. Low hills are rumpling away from the road, capped with green, like a body sleeping under blankets, and the only thing shattering that image is when the bright bones of the sandstone break through to the surface. It's wide country, mostly open and flat, and even something as simple as a wind farm or a railway marshalling yard is a distraction and almost a relief.

The road signs are a compendium of wounds from different types of ammunition: some dented with fistfuls of shotgun pellets, others blown clear through with the big holes from high-caliber rifle ammunition, the kind of blasts that leave ragged, sharp metal on the back sides of the signs. Then, there are the occasional small divots of .22 ammunition that look like someone's little brother trying to copy everyone else.

In Guernsey, there's chain link and barbed wire around a familiar theme: the military economy. You can see the Humvees and heavy trucks through the wire, and Camp Guernsey advertises itself online: "Camp Guernsey was built on the tradition of the frontier forts of America's early years. Frontier forts were often the vanguard of defense in the American West. Camp Guernsey continues this tradition by providing realistic, combat-based training opportunities for continental and deploying American forces. Customers from all branches of the Department of Defense, other federal agencies, Wyoming state and local agencies, and civilian entities, train here."

But it's nothing like a frontier fort at all. The forts Dodge saw were little more than stockaded trading posts, the American troops he met more of a threat to Dodge's animals and equipment than the Native Americans.

Camp Guernsey is 78,000 acres of military training area, live-fire military ranges, and military airspace. Everything from IED training to heavy missiles.

The American military pops up everywhere across the western states: weapons caches in the Nevada desert, all in evenly spaced bunkers, guarded by barbed wire and video cameras; dusty soldiers and their heavy packs, swigging water from one-litre plastic bottles and incongruously filling the elevator in a Las Vegas gambling resort, heading upstairs to bivouac in king-sized beds with high thread count sheets. There are flatcar trains hauling miles of desert-dusted trucks and artillery; sudden brightly lit night-time airfields lined with fighter jets, cockpits open and waiting for the arrival of pilots.

Unlike the old frontier forts, travellers aren't immediately welcome. It's guardhouses, video surveillance, and wire fences — but also, clearly a huge economic force, with the military quarters, the grid-pattern blocks of family housing, the manicured lawns, even the freshly painted fire hydrants.

After the base, the road out of Guernsey wends between chalky, sandy crags — the stone, where it juts out of the plains and starts to climb, is shouldered by trees and scrub — the plain itself is chewed down to stubble by cattle.

We cross the North Platte on a bridge that's more dike than actual river crossing, "No jumping or diving from bridge." The river is so shallow that "No Diving" seems like it should be obvious.

◌◌◇◇◇◌◌

June 28, 1849

As usual, started early and travelled 4 or 5 miles where we struck the road leading over the mountain, distant from the fort about 60 miles. At this point the road appears like some great thoroughfare — it is so worn. The morning is a splendid one & as the riflemen came galloping past with some ladies on horseback accompanied by the officers, the scene appeared grand and enlivening. For a short distance the road was smooth and good, but soon began to descend quite fast into a valley where we crossed a fine creek with plenty of timber on its banks. Passing about 50 ox teams, we bore to the right & began to ascend again. Near the creek were a large number of very large deer horns, the largest I ever saw — when standing upright a man could very nearly walk under them without stooping. We soon came to a rough road, and steep. Passing along a little way we came into a place different from any I have yet seen. High and broken ranges were on either side, & in front of a high ridge of rough broken rock piled upon rock, through a gap in which the road passes, in the hollow there runs a vane or streak of earth resembling in colour brick-dust, having the appearance of having been burnt.

Note: The earth and rocks at this place show plainly the effects of volcanic fire & present to the Geologist a broad and inviting field for inquiry.

The soil is sandy as elsewhere & is covered with artemisia and cactus, the latter of which was in full bloom. After passing over this red earth, just at the top of a little descent, there is a white substance in the road, which in appearance resembles saleratus or soda — but it is not either. It appears to have been the very mouth of some former volcano. Directly in the road is a solid mass or rock of it, the surface of which is pulverized by the passage of the wagons, & exactly resembles lime, except that it glistens like the grit in marble, when broken. Passing through a dry creek, down which, a short distance to the right of the road is a good spring — the road leads over a succession of steep though not very large hills, which are rough and stony — very bad for animals' feet. This is the roughest road over which we have yet passed.

∞∞∞∞∞

The North Platte River winds and oxbows — if you were to try and follow one bank of the river, it would add miles to any trip, especially between Fort Laramie and Guernsey, where the river's track opens up wide into a web of veins and arteries and capillaries that meander away and then together again, courses carving through malleable flatland.

The river's edge shows that its topography is regularly altered; it's shallow and sandy, stumps and logs suggesting that some of the places now underwater were shore-side property not all that long ago.

We reach Register Cliff just on the backside of Guernsey, the cliff's high sandstone faces full with the names of different emigrants carved deep into the stone in block letters, the tops of the cliff faces overhung by the wattle adobe-like nests of the cliff swallows.

On the cliff itself, there are many names, some old, some even older, and some almost brand new. It is the perfect time to be here, the sun slanting down in a way that highlights the names with deep shadow, even the ones so worn away as to have become almost illegible. Scores of them, written and overwritten, Houston and Kennedy and Rook, Willard and Patrick. Some surrounded by carved boxes, some fitted in tight between other, older names. The setting sun brings the names out larger than life: 1849, 1852 — some from the 1970s, the 2000s. Where the older names are, the rock face has been contained behind a tall wrought-iron fence in some places, behind newer chain link in others, to keep new scribes away from the historic surfaces. But the wind and weather get through, and the older names are fading anyway.

How old does graffiti have to be to become history? Why is the desire to carve a name into a soft cliff personal aggrandizement now, but a historical feature if it's still there around 160 years from now? Is nobility as simple as time?

Jackrabbits pop up and sprint away as we follow the edge of the cliff, looking for Dodge's name.

There is a type of man you meet on airplanes, the kind who holds up all boarding passengers while he folds his overcoat perfectly — and still calls it an overcoat. Leslie and I call him and his ilk "a man of a certain age." At Register Cliff, we meet one of these. Clearly gripped by the history in front of us, he asks Leslie if she would have chosen to come across the Great Plains by oxcart for the sake of her religion, the way the Mormons did. She pauses for a heartbeat; "As a woman, it wouldn't have been my choice. I would have been obligated to follow." Alone with us in front of the sandstone cliff, the man still manages somehow to melt away after that short sharp exchange.

We give up our search, empty-handed, trudge back to the car.

The cliff is fading with the declining sun: huge cottonwoods, surely hundreds of years old, throw long, fat shadows beside and across the road, so we travel through flickering light and dark stripes. There are cattle next to the fences, knee-deep in the river, head-down on the grassy, marshy delta islands.

Above Guernsey and at Glendo, ahead of us, the river is impounded again, creating twin huge reservoirs for hydroelectric power, and as the river slows behind the dams, the silt drops out, the lakes far clearer and still than the active river. At Orin, above the reservoir, the water is the colour of sand itself: after it spills into the great lake, satellite photos show how the silt fans out and fades away. At the other end of the reservoir, past the spillway and powerhouse, clear water starts to move again, picking up stray silt and heading back toward opaque.

✕◇✕◇✕◇✕

June 29, 1849

Started early and passed several companies with oxen and one camped. The road is quite smooth and good, though there are many steep hills. During the forenoon we crossed three or four creeks, following the winding course of the road over the hills, & stopped at noon by a fine mountain stream, having travelled 12 miles. No grass anywhere — nothing but sage & weeds! Since coming into the sage district, we find the ground almost covered with a kind of large reddish-brown cricket, destitute of wings, & feeding upon the sage and cactus plants. Except for a few sage cocks — a bird much resembling the prairie hen, but larger — & occasionally a deer, we have not seen any kind of game since leaving the Platte. The varieties of flowers are small, though there are a few beautiful ones. I find our present much the pleasantest mode of travelling. When we stopped with the army on the evening of the 27, they buried an Officer — his rank I did not learn. He was buried with the honors of war! Poor fellow! In serving his country his bones are left to rest on the rugged peaks of the Rocky Mountains, where without inquiry from those for whom he died, they will return again to their mother earth! Oh it is a sad thing to die thus far from home and from friends! Just as we were ready to leave, Gov. train came along, & we fell in & travelled with them. The sun shone intensely hot, & the road was filled with loose sand from 1 to 4 inches in depth, which not only made it hard drawing, but also raised such a dust as to fill our eyes & even obscure the road. Many of the Gov. teams gave out and they were obliged to turn them out at the side of the road till night. Some of the mules lay down in the road, & all the efforts of the drivers with whip and spur could not move them an inch. Camped on a bottom where a nice stream comes down from the left and empties into the Platte, which here is a narrow, deep, & swift stream, & not near as muddy as below. Where we camped the grass was eaten off as close as though it had been sheared.

June 30, 1849.
Our mules have found no feed, we travelled on about 5 miles, where finding a little spot of grass, we stopped, till the Gov. train all passed; when moved on through the sand till we came up with them camped for the night. It being not more than 3 P.M. we moved on about 7 miles & camped with some ox teams from Illinois. Close below us some emigrants have built a ferry, whereby finding our own ropes and giving them $2.50 for the privilege of working our passage, we might have crossed. Grass is out of the question — what little there has been is dead and dried up, & there is scarcely a particle of green to be seen! Of all the barren looking places that I ever saw, this is the most so. Our mules can hardly live & that is all; & even they are becoming tired and poor. As before, the day has been extremely warm, and the sand plentiful & deep.

On the evening of the 28th, a man was found in the river near here, supposed to have accidentally drowned in looking for a good ford.

Now we begin to see hard times we expected — and if any there are who thought to make this a pleasure trip, now is the time they will find themselves very much mistaken indeed.

∞∞∞∞∞

We're heading for Douglas, Wyoming, and another reunion with the North Platte River. There are deer at play on the climbing plateau of the flatlands, mountains appearing in a long and hazy row along the horizon. One hundred and sixty years ago, before roads were blasted through, the mountains blocked the way and pushed the emigrants north to passes where the climb was at a tolerable and steady rate. alkali ponds are appearing and disappearing on both sides of the road, leaving white soil scars where they've filled, stood, and dried.

The light is fading fast, the sky going from denim blue to orange to bruise, and we're more than a little relieved when the lights of the highway hotels pop up over the horizon. It's chain hotels tonight — we've left it too late to find our way to our favourite, the worn motel strips that still huddle along what used to be the main highway.

I find out the next day on foot that the old highway would be Business Route 25, still home for both the 4 Winds Motel and the Plains Motel and Gift Shop, the kinds of motor hotels that used to have their own postcards, where the pictures on the front are the motels themselves. The motor hotels are still there, fading, but the cars and the customers have moved to the bigger, faster roads.

If we'd arrived with more daylight, we'd have chosen the Plains. It looks more like our kind of place than the Super 8.

∞∞∞∞∞

July 1, Sunday, 1849
Started late and drove up to the Morison ferry 6 miles, distant from Ft. L. 120 miles. The road is sandy but good. At this place a couple of emigrants have set up a forge at which they will coin money faster than many will in California. For making shoes for one ox they charge $4.00 & for merely nailing on a mule shoe they charge $4.00! Mr. Ewing is selling almonds at $6.00 per pound, raisins at $2.00 per pint, sugar $2.00 per pound, & molasses $45.00 per gallon. The ferry is nothing but a couple of dugouts on which they will <u>help</u> take your wagon across for $3.00, the team being compelled to swim across! Not being able to cross today on account of the number of teams there, & there being no feed near, we drove out

to the foot of the mountains about 4 miles & camped on a pretty little stream coming down from the Mountains where we found plenty of wood and some grass. There is no other company within 3 or 4 miles of us & we are running considerable of a risk especially while I am writing this, as D. has gone over to the ferry & left me here alone; not knowing every moment but the next thing that will greet my vision will be a band of the thievish Crow Indians! Well let them come! Before taking me, they will be obliged to take the contents of two good rifles and two pistols which <u>may</u> not be bad to take. We are lying here to recruit our mules which have had pretty hard fare & to see where the Gov. train crosses, that we may cross with them.

∞∞∞∞∞∞

There are three Poles at the Super 8 in Douglas: father, mother, son. The father without a word of English, in a beige vest with a big American flag on the breast and military badges, and he's wearing 1970s sunglasses with earpieces that wrap right around his ears, like they're meant to stay on even in a bar fight.

The mother unspeaking, but clearly with enough English to word-lessly provide more credit cards, ID, pursed lips like she's expecting trouble and doesn't want to be the one to start it. The adult son in a brown T-shirt, trying to problem-solve language barriers and declined credit cards.

They ask for a restaurant, refuse Mexican food, head for a steak-house instead. The front desk clerk stays cheerful; the lobby is little more than a kiosk off a hall, the space even smaller because it's got the obligatory free breakfast set-up: the waffle maker, the three tubs of dried cereal, the coffee machine. This is a country of endless huge waffles, as thick as ocean sponges. Plastic forks and knives, Styrofoam plates. There are two small tables, topped with the hard plastic that dropped things bounce off and slide from.

And the hotel phone is ringing, ringing, ringing, with the nagging insistence of a fat circling housefly.

The clerk's son, six or seven years old, is at work with his mother, flitting around, messing up the desk, and the whole room is supercharged by the constant sound of the phone.

At the Mexican restaurant across the street, the La Costa, bright light-blue murals stretch across the front wall. There are a dozen conversations worth eavesdropping on, but I am too tired to catch more than a few words and to thank goodness for shredded spiced beef. Leslie, though, is alert enough to catch a thorough mansplaining of American politics from a young man in a loud group two tables away. It's the first talk of politics we've heard since we arrived in America — and it's just two months shy of the U.S. presidential election. Dodge has had more to say about politics by this point in his journey.

"Of course it's illegal," the loud young man opines confidently. "Everything is illegal in Massachusetts."

The last of the light drops away, dusk to night happening in a handful of minutes like someone turning a sign around in a shop window. Geographically, as we get ready for bed, we are closely aligned with Dodge's location in the diary: as always, Dodge is in another world entirely — one where even U.S. government soldiers are a danger.

∞∞∞∞∞∞

July 2, 1849

'Tis noon and all is well. Neither red man nor white has molested us — the selfsame Providence which heretofore hath protected us, is with us still. Yesterday for the first time I lost track of the time — mistaking Sunday for Saturday. The place where we are encamped is most delightful indeed. Just behind us tower the lofty summits of the Rocky Mountains, with their steep sides covered with the shrubby cedar, giving them a very dark appearance from which originated the name "Black Hills." Through a little valley, foaming and tumbling comes a littler stream clear as crystal from the mountain, dividing just before reaching us into two channels and uniting again just below, thus forming a beautiful island; near the center of which, under the shade of some large cottonwood trees is our camp. Here we have everything we want — plenty of grass for our mules, the best of water & any quantity of wood, and nobody to molest or interrupt us! Oh 'tis delightful! One thing only is wanting to render it a miniature Paradise — Home — friends! Oh would to Heaven, that for a moment they were here! What to me is all the gold in California compared to them? 'Tis nothing — a mere shadow, a glittering toy that has turned the brain and ruined the souls of more men than ever fell by any other evil.

Still that restless spirit must needs excite me to join in the foolish enterprise. Oh foolish youth! How might you have enjoyed the smiles of loving Sisters & doting Parents. How might you have made yourself happy with the warm approbation of a numerous circle of anxious friends! But no, the bright prospects which in the future shone fair — the tender endearments of the friendly social circle — these all these; aye more even Home, Parents, & Sisters — all, all are sacrificed! And yet, who knows but that 'tis best. That power alone knows that didst light out of darkness bring — and quietly will I wait its guidance now.

The forepart of the day was spent in washing — shooting at a mark — melting bullets, cutting patches, reading, etc., etc. Toward evening we hitched up and drove over to the ferry where we found the first division, the second being 4 miles above at another crossing, and the third some 14 miles behind at another. Hoping to cross in the morning we camped near the ferry, though the ground was bare of grass. About this time Dickerson got a notion into his head that he might do better with the Guide, Wilcox — who is a very clever fellow — & therefore tried to get me to pack, pretending to be somewhat dissatisfied.

July 3, 1849

I spent the morning in seeing what I could do with the Gov. Officers, and also the prospect in regard to packing. Not being able to effect anything, and not liking to pack from here alone, we concluded to go on until our boys should overtake us, & then I would pack if he desired it. Before noon I got my two mules shod on their fore-feet, which cost me $3.00 — myself finding the shoes and nails! We then moved on to the upper on 2nd Division, where we found splendid grass. Gov. having chartered the ferry we could not cross till they were all over, nor did we care, while we had such feed. Spent the afternoon in covering my canteen, which is much better keeping the water very cool & nice. Had a talk with the guide and found that I was well acquainted with his acquaintances in New York. The day has been fine, & the evening is delightful. Much dissatisfaction exists among the soldiers on account of maltreatment by the Officers, most of whom are a set of drunken rowdy characters. Already there has been enlisted in this regiment near 4,000 men, & now they do not number 400! One company has but 14 left; and when they reach Ft. Hall probably nearly all will desert. A band of some 30 of the deserters, led by one Dick Murphy of Company 1, are camped but a few miles back in the mountains — their fires being in plain sight; yet such is the feeling among the soldiers that the Officers dare not attempt to secure them. Many of the Officers are afraid to risk their lives in the hands of the soldiers, many of whom would be glad of an opportunity to pay off their old grudges.

Nearly every night the deserters enter camp and carry away provisions, arms, & horses, — they have taken the very best of the Officer's horses, and they cannot prevent it, nor dare they even issue the revolvers, knowing that as soon as they are obtained, the larger portion of them would leave at once. Many of them are Germans who can scarcely speak or understand English at all. By a soldier I am informed that the deserters intend forming themselves into guerrilla parties, & when they get beyond Ft. Hall, to prey upon the emigrants.

◇◇◇◇◇◇◇

The next morning, I find out why the phone is ringing so constantly at the Super 8.

The same clerk is still working behind the narrow desk, her son eating cereal from the narrow breakfast bar while she's trying to solve an overbooking problem, going through every hotel in Douglas, through nearby Casper, looking for rooms. Finding none.

When she puts the phone down, it rings again: "No," she says when she picks it up, "We're fully booked."

"For tonight?" I ask when she's done, curious, knowing the hotel had been almost empty overnight.

"No," she answers, "For next year. For the eclipse."

That eclipse is set to travel almost directly over Douglas, with "totality," the point where the whole sun is covered by the moon, arriving at 11:25:45 a.m. Mountain Time. The total eclipse will last a mere two minutes and 22 seconds — barely a third of the 6:59 it takes, for example, to play Bonnie Tyler's original version of "Total Eclipse of the Heart" — and so many people have planned to be in Douglas that there is not one single hotel room left, even a year in advance.

Why do we benchmark our lives by saying "I was there" when something unique or astounding occurs? What's the value that it adds? Why do we spend thousands of dollars to be at a last concert or a farewell tour? Why do we seek out the bigger-than-us with such religious fervour? Why do we quest to be present for rare birds, for great walls coming down, for massive marches?

It's like we're deliberately hanging our own smiling pictures inside the frames of world events.

Maybe the truth is we're all just barnacles, trying to anchor ourselves to something with enough weight or heft to hold us fast. Does being there, being part of something, fulfil some need in us, some need to fit precisely in the larger firmament? Are touchpoints an affirmation of shared humanity? "And yet, who knows but that 'tis best." Maybe I'm just lacking Dodge's faith.

But I can't help thinking: mathematics and planetary motion will combine with absolute predictability, and total darkness will descend on a crowded Douglas.

The same total darkness that there was when we drove into town. The same total darkness that similar sorts of immutable laws of nature and planetary motion bring to all of us at least once every single day.

Except we called it night, are used to that, and don't go even a mile out of our way to find it.

∞∞∞∞∞

July 4, 1849

This is the "Glorious Fourth" and a most glorious morning it is too! The sky clear, and Old Sol sends down his rays in a manner most delightful. No prospect of crossing today, Gov. train having bought the ferry which was built by the DuBuque Co. of emigrants at this place, & it will take all day at least for them to cross.

An Officer just rode up enquiring if we had seen any men pass during the night — four more teamsters having deserted, taking with them the four best mules in their teams! Change, change — is the order of the day — even as my ink is changed in colour so is nearly everything except the immutable laws of nature, changed. The Officers have changed their opinions — that is if they ever possessed ideas sufficient to form an opinion. Instead of crossing here they have taken the dugouts down to the lower crossing & intend to cross there. Waiting till the last of their wagons were out of sight, we followed, hoping to get across this evening, but when we arrived, we found part of them across, & the rest camped by the ferry — and although the evening was extremely quiet, they were doing nothing, & the boat was lying idle! Seeing the boat idle we were much in hopes of being able to cross — but after searching a long time for the ferryman in vain, we were compelled to wait till morning, with not a particle of grass for our mules! In the morning we were informed that we would have to wait till Gov. train was finished — which would probably be about 4 o'clock in the afternoon.

The North Platte River at Douglas. I feel like we have crossed that river a hundred times, as many or more times than Dodge himself, and each time it's different. Out on foot in the cool September morning, and Douglas is like any western city with access to water: lawns and trees and green, and here the river is like an eastern river, crossed with rocky shoals and riffles, large boulders poking up through the water. At this time of year, at least, it's clear and clean. Willows right down to the edge of the banks, and signs about fishing regulations and how and when the boat launches can be used.

The bridge to the fairgrounds for the Wyoming State Fair has arched steel railings all the way across, like waves. It also has several bedrolls hidden under it, too, tucked up tight against the abutments, with no sign of their owners. In the Riverside Park public washrooms, there's a shirtless, pants-less man washing up in the sink. It might be 165 years later, but there are still people sleeping under the open skies and using clean water wherever they can find it.

There's a flatbed pickup truck in the gas station that's been refitted to unroll a mile of barbed wire off each back corner — fencing made manageable from the driver's seat. It can string fences faster than Dodge's group could travel, closing off open prairie and leaving only a brief tang of exhaust behind it.

The green grass and trees end exactly, precisely where the irrigation must also end; the divide between green and beige is drawn as sharply as if it had been done with a ruler.

The sagebrush and cactus are just waiting, biding their time. Only the green of the riverbanks will be spared if the water stops being delivered.

In Casper, we re-provision, the big-box stores nestled tight to the highway again. What are these towns even for anymore? Just houses for the staff of highway-big-box stores? Homes for the cleaners stripping mattresses at the Super 8? We get coffee at a McDonald's, and the pickup truck next to us has what looks like a gun rack in the back window — except it holds a highly-varnished baseball bat with the black script legend "Ready when you are."

Gas. Re-inflate the low tire. Wash the windshield. Buy beer in a roadside liquor store that's also a bar with the convenience of a drive-through: Taylor's Liquor is split in half by a counter, so one side is a sports bar, the other, a "package store" for full-bottle purchases. When you've made your selection, the bartender turns away from his morning patrons, walks over still drying a glass with a dishtowel, and takes the money for your purchase. Full service, in all ways. It is 10 o'clock in the morning, and there is a patron on the bar side who is tilted so far forwards that, if his face was any lower, his cheek would be pressed against the bar top. Sports highlights battle each other from competing flat-screen televisions.

The difference between the cool dark inside the store and the hot bright light of Wyoming mid-morning is like a body blow. You lower your shoulder to push out into it, blinking.

<hr />

July 5, 1849
Accordingly, I hitched up and drove back 2 or 3 miles to find grass. Yesterday I made an arrangement with Dickerson by

which he is to assume all the risk of the wagon breaking or giving out, & I am to do the cooking & tend to the team. He is a vacillating quibbling sort of a fellow & not very agreeable — or easy to get along with. In crossing yesterday, two soldiers were drowned, and the Officers instead of making any active exertions for their rescue, merely remarked that the d-m cusses ought to be drowned! The Officers are a drinking, overbearing, insolent set of fellows, & they mistreat the men, both soldiers and teamsters shamefully, often striking and abusing them in a beastly manner — causing them to be tied and flogged for no worse crime than simply looking dejected! The expedition is very badly managed, & the men continue to desert daily.

Instead of being an assistance to the emigrants, they are a nuisance — no one can camp near them but he is in danger of having stolen from him everything he has — especially larriettes and pickets — they have stolen one of mine and cut several more — even our animals we are obliged to watch more on their account than of the Indians!

Here as before the country is broken and mountainous — the soil sandy and barren. Nothing scarcely grows here except the Prickly Pear and wild sage. It has been frequently said that mules would readily feed and live upon the sage, but I have not seen one touch it yet, and they have had some pretty hard times for grass too. They live upon the few spears of grass & weeds, growing among the sage, gnawing it clear to the roots. The mountains run parallel with the river, about 4 miles to the south of it — the intervening ground being cut into separate ridges by the streams flowing down the Mts. into the Platte, & also covered with sage, which grows in bunches, with stalks frequently as large as a man's wrist. It very much resembles a potato field except that the hills are larger, making it very difficult driving a wagon over it. In the valley between the

river and the Mts. may be found a little grass on the border of the little streams. Down with the book! Away goes
one of the confounded mules, making a straight wake for
the river ¾ of a mile off. Perhaps 'tis dry — no doubt, but
see, the contrary thing will not drink now it is there! Of all
animals that ever were created, I do believe the mule is the
most obstinate & provoking. They will neither lead nor
drive with any kind of decency — & where you do not
want them to go, there they will! They alone are enough to
spoil the temper of any man except a Philosopher — and
it is very few of that class of beings who are to be found
engaged in such an expedition as this! None but those who
are inured to toil and fatigue ought ever to start on a trip
like this, & if any wish to preserve their finer and more
acute feelings uninjured, I would advise them to stay at
home. Let men who have no care for home or friends —
whose only God is gold — & whose only recognition of
right is might — let such men go. But the man of refined
taste & of warm social feelings, I would say should stay at
home. 'Tis done! And toiling through the sand again we
go. After so long a time we have at last got across, safely,
though the mules did not much relish their bath at first
— they being compelled to swim across. We moved on
through heavy sand about 2 miles and camped close to the
river on a small bottom where once there had been grass,
but which was ere this numbered with the things that had
been! Very fine weather indeed — days hot — evenings
clear and nights quite chilly.

∞∞∞∞∞∞

It's hard to explain the monotony and endlessness of the sage desert
— harder still to imagine walking through it for days and weeks on
end like Dodge did, heading for California. The heat, the flies, the
days on the trail just looking for a good source of the necessary trio

of water, wood, and grass. Water, wood, and grass: when they find all three, it suddenly becomes a good day, a paradise.

Wyoming — and Nebraska before it — now specialize in the equipment graveyard, the rows and rows of trucks, military surplus, farm equipment, old cars, all laid out in blocks. As if at any time, someone might come up and ask for a suspension part from a deuce army transport, and you'd not only have it but be able to ask your price, the way Dodge saw suppliers asking $45 a gallon for molasses.

It's dry enough here for the old trucks to stay in a rustless stasis: dry enough that we drink litres and litres of water every day and have gallons of it in the trunk. Filling the water jugs is an every-morning chore before we head out to the car. For us, it's as close as the tap, clean and constant. For Dodge, it was none of those. I can't help thinking of that every time I lift a bottle to drink.

Every electric sign on the highway warns that there's a high fire risk; it's easy to imagine a windswept fire leaping from greasewood to greasewood, sage to sage, crowning its way across the desert, growing by leaps and bounds and filling the sky with smoke. And this is September, the heat already tailing away fast in the evenings.

◇◇◇◇◇◇◇

July 6, 1849
Got under way early! Here the hill approaches close to the river, which makes the road take off over a steep hill where the sand is 4 or 5 inches deep — making the drawing very hard. After going a little way over this, the road again makes down to the river which it follows for about 8 miles & then turns off to the right over the high hills. The road is good though a little sandy & at present is strewn with dead oxen, which creates a most unpleasant stench. We have passed much as a dozen this forenoon. There is no water after leaving the river for 25 miles, except some few springs, which are so strongly impregnated with alkali as to be dangerous to use. We passed a couple of

puddles soon after leaving the river, the shores of which were white with the deposits of saleratus. . . . There is no grass on this hill & [it] has a very barren appearance indeed. So far as we can see not a green object meets the eye except a few small weeds. No wood, except occasionally — a few — trees in the hollows. The country is rough and broken, presenting a great variety of ridges, hills, ledges, etc. The strata of rock mostly lie in a slanting position, showing conclusively the effect of volcanic action. Road smooth except holes made by the quicksand giving way, of which the road has been full for the last 100 miles. This afternoon we passed a ledge of rocks set up edgewise rising to the height of from 10 to 30 feet and making a wall 75 or 100 rods in length. The road passes over the lower or eastern end of this ridge, just where it disappears beneath the surface. During the afternoon there arose a strong wind which blew the dust & sand into our faces so that we could not see where to go. At noon we gave away all our water to some of the Officers & ladies expecting to get some again soon, but did not, so we suffered most severely for the want of it, till dark when we reached a little stream running from a spring but which contained so much sulphur & other mineral qualities as to render it nearly unfit for use, although it was very cool. No wood here and the grass all eaten off. We saw vast numbers of dead cattle — eight in one place, and they are strewed all along the roadside — killed by drinking this water.

July 7, 1849
Our mules having had nothing to eat, we started without waiting to get breakfast, hoping soon to find grass. In 3 or 4 miles we came to the Willow Spring. This is a fine large spring close to the right hand of the road and is the first

good water after leaving the river 25 miles back. 3 or 4 miles farther we found a boggy spot with a little grass and stopped. There is a small stream and an excellent spring to the left in the swails. At 4 P.M. we started and passing large numbers of dead cattle, drove on through heavy sand and camped with a Co. a little to the left of the road. Just beyond a little stream that puts off to the south. . . . During the day one of my mules was quite sick from drinking too much water at the sulphur stream where we camped the night before.

◇◇◇◇◇◇◇

We pass just below the Willow Spring on the 220, take a turn to the left onto Pathfinder Road just past the marina and a man-made lake behind a dam at Alcova — and we get out of the car to be stabbed in the feet and ankles by hidden cactus spears.

It's just a rest from driving, a chance to stretch our legs, a break from the constant cars and the steady passage of the dust and sage. Behind a hummock, I pee into the hot dust and the powdered rock, and sand — like flour in its consistency — rolls over as if leaping thirstily into the unexpected liquid. Leslie's having a smoke.

Looking west, a long line of hills darkens the horizon.

Leslie, one hand over her eyes, spots a dusty pair of ruts cutting through the sage to the west, die-straight, and says it might be the trail, two-wheel tracks heading off toward the horizon, right where the trail would have had to have dropped down from Willow Springs, away, finally, from the North Platte and heading for the Sweetwater River.

I think that's pretty far-fetched: stop the car at random and just spot a road and decide it's a 165-year-old wagon trail. But I don't say that out loud.

The ground is full of quartz and rocks that look like beach stones, along with flattened, rusted (annealed, really) tin cans of indeterminate age. All manner of castoff and unidentifiable things. The more I look, the more I start to agree that it doesn't take much imagination to superimpose the emigrant wagons on two ruts heading away from us. In the middle, directly in front of that trail heading west, I spot a huge, flat dome of rock nudging up out of the desert. So obvious that, if this is the trail, it will be an obvious landmark, something Dodge is bound to name. I'm right about that part, at least.

∞∞∞∞∞

July 8, Sunday, 1849

Again the day of the week had like to have passed unnoticed! So little is the Sabbath regarded by any here! For shame! Leaving camp we passed down this stream, taking a new route to the Sweet Water, distant 7 miles. Passing down the valley of this stream we found several companies encamped recruiting their teams — passed one grave also. Having some anxiety to ascend the summit of some of the various peaks which are to be seen here, I accordingly struck for one a little off to the right. It did not look to be more than a good sized hill, & but a little way off, but by the time I arrived at its base, I thought the distance to be "some" at least! & as for climbing it, that was easier talked of than accomplished. Determined not to be foiled, I commenced and had proceeded but a little way when all at once I found myself on the brink of a fissure some 30 feet deep, and the place where I stood so steep that I could go no further, so smooth that I could scarcely stand where I was! With great difficulty I descended, during which operation I liked to have torn my pants entirely off! Finding the path impassible, I then went back and crawled up one of the fissures where the rock on either side was far above my head, and so narrow at the bottom as to be scarcely wide enough for my foot without wedging fast. After a tedious journey of some length, I finally reached the top, where I was richly repaid for my toil. Here large masses of huge rocks larger than a church piled one upon another in the utmost confusion, while smaller ones are piled in every possible shape & form showing plainly the effect of volcanic eruptions. Letting myself down on the opposite side I soon overtook the team & after passing a bottom covered with a white incrustation of Saleratus and nitre, we soon came to a small pond, the water of which had dried away leaving a crust of almost pure saleratus, which in the distance resembled ice. Soon after passing that we struck the Sweetwater. Here is the famous Independence Rock just to the right of the road which here runs close to its base.

∞∞∞∞

Our next stop, a short time later, is at the Independence Rock Interpretive Center. Leslie points at a photo of the trail, exactly where we had stopped, and she is right, again. We were scuffling around in the desert exactly where the trail ran, our feet in the same place as his feet in 1849. It's almost like a physical shudder, every time it happens. Every time I can know for certain, for absolute certain, that my feet and his are on the same ground, that my eyes are staring out at the same line of horizon, that the dust is, at least to some measurable degree, the same dust.

∞∞∞∞

July 8, 1849 (con't)
It is large conical, oblong, granite rock, perfectly bare — except its crop of inscriptions, which is very great — nearly every person that passes putting his name, with paint or by engraving. The sides of it are completely covered. Wishing to be as foolish as the rest, we camped just against the foot of it & proceeded to add ours to the already numerous catalogue of adventurers. Several parties are camped near us.

∞∞∞∞

A big owl launches itself out of a scraggly cedar on the back of Independence Rock and flies directly over me, its wings soundless. A discarded snakeskin tumbles by; my eyes at first see only a discarded plastic bag, until the shape makes itself clear.

It was named Independence Rock because it was a waypoint: in order to get to the goldfields before the weather turned too cold, emigrants had to have reached the rock by Independence Day, the Fourth of July. Dodge was five days behind that schedule. The rock stands out alone on the desert floor, its shoulders visible for miles, almost to where the trail wends out of the hill country at Willow Springs.

I'm watching for rattlers around my ankles, while keeping an eye open for Dodge's name on the rocks. A trail goes all the way around. At the end, where the trail passes with the rock to its right, where Dodge said he camped, the ground is uniformly damp and there are some reeds that suggest water is not too deep below the surface. The Sweetwater River curls a mere stone's throw away, small oxbows and bends and curves. Standing on top of the rock and looking east, you can see the white trail markers and the trail itself, heading back across the sage to where we stood on Pathfinder Road. The most common sight around the huge stone is older men in khaki shorts with sensible, sun-protecting hats that reach out over their ruddy ears, talking loud, explaining the obvious to the air. Wives and other family members trail along behind, paying half-attention. I am wearing a sensible desert hat: my khaki shorts reach almost exactly to my knees. I am a familiar trope in my own story.

We make our way around the entire rock, searching for the spot with his name.

Dodge's name, though, is elusive.

I don't find it. He's not completely clear whether he carved it into the rock or wrote it with grease and tar, as others did. By date, he would have been among the earliest of the names, though he said plenty had left their mark already.

◇◇◇◇◇◇◇

July 8, 1849 (con't)

A rather romantic, yet sadly tragical affair came off here a day or two since. There appears to be an old man & daughter from Missouri travelling in a Co., & the daughter had two suitors, one of whom the father did not like & accordingly forbade her showing him any encouragement, which highly incensed the disappointed one. A day or two since the father and both young men went out hunting & not returning at night, next morning some of his party went in search of them, when they found the old man badly wounded by shot in the back of the neck! One of the young men has not been found & the other was putting on ahead, when he was overtaken and brought back to the Rock, where a jury of emigrants was called and a trial held. Though nothing could be proven for certain, it was fully believed that he had killed his rival, & then shot the father and left him, as he supposed, dead! On the strength of this he was compelled to leave and return to the "States." He passed us today on his way back. Since writing the above I have learned that the case is not as stated there, but as follows: The old gentleman alluded to had with him two daughters & their stepmother who was far his junior in years. There was also a Campbellite preacher who had two sons. This preacher & the old man's wife became rather more intimate than was proper, when it was agreed that they would kill the old man — the preacher take the wife, & the young men take the sisters, and proceed with the old man's team to California! Having made their arrangements, they invited the father of the girls to go out hunting, when they shot him! Seeing him struggle, they advanced to finish their fiendish work, when he, seeing their purpose, pretended to fall back dead; whereupon they turned and fled. They came into camp as though nothing had happened. About midnight, the wounded man came into camp in a frightful condition, having received nine buckshot in his neck and body! The men fled, but one of them was taken, & after a sort of trial delivered to the Gov. Officers, who let them go! The females I am informed are with the soldiers — the Co. taking the old man along, though it is uncertain whether he will recover or not.

∞∞∞∞∞

Dodge is clear: the story changes with the teller.

There's a granite trail marker with a metal inset plaque, and below it, the inscription "To all the unknown pioneers who passed this way to win and hold the West. Placed here by Troop 21, Boy Scouts of America, Woodmere, Long Island, New York. Charles A. Jewlett, Scoutmaster."

"It's not that simple," I want to scratch into the metal. Because it isn't: not at all. The winners get to pick who the heroes were and write the commemoration. But they're only overwriting the names of those who learned the same ground — and lived on it for generations — before them.

∞∞∞∞∞

July 9, 1849

This is a beautiful morning, & having breakfasted in the shade of Independence Rock, we rolled on. Nearly all are disappointed at the appearance of the Rock. It does not, at first sight, seem to be very high nor very large, but by the time that a man has walked around it — has ascended to its summit, & read all the names on it, he will begin to think it considerable of a stone! It covers an area from 3 to 5 acres — rises in an oblong conical form to a height of over 300 feet & has not a shrub or plant on it. It is perfectly bare & incapable of being ascended in

169

front, though on the S.W. side a man may climb it with ease. Very few of the many names on it are engraved — most of them being merely painted or daubed on in a very awkward manner, with tar, paint, or the grease used on their wagons. Crossing the Sweetwater soon after leaving the Rock, and proceeding 5 miles we came to Devil's Gate — a curiosity well worthy of notice. It is a gap where the river passes through a granite ridge, the rock on both sides rising 400 feet. The road lies along the river valley, on either side of which rise numerous peaks and ridges of naked rocks of all shapes & sizes, some of which are more than 1,000 ft. above the river. Most of them are perfectly naked having no grass or timber except an occasional cedar shrub growing out of a fissure in the rock. For several days we have had a very strong wind from the W. & S.W., which with the cloud of sand in which we are continually enveloped, makes the travelling very tedious indeed. The road is so filled with loose sand that it is very hard for the teams — that the wagons are all shrinking up. Spokes, tires, etc. are working loose, & we are compelled to wet them often. Even a painted pail kept constantly in the shade has shrunk so as nearly to fall to pieces!

◇◇◇◇◇◇

July 10, 1849

Moved on and soon found ourselves behind a train of about 75 ox teams, which we could not pass for the sage. The sand blew in our eyes, almost blinding us, all during the forenoon we had a most disagreeable time. I paid $1.75 for a pair of goggles, which in the States could be bought for $3.00! At noon Dickerson got mad, and wanted to fight, at which I merely laughed. We are travelling over gradual hills, with a smooth road, but filled with loose sand. . . . Game plenty but it is frightened back into the hills by the continual passing of trains. Deer and antelope abound with frequent signs of buffalo along the S.W. Bear are also quite numerous, but are not found near the road, they keep in the hills or in the high sage at the bottom of them, where it is rather dangerous to come suddenly upon them. We have not seen an Indian since entering the Crow territory, though we saw yesterday where a large party had been not more than a day or two since — the region of the country in which we now are is considered the most dangerous of any on the route.

Yesterday noon Dickerson got mad at nothing — except it was the operation of some brandy which we had been drinking — and swore he would throw my things out & leave me there, some 15 or 20 miles ahead of the Gov. train & no camp near! I had made arrangements to go with Dr. White, from Ft. Hall, where he intended leaving the Gov. train, directly through to the diggings, & was only waiting for them to come up that I might join them. Dickerson having understood the arrangement agreed to wait for them if we did not meet part of the Dr.'s Co. (who had gone ahead) returning. Now he refused to wait, & even declared he was going still faster, swearing at the same time that he would throw out my things & leave me there alone! I told him to do so if he chose, when he seeing that I was not afraid to remain & that I would of course take my team, which would render him unable to proceed, one of his mules being about used up, he proposed that he should go on, which I consented to. . . . We got ready for a start when he commenced swearing at & abusing me most shamefully, all of which I took perfectly cool, which so exasperated him that he jumped down from the carriage determined to fight any person — but that he could not frighten me, and if he wished, to strike me as soon as he pleased! My coolness seemed perfectly to exasperate him, and he proposed to fight me with weapons! He had two pistols, one of which was loaded, & a dagger all within his reach, while I had no weapon of any kind about — having used my belt knife to cut meat and left it in the box which was then locked — nor did I wish any but told him again that I would not fight except in self defense, yet if he wanted to shoot to do so as soon as he saw fit. Finding that he could not provoke me to fight and having exhausted himself in his fruitless efforts he finally drove on. During the afternoon his mule gave out, and mine were compelled to draw the whole, nearly. After stopping at night he proposed to trade me a gold watch for one of my mules, which I consented to do provided he would wait till I could see if the Dr. would consent to my joining him with but one mule.

Chapter 9

The Continental Divide

Near Lander, we turn onto the 28 to climb to the South Pass, the gap in the Rockies that the emigrants have been aiming for. It's the lowest point on the Continental Divide — on the eastern side, rivers flow toward the Atlantic. On the western side, toward the Pacific. The Rocky Mountains here are not like their northern counterparts: I expected sharp peaks with treed sides, gashes of fanned-out fallen rock from landslides, snow-capped peaks late into the summer. Most likely, a narrow gap for the wagons to work their way through, the typical mountain pass of movies. But these are flatter, lower, rounder mountains, at this point barely discernible as a range. There are snowy peaks in the distance, but they seem detached from where we are. This horizon of mountaintops — they seem, well, tired, disinterested, old.

The next moment, things change. You can drive for miles in Wyoming without seeing anything but sage, and then all at once the whole place cleaves right open with beautiful geography and heart-stopping geology.

There's a spot past Sweetwater Station where the hills fall away by hundreds of feet. It's still well before the South Pass but has the feel of continents shifting that I was expecting from the pass itself. Off to one side, there is a great sea of change in the land, from flat sage desert to white, white cliffs. I startle an antelope, which springs like a gymnast from dirt pile to dirt pile, kicking up clouds of dust everywhere it lands, before it turns straight downhill and disappears.

⊰⊱⊰⊱

July 11, 1849

Next morning (Dickerson) was very sick with a nervous headache — the effects of his anger last night — for which reason we remained there. Where we camped about 25 or 30 miles from the Rock, the valley of the Sweetwater is narrow, affording only here and there a spot of grass, all of which have been camped upon till the grass is eaten to the very roots! On both sides of the river, and in many places directly from its banks, rise mountain ranges of rough huge naked rock, several hundred feet in height. Some of the peaks are covered with stunted cedars which give them a black appearance, hence the name "Black Hills." The river is much clearer than the Platte of which it is a tributary, & is from 1 to 3 rods in width and about 2 or 3 feet deep — what in the States we would call a good creek. At this place we used buffalo chips for fuel, and they burn well, there having been no rain to wet them for several weeks. We have a strong wind from the S.W. which commenced about 9 o'clock A.M. and continued till night. It is very disagreeable, & I am told by old mountaineers that at this time of the year it almost always blows in this direction & manner. It blows very strong, often upsetting our dishes, spilling our coffee, & filling everything — eyes, mouth, ears, dishes — with sand! Goggles are indispensable here. Already we have passed 280 dead oxen since leaving the Ferry & a Mormon who has just arrived from the Salt Lake says there are upwards of <u>five thousand</u> lying between that place and the Ferry! Every day we pass wagons & other things thrown away & destroyed for want of teams to haul them — & still the grass is not sufficient for what teams there are! We have passed several Companies who have stopped to set their wagon tires, cut off the bodies, etc. — one lies near us repairing theirs. A large portion of the emigrants, especially those with ox teams, have about concluded to take the Oregon route.

Dickerson remained sick, grunting & groaning frightfully all day. He was even unable to get out of the wagon, & had to be waited upon like a little child; all of which I did with pleasure, thankful that Heaven had given me a spirit that took delight in repaying evil with good — and still, the ungrateful wretch, that very evening got mad at, & cussed and swore at me most shamefully — simply because I succeeded in shooting a ball through a card loosely stuck in the end of a stick; for which he said he would give me $10.00 if I would accomplish the feat! The money of course I would not have taken. At night we were again alone and compelled to watch our mules. Early in the evening they were frightened by an Indian or some wild animal, we could not tell which, & one of them broke loose, which frightened Dickerson very much. I sat up most of the night which was very dark and chilly — making it seem long and dreary. Many men would say that I am a fool for putting up with Dickerson's treatment — but what need I care what the world says while my conscience approves.

July 12, 1849
During the night the wind changed to the east from which it blew a gentle breeze during the forenoon. Leaving our camp, we crossed the Sweetwater and took up that stream, the mountains shutting it in so close as scarcely to leave room for a wagon to pass. The road is smooth & not quite so much of deep sand. . . . The ranges of naked rock present some grand sights indeed. After proceeding about 3 miles, for the first time we saw snow on

the top of a ridge off to the left several miles. The sun is shining intensely yet it was sufficiently cool to require a coat on! After passing some most interesting looking ridges for 2 miles further, we camped near the river, as the Guide informed us that we would find no grass for 16 miles, and also to let the train come up so that I might complete my arrangements with the Dr. Directly to the west of us some 25 or 30 miles rises a range the tops of which are now covered with snow, presenting a splendid appearance. Joined the Dr. and transferred my loading to his wagon. Dickerson mad again, & wanted to fight as usual. Evening very cool — requiring an overcoat.

July 13, 1849
Put my team in with the Dr.'s & rode a horse of his — moving with the 2nd Division of the Army, of which the Dr. is surgeon. Leaving camp we crossed the Sweetwater & took over some long high hills 16 miles when we again crossed the river, and finding the grass all eaten off passed over another hill 5 miles, & again struck the river & camped. Found good grass across the river, but no fuel. Here we met the boys whom the Dr. had sent on to recover his share of the stock in Capt. White's Co., who was making off with it as fast as possible. Weather extremely hot during the middle of the day.

◇◇◇◇◇◇◇

You can't pick your family: Dodge is finding that, even if you can pick your travelling companions, it doesn't always work out well either. Travelling has a way of pressing home that point, the sheer closeness of contact magnifying small irritations. Leslie and I have our moments: we're not talking about dissolving the company, but like Dodge, we sometimes need to head out on our own individual explorations.

The climb to the South Pass is a constant uphill grade. We travel alongside a great red stone gash in the hill, a sheered-off cliff where the road follows its contour. Later, from above, the red cliff is like a great tear in the earth, though the sight of it, as huge as it is, reminds me of the white curve of a nail bed on a fingernail. There are few other cars and I worry for miles about a single Honda pulled off on the opposite shoulder in a place no car should be stopped, about whether the driver might have been in trouble and needed our help.

Down below us, a small river also follows the contour of the rock. Here, it's not a river that has carved a route, it's a river's route dictated by abrupt geology that bends the river to its will.

⬦⬦⬦⬦⬦⬦

July 14, 1849

Remained at that place. We were not much pleased at this way of getting along so slowly, but the grass being good, our teams are recruiting. Nothing unusual occurred. Spent the day preparing and arranging matters to form a separate mess of us boys — cleaning our arms, washing, etc. Gov. people busy shoeing their animals. Very warm indeed. Hundreds of ground puppies and squirrels all along here — easily shot. Spent the afternoon in constructing a portable table for Mrs. White.

July 15, 1849

Left camp very early, & after following the river 4 miles, turned to the right over the longest and highest hill that we have yet passed. The road, most of the ascent was very smooth, except loose stones, but on or near the top we crossed several ledges of rough rock protruding edgewise from the surface, forming a spine or backbone as it were to the range over which we were passing, making the road very rough! Large isolated rocks are seen protruding from the surface in various directions, & no vegetation of any kind to be seen. The everlasting sage! Numerous dead oxen, wagons, harness, trunks, beans bacon, and almost everything usual in such an expedition is strewn all along the road! The day has been extremely warm, & yet ahead bearing to the right could be seen the Wind River Chain with their tops covered with snow — forming a most pleasing contrast to the burning sand beneath our feet. On the summit we passed a couple of excellent springs — one on the left — & a much better one on the right — they may be found by the little stream running from them. Near the spring is a couple of ponds to the left, the water not fit for use. 12 or 14 miles from the river we crossed a beautiful stream of cool water descending from the snowy peaks & emptying in the Sweetwater. A few miles on we camped on another fine stream. Plenty of willow for fuel — grass all eaten off. From the top of the large hill we crossed may be had a very extensive view of the surrounding hills & mountains — some of the highest can be seen at a distance of 75 miles off — probably farther.

◇◇◇◇◇◇◇

The range has more in common with hilltops than anything else: still rolled round and saged-over, no sharp rocks or cliffs.

The South Pass itself is anticlimactic when it finally appears; a swale cut into the hilltop climbs and climbs and climbs until suddenly you are at the top, and then the angle simply changes, and instead of going up still further, you start to descend. At the very top, although the communication towers give away the fact that you're finally at the highest point, the pass is more like a dip between adjacent hilltops.

Both sides of the path upwards are treed, a sign that the high lands have brought more rain: once through the pass, the desert plain returns abruptly, beige flatlands out in front of us again to the next horizon of high ground. All that hard upwards work for the emigrants, just for a broad vista of more of the same.

<><><><><>

July 16, 1849
Day cold and stormy — fine for travelling. All the men wear their overcoats though it is the middle of July. Left camp and struck the Sweetwater to our left & crossed it 4 or 5 miles from starting. Here we took our final leave of the river and passed up a very gradual ascent with a smooth road for about 9 miles [to] reach the summit of the famous South Pass. It is difficult to tell the precise summit — indeed there is nothing at all to attract the traveller's attention except a few fine peaks off to the left, & the snowy peaks of the Wind River mountains to the right completely enveloped in rain & mist at this time. Passing the summit, we began to descend gradually & in about 2 miles came to the Pacific Spring off to the right, where rises a small stream or tributary of the Colorado, which empties into the Pacific Ocean by the Gulf of California. The road beyond the pass was strewn thicker than ever with dead cattle! Bearing to the left of the road we camped in a little hollow, where we found water, & grass, but no wood.

<><><><><>

The map lures us off the main road onto a network of small, interconnected dirt roads, heading for the tiny community of South Pass City. On the way, we pass the huge headworkings of the Carissa Mine: gold brought the population of South Pass City to 2,000 people at one point, and the end of that gold also drained the place. Dodge and the other emigrants passed almost directly by. Twenty years later, huge gold deposits were found there.

What remains of the town and mine — and what's been later rebuilt — is now a state historic site and a strangely empty, lost-in-time collection of huddled buildings. There is little to do except to look at what buildings there are and turn the car around. We have to double back: the other route out of town warns of four-wheel-drive-only hazards, and we're leery of getting stuck. It's a disconcerting spot, wide-open on all sides, with the buildings tucked into a little valley in the hills barely sheltered from the wind. You can imagine being pinned down for days by inclement weather. The original site of the town was where Dodge left the Sweetwater for the last time — the ninth time the trail crossed the river — and headed nine miles to the Pass. Later called Burnt Ranch, it became a stopover for people on the trail only a few years after Dodge passed through. Some historical accounts suggest there was a trading post there, run by Jim Bridger, also the founder of Fort Bridger. Dodge doesn't mention it, a curious omission given how few spots there are on the trail with any established habitation.

We get back to the highway without cut tires, despite the rough roads, and reach a small interpretive site with clean bathrooms, surrounded by the most amazingly lush-green irrigated grass.

At the edge of the grass, there's a four-bar split rail fence, and behind it, a small herd of black beef cattle stand in a hoof-bald patch of sage and dust and cactus. The cattle are forcing their heads through the bars of the fence, turning them sideways to fit their horns through. They've eaten a narrow runnel of the greener grass on the other side of the fence, every single scrap they can reach, right down to the roots.

◇◇◇◇◇◇

July 17, 1849
Train left camp in good season but two of the mules being gone & the Dr.'s horse, which we found in a soldier's possession, it was late before the baggage wagon got under way. Road smooth except loose stones, gradually ascending for a few miles, then slightly descending. Weather hot — nothing but wild sage to be seen in the shape of vegetation, except a few cedar shrubs near the

base of the Wind River chain, whose snowy peaks are nearer to us than at any former time. Made 20 miles & camped on the Lower Sandy. Grass rather plenty, but coarse, with plenty of willow bushes. Rabbits and ground dogs are plenty. Peter, the Dr.'s black boy, came very near being killed by falling under the wagon wheel. Saw Holcombe, Ingalsbee, Chapman, & Fred, & learned from them that Ebon & Low are yet behind — Lewis was with them, but Churchill had left them. They remained at Ft. Laramie ten days after we left.

July 18, 1849
Moved on to the Big Sandy 8 miles and camped. . . . The Big Sandy is shallow and full of islands & sand bars, and like the Platte, Sweetwater & Lower Sandy, its waters are completely full of fine sand. The snow peaks to our right are yet in sight, though receding. Grass ordinary, with some willow. Sage hens quite plenty.

In Rock Springs, Wyoming, at a roadside place named Bomber's Sports Bar, the clientele is at the video gambling machines and the air is thick with smoke. Everyone playing the machines is male, and there are codes you have to know about casinos to understand; the ashtray left on a machine means someone's playing that one, they're at the bar for another drink or in the bathroom, and sitting down to play — even though no one's there — will mean big trouble, especially if you are lucky enough to cash out a big win, a win that someone else believes they have been working toward by pumping in $20 after $20.

There's a big hotel in the downtown that we see heading in over the railway tracks on the 430 — we head for it, but it's another empty and closed business. Every sizeable town we pass through has an anchor hotel at the centre of the downtown — they're all closed. This time, it's the Park Hotel — once considered a hub for commercial travellers on the Lincoln Highway, now a symbol of the death of downtown. The lounge appears to still be open.

We end up in a typical Days Inn, directly next to the highway, the kind of two-storey motor hotel that the 1970s forgot. One whole side of the room is glass; the floor is covered in brown carpet that runs all the way to the back of the room, and then up the wall to counter-top level. The bar fridge is set right into the carpeted wall. The sink is in the bedroom, a small bathroom has the shower and toilet. It's the kind of place that makes you expect to hear a thin, tinny set of Abba songs playing. Across the parking lot, there is a closed swimming pool, the deep end filled with dirty water that's left a crusty ring as it recedes in the heat, the shallow end boasting a drift of dead leaves.

We eat at Monty's Bar and Grill, then I walk directly into the attached casino. I win a little, but it's hard to stay. The main prize in the low-ceilinged room seems to be despair, and the cigarette smoke moves down the walls steadily, constantly, like fog rolling in.

Later, Leslie steps outside the hotel room for a late-night smoke as a cowboy steps out of an adjoining unit: the real deal. Straight-legged jeans, rodeo shirt, big belt buckle, cowboy hat. Everything but a rope lasso. He's the Marlboro Man's skinny younger brother. The Winston-smoking cowboy Leslie's wanted to meet since she was a teenager in Pennsylvania during the height of the rugged western cigarette advertisement.

And here he is, at the Days Inn in the room next door. Except she's in pyjama pants and an old shirt, post-shower hair and no makeup.

He doesn't have a horse. Instead, he's driving a big, square-backed U-Haul, today's wagons and team for people making trips to a new frontier. We've seen them constantly, all trip long. Leslie once hauled one 4,789 kilometres east for a new life with me: together, we drove a huge box-back U-Haul with her mother's furniture 780 kilometres through the Adirondacks and a raging wind and rainstorm from Pittsburgh to a life nearer Leslie's brother in Cary, North Carolina.

Leslie can do little more than watch the Marlboro Man's cigarette burn down until he stubs it out and turns back into a room that is undoubtedly laid out exactly like our own. Then, she phones her high school best friend Cathy, a friend who's closer in many ways than family. Cathy's the only one who can truly commiserate, the one who knows Leslie's penchant for cowboys.

Expectation, meet reality. Life can be cruel.

∞∞∞∞∞

July 19, 1849

Started at 5 A.M. & crossing the Big Sandy a few miles from camp, travelled 17 miles without water, though the river was not far from the road, and after having made over 20 miles, camped again on the Big Sandy. Grass poor — bushes a little way off. Weather fine, roads smooth except loose stones and sand. Toward evening the wind blew strong, & in half an hour after pitching tent, our blankets were completely covered with sand! Today I found a lot of beautiful stones, mostly quartz — some carnelian. Near camp to the right of the road we saw a hill covered with the greatest variety of curious stones I ever saw. It was a perfect museum.

∞∞∞∞∞

We're collecting rocks too, rough sandstone and chert that's been knapped into sharp edges where it has been broken out of rock cliffs, white crystals of quartz and fat round balls of pumice that weigh startlingly less than they look like they should. It's not only this trip. I've got paper bags of agates and amethyst from Scott's Bay in Nova Scotia, long sheets of orange crystal, and a snatch of fossilized tree bark from a tidal beach on the Fundy shore. My collection lacks Dodge's order: the only index of what came from where is my memory. Leslie's collecting too, but her collection is less formal: a sandstone desert rose and polished stones from stores, other scattered rocks that she sees something in, but I do not. Our collection — and our luggage — gets heavier every day.

We drive through fading towns like Eden Valley. There are still big ranch plots, surrounded by their strange crop-circles of irrigated land, but fewer people. The farmhouses now are flat ranches, but also their own sort of outpost forts: they oversee miles of ground where there is nothing to see except the land and the fence lines. There have been so many dying downtowns: boarded-up storefronts, for rent signs, empty old-school hotels away from the important interstate intersections.

Sometimes, I feel like making the choice to stay in a particular run-down hotel is like tossing a last thin lifeline for a borderline business, offering up one last little scrap of hope and a few more days before what seems like an inevitable end.

All day, Leslie's been reading the diary out loud from the passenger seat, and all day, the landscape has been unfolding just as Dodge describes it. It has become eerie. If we had found his name on Independence Rock, I think I would have looked hard over my shoulder to see if someone was there. Trite to say we're being directed, but too many times, things have happened by chance on this trip. We trip into things: the caves at Blue Mounds, where we stopped by chance, the Robidoux museum in St. Joseph, the driving break at Pioneer Ranch that turned into a cameo appearance by our own private section of raw pioneer trail.

Horses and black beef cattle are working over the sage lands, eating every blade of grass that grows anywhere between the sage.

Next, Green River.

⬦⬦⬦⬦⬦⬦

July 20, 1849
This morning we started just as Old Sol peeped above the horizon, and having a good level road we soon reached Green River, a distance of 10 miles. There we were obliged to stay all day waiting for the teams to be ferried across. Grass short — wood plenty — Green River is a deep and rapid stream much larger than either other we

have passed, except the Platte. To the right of our road today are some interesting hills, from which were washed down a great number of pebbles of every variety & hue, completely across the plain below.

This has been decidedly the most unlucky day that I have yet seen. In the morning I lent my gold pen to Col. Cuen who has persuaded himself — and it may be others also — that he is somewhat of a poet, together with my ink — the pen he has lost, and spilled all my ink — leaving me nothing but a pencil! Confound it, it is too bad!

July 21, 1849
Crossed the river and moved out 8 miles & laid there till next morning. Express from Ft. Hall arrived. Myself quite unwell for several days past — much worse today — mosquitoes are terrible indeed. Grass short, wood enough for fuel. A little storm in afternoon. Two of the greatest luxuries on the trip are pickles and molasses. Butter, cheese, & indeed nearly every kind of food can be taken as well as not. The worst of all diseases is a kind of dysentery — such as the Army of the Rio Grande suffered so much by — brought on by want of proper diet and by exposure.

NOTE: The ferry by which we crossed the Green River is owned by private individuals — price $4 per wagon — flat boats.

<><><><><><>

I have the foolish idea that if we stop in just the right spot, we might actually find Dodge's pen, as if our two trips are so close that it's like retracing someone's trip to the grocery store to find their lost glove. There is absolutely no reason to even imagine it's possible, but in my head, I can see a glint of gold in the dust, and can imagine sweeping the sand away, spotting the pen's barrel, feeling that upwelling in my chest that comes with found treasure. I can't shake myself of the possibility and can imagine spending a whole day in a search that can't possibly succeed.

We come into the town of Green River some 20 miles south of where Dodge forded the river. We're travelling along the sides of high, eroded cliffs, sometimes through road tunnels punched straight through interfering cliff faces. We see the Tetons now at regular intervals, solid rock punching up like peg teeth in the plain. In some places, side roads meander away down the centre of vertical canyons, enticing diversions.

We stop to walk among the sage, the cliffs shot through with different colours, and sit atop banks of broken stone that has sheared away from the cliff face and come to rest as steeply as it can without sliding further. Every step you take upsets that order. It's easy to feel that, just by walking there, you are fundamentally changing things for years. Small desert plants are at the end of their bloom, the air is redolent with the smell of the heating valley, and there are scores of rabbits, always ready to startle you by bursting out of cover at your feet.

There is a startling collision between the natural and the artificial. Off-road drivers have picked the steepest parts of the slopes below the Tetons to test their hill-climbing abilities, so tire tracks run up steep inclines all around us — tire tracks that, in this climate, are probably close to permanent. Up close, the rock is etched by wind and sand, eroded, pocked, and carved.

Then, there's the hotel. Nestled directly beneath a pair of the most impressive Tetons, a four-storey Hampton Inn and Suites boasts an "indoor pool and casual lounge, plus free Wi-Fi and hot breakfast." The building is, at least, the same colour as its surroundings, except for the tonsure of bright green grass around it, but if the intention was to blend in, it's a complete failure. The scene is jarring, like someone decided to Photoshop a hotel into a postcard as an advertising promotion. Like the Tetons were made to promote the hotel. Like graffiti on a painting.

On the other side of the river, an endless train uncoils itself through the valley.

We cross the Green on an unremarkable four-lane highway bridge. No waiting for ferrymen. No toll. We don't even stop to see if some's scrawled their name on the concrete with axle grease from a wagon.

∞∞∞∞∞

July 22, Sunday, 1849

After leaving the river we passed through a most extensive village of prairie dogs. Soon after we came to some most interesting appearing hills mostly on the left of the road — they were composed of strata of various colours — blue, red, yellow, etc. at the foot of which may be found a most extensive and interesting variety of geological specimens. We picked up some beautiful specimens of Quartz of variegated hues & several pieces of petrified wood and bark. Touching Blacks fork we passed on about 4 miles and camped at Ham's fork, a tributary of Blacks fork, which is a tributary of Green. Grass pretty good — plenty of wood & some beautiful fish were caught here.

July 23, 1849

Crossed Ham's fork, & passing a short distance over a gentle ascent bearing off to the left we soon reached & crossed Blacks fork. These are both fine clear streams, the former 1 1/2 and the latter 3 ft. deep. Just before crossing Blacks fork, we left the road and took another trail bearing to the left, which had not been travelled before; thereby saving 10 miles. After passing a number of these variegated hills such as we saw yesterday, & travelling 16 miles from our starting place, we again crossed Blacks fork & camped in fine grass — there having been no teams there before us. Plenty of bushes for fuel.

Today we had a greater excitement than ever before in camp. There was a half breed and a Walla Walla Indian who came into camp with dispatches from Oregon travelling with us on their return. This morning the half breed was quite unwell, & seemed to have got the idea that someone was determined to kill him! To favor his health he was put into one of the wagons, where he appeared very uneasy from fear. Wilcox the guide was with him, singing and talking very socially — he called Wilcox his good friend etc., when of a sudden, and without any apparent cause he placed his pistol against the base of Wilcox's brain & discharged it, killing him instantly. Snatching Wilcox's revolver from his belt, he sprang from the wagon & started to run. A soldier took after him, he having by the time hid in a little ravine. An Officer rode near his hiding place when he sprang up & giving a whoop fired at him, the ball passing through the neck of [the officer's] horse! Soon he was shot, first in the breast and then in the forehead, either wound being mortal. He was searched but nothing found to give any clue whatever to his mysterious act.

I retained a brass breastpin which Wilcox wore, as a momento of the sad event. He was a fine fellow & liked by all — the greatest indignation was exhibited by all toward the whole Indian race, & it was with difficulty that the men were restrained from killing the other Indian, on the spot. The general opinion was that the half breed was insane.

Of all countries this is the most barren — not a tree or shrub except a few bushes along the streams — not a berry of any kind, nor fruit have we seen — nothing but the everlasting sage. As for game there are plenty of prairie dogs, some sage hens & frequently some of the large Jack Rabbits are shot. Other game is all frightened from the road.

Seven o'clock P.M. Poor Wilcox! We have just buried him to the right of the road, on the bank where we cross B fork again in the morning. How little he thought of such an ending to this day, as he sat talking and laughing this morning. But such is the brittle thread upon which hang suspended the lives of these mountain men, who, impelled by some unaccountable feeling, forsake the pleasures of civilized society for that of the savage, where the rifle is the only <u>passport</u>, and might not <u>right</u> is the arbiter of life and death! It is an awful thing to die thus, far from home and friends! Heaven grant that whatever may be my fate while living, that I may at least die among my friends.

∞∞∞∞∞

The Wilcox killing resonated with other emigrant groups as well — the guide was well known. Dodge had been only a few days ahead of a group of better-financed emigrants travelling on a paid wagon train called the Pioneer Line, the travails of which were recorded in the diaries of Bernard J. Reid. Reid mentions "the Wilcox tragedy" as well. At least one other diary, that of Niles Searls, suggests that Wilcox's killer knew him from Oregon, and that the murder was done out of revenge for something that had happened in that territory. We can't shake the suddenness of Dodge's description: Leslie was reading the diary out loud when it dropped on us suddenly, as if it had happened in front of us. That's coupled with the offhand way he talks about it, about every death, footnoting that death was commonplace and could be expected at any time.

∞∞∞∞∞

July 24, 1849

By dint of perseverance, I have at length got some ink again. Crossed Blacks fork & followed up it on the left bank till we reached Ft. Bridger, about 18 miles. The fort consists of a few log houses arranged so as to form a hollow

square — it is merely a trading post. Saw several Snake
Indians — one gave me an arrow. Grass good — plenty
of bushes — several small streams from the snow-covered
Utah range come down and empty into Blacks fork near
the fort. Pre-paid $3.00 for carrying a letter to the states.
Boys traded their horses for ponies.

<><><><><><>

At Fort Bridger, most things there on display, and most of the fort
itself, arrived well after Dodge passed through.

He saw a small stockade and two traders' cabins, one with a
blacksmith's shop. His account of the place is as good or better than
anything the museum has. Jim Bridger and his partner, Louis Vasquez
had seen a great opportunity in the emigrant trail: they knew that, by
the time the travellers reached that point, they would need a range of
services and supplies they could only get from a trading outpost. As
Bridger himself wrote, "I have established a small fort, with a blacksmith shop and a supply of iron in the road of the emigrants on the
Black Fork of the Green River, which promises fairly. People coming
from the East are generally well supplied with money, but by the time
they get here are in want of all kinds of supplies. Horses, provisions,
and smith work bring ready cash from them, and should I receive the
goods hereby ordered will do a considerable business with them."

Joel Palmer wrote about the fort in 1845, saying, "It is built of poles
and dogwood mud. It is a shabby concern." In 1846, John McBride said,
"We arrived at Fort Bridger so called by courtesy. It is only a camp where
some fifty trappers were living in lodges. A single cabin of willow brush
covered with earth composed the fort. . . . A brisk traffic . . . went on."

Today, the Wyoming parks service sees the same brisk traffic, and
one-half of a reconstructed Bridger trading post is a gift shop. "The
past comes alive through costumed interpreters, museum displays, and
a reconstruction of Jim Bridger's trading post" — so the brochure
says. There's sugar candy, replica telescopes on leather lanyards, fake
trade goods. All of it cheaply produced, making it the same kind of

goods that soldiers on the emigrant trail regularly handed out to the Native Americans they needed to curry favour with.

The trading post still does "a considerable business" from customers with "ready cash," customers who wander away happy with rock candy on a wooden stick, a fistful of polished rocks, or a modern arrowhead manufactured on an assembly line a continent away.

Bridger would be pleased.

⬦⬦⬦⬦⬦⬦⬦

July 26, 1849

Started early and travelled 23 miles — most of the way through a kind of mountain pass or defile — following the valley of Muddy creek except that we left it occasionally to avoid the hills. The road is rough and hilly filled with loose stones & ravines — the peaks on either side often rising very abruptly & presenting some interesting appearances. At noon I climbed to the top of one very steep several hundred ft. above the road, from which I had a fine view. In a crevice near the top where I could but just climb I found a hawk's nest — the old ones meantime flying around my head in great fright. We nooned & took lunch under the shade of some cedars part way up the hillside, a beautiful place — bunch grass fine here. Some very steep ravines & hills — hard travelling — seems much more like being in the mountains.

⬦⬦⬦⬦⬦⬦⬦

One of the pitfalls of the American road trip is the near-total ban on stopping on the shoulder. I see things I want to get a closer look at, but regular road signs warn that no such voyeurism should be attempted.

There are abandoned and tumbled-down houses I want to see inside, windows I want to peer into. Dodge was on this ground, writing of not wanting to die, like Wilcox, far from home and friends — yet we pass so many houses that, for lack of a better description, have died themselves. When you do find a way inside, it can seem as if their abandonment was near-instantaneous. A dishcloth still hanging next to a sink, stiff with age. Wallpaper with roses that someone chose and hung. Plates and a cup waiting on the drainboard to be placed back in the cupboard — while all the cupboard doors have been ripped from their hinges and lie like broken shells on the floor. A bedroom, the air fetid and still, with a bed and mattress where the sheets and blankets are thrown back as though someone left in a hurry and inexplicably never came back. Home, interrupted.

But more than that. Sell a house, move, and that place is caught only in memory's amber — yours, and the people who lived there with you. Go back when someone else has moved in, and all that catches your eye are the things that are different, that are wrong. The neighbourhood may have stayed the same, but it's moved on from you.

I feel as though every year strips away connections. It's piercing when both of your parents have died, and you realize, all at once, that their great storehouse of information has winked out irretrievably. No picking up the phone for a quick call to ask if you're remembering something right — no way to ask who the person is, standing on the left in a photograph. Children grow and satellite out into their own lives and directions, their own trains, switched over and running now on new tracks. Communities work differently today: focusing on the nuclear family means connection ends at the curb, where you put the garbage out for weekly collection.

Out here in the empty prairie, the car ticking as it loses heat on the shoulder, Leslie and I, the only sets of eyes and ears that are open and recording, look for traces of a world that has all but vanished.

And I know, all at once and absolutely, that ours will vanish, too.

Every stretch of land, no matter how parched and worthless looking, is fenced. How is it that everything is owned by someone, perhaps part of a ranch so far away you can't even see it? Often, you see no more sign of that owner than faded tire tracks in cracked and dried-up, dusty mud. No way to know when the parallel stamp of tire marks was made. But owned, it is.

At one spot, a wire fence strung between broken, rotted posts, the barbed wire almost to the ground, with a brand-new "No Trespassing" sign hanging from it just above the desert dust.

⟡⟡⟡⟡⟡⟡

July 27, 1849

Started at 5 A.M. and continued along the valley of Muddy creek, followed it clear to its source, which is several springs of the finest water, cold as ice. A few miles up a smooth steep ascent & we stood upon the ridge of the Summit Pass — over 8,200 ft. above the level of the sea. The night was extremely cold — prevented me from sleeping toward morning — ice was frozen in the buckets thicker than glass! Mules shivering with the cold. The narrow bottom up which the road leads to the summit, was of black loam, luxuriantly covered with a growth of grass, wildflowers, contrasting strongly with the barren hill-sides around us! On the left near the top of the pass is a poplar grove of bushes, on some of which were carved the names of persons who had formerly passed, some in '45 — cut mine with the date.

Reaching the summit, the road turns to the right and follows along the top of the ridge a little way, then turns to the left down a long & pretty steep hill — smooth except loose stones. . . . At the foot of the hill, the road turns to the right & winds along the base of the mountain, by the side of a dry ravine with occasional pools of water — a few miles on are two very bad places for wagons — road rocky & sideling . . . . Turning & winding along the bottom of this gorge for some 12 or 15 miles from the pass, we at length emerged into the broad valley of Bear River — crossed a couple of mountain streams & proceed 2 or 3 miles through the sage, we camped by the side of the first division on the river bank. Grass good, on the opposite

side, no fuel but sage — river like Platte, banks clay &
bad! Sage hens very plenty. Myself ailing yet.

The road appears new — nothing but the 1st Division
scarcely having passed over it — nearly all the emigrants
have gone via the Salt Lake.

∾∾∾∾∾

For us, it's a long, steep run down into the Bear River valley, the off-
ramp for Bear Lake and the right-hand turn away from the Salt Lake
City route. It's a simple turn, but a key point for keeping on Dodge's
part of the trail. The Mormon Trail continued on to the Great Salt
Lake, while the Oregon Trail bowed upwards to the north to the Bear
River before turning west again. Arriving at the outer edge of a town
means finding grass again, watered lawns in sharp square boxes, all
that groundwater pumped up from aquifers, diverted from rivers, just
to have something to mow. The edges of every span of yard marks a
quick trip back to sage.

The turn into Evanston feels like it should be important, a great
divergence of two different streams of immigrants, one set travelling
for religion, the other, for imagined riches. Instead, it is the height
of nondescript, right back to truck-stop America — gas stations, rest
services and showers for truckers, a brilliant-green park dotted with
giant RVs.

The desert held back at the town limits.

For now.

∾∾∾∾∾

July 28, 1849
Today we lay over to rest the teams — spent the day in
getting the mules shod — mending camp stools — cast-
ing bullets, cleaning guns, etc. Large numbers of young
ducks were killed by the men — weather fine — mornings very cold — midday extremely warm. The Brass
Band of the Regiment gave a grand serenade at the tent of

the different Officers, the Dr.'s among others — the girls had a fine time waltzing on the grass! It really seemed like some holiday festival. How strangely melancholy are the thoughts which such scenes give rise to here in this desert region! Ah, home & friends and loved scenes, how they flitter before the imagination!

July 29, Sunday, 1849

Moved only 8 miles to give the 3 divisions time to separate again. Beautiful camping place — splendid grass — wild rye 2 ft. high in head — mules like it very much. Griffin broke wagon tongue — carelessness. He and I spliced it & moved into camp. Here the other or commonly travelled road, Sublette's Cut-Off, comes into ours & several emigrant trains are just ahead of us — among others the Pioneer Train. This morning some of the train saw a herd of 150 mountain sheep.

Just after leaving camp we crossed a stream 12 or 15 ft. wide — the whole of which came from a spring not more than 50 rods above the road, on our right. It was splendid water. The mountains around this valley are not as rough & broken — but present a much smoother & less abrupt appearance — here they are dotted with green spots, which interspersed over the red soil give them a very singular appearance.

∞∞∞∞∞

We are passing Dodge at touchpoints now, joining up at crossings. The trail is something like 2,100 miles long, depending on which route the miners took. We'll end up with more than 5,400 miles under our belts, trying to reach as much trail as we can. Dodge and his fellows will follow the Doctor's advice and take the Hudspeth Cutoff, heading west instead of angling north, and skipping Fort Hall in the process. They are focusing on cutting distance, but Fort Hall, a Hudson's Bay trading post, is the last established trading post before reaching the end of the trail in California, one of the few spots left for any possibility of resupply.

We can't cut the same corners Dodge does: there's just no straight shot through. We will be forced to square the box and head instead toward the Snake River.

We are just into Idaho, above the looping muddy river oxbows of Thomas Fork, pulled onto a dusty shoulder, looking at the display signs for the Big Hill, one of the steepest drops on this part of the trail and the site of many wagon accidents. We've come up Route 30, through a gap blasted into the rock alongside the river. The pull-off is laced with garbage, empty coffee cups, water bottles, chip bags. Used condoms have been flung on to the dusty verge. Who would set up a tryst at a lay-by, barely more than a paved road-widening in the sagelands, next to two historical plaques?

A long-running trail of oil marks the pavement, coming to an end in a large pool, now soaked deep into the pavement, a sign that someone's car or truck failed directly in front of the commemorative signs. Someone's trip halted, at least for the time being. A broken-down car seems even more confounding than a broken wagon tongue. Unlike Dodge, the driver of the car probably lacked the skill — and almost certainly the parts — to do the necessary repairs.

‹‹‹‹‹‹›››

July 30, 1849

This has been a great day for small events. The morning was very cold — frost & ice — started early, travelled 17 miles N. & N.W. along the base of the mountain by the side of Bear River & camped at its northern extremity where Thomas's fork empties into it, & the river turns to the S.S.W toward Salt Lake. Taking my rifle, I mounted my mule & followed along the river shore to kill some game — saw plenty of ducks — curlews — sage hens, a few geese, crows, and hawks — shot nothing but a couple of hawks. Get into a swamp & had great difficulty in getting out — had to wade near a mile — some of the way belly deep to my mule — who was very obstinate. Saw some emigrants who came via "Sublette's Cut-Off." A portion represent the route as extremely bad — others do not, first 50 miles road splendid.

Forty miles no water — plenty grass all the way — ascent and descent of the summit very steep. Two routes down — in the shorter is a precipice 20 ft. perpendicular down. . . . A wagon was blown over the precipice to the right of the ridge and was dashed to pieces. During the afternoon passed Pioneer train — man very sick — saw several Snake Indian Papooses carried in a sack on the horse's shoulder like a pistol in a holster!

Dodge crossed paths with the Pioneer Line on July 30th, with Bernard J. Reid of the Line citing the same scene in his diaries: "The papoose done up so curiously fastened on a board and hung to the saddle horn." Working my way through other diaries — and the trail guides, which excerpt still more diaries — is like setting waypoints. Every time I see something from other travellers that matches what he's writing about, that builds on it or echoes it, Dodge's trip, his words, get worked into a larger, more significant firmament. The other accounts don't as much verify what he writes about as they but solidify it. Like a series of experiments, confirming the same hypothesis.

Meanwhile, the desert slides by outside our windows, miles without anything except open plains, scattered haughty Tetons, sage. Saw deer, cows on the road, more sage. Dodge ticks through the same repeated things, metronomic. The trip, for the emigrants, must have been beyond monotonous — and at the same time, perilous for a host of reasons but partly because of the lack of clear direction. We have accurate maps: we know exactly where we are, where we're going. Dodge and other emigrants were working from incomplete handbooks for directions, competing routes and cutoffs, incomplete information about which route is the shortest. Even the number of miles they have remaining is like a lottery, random numbers that change every day. Sometimes, the remaining distance seems short: those hopes are often quickly dashed.

∞∞∞∞

July 31, 1849

Crossed Thomas's fork — bad crossing — then ascended a very steep hill, turning to the right from the river. Descent very steep. Passed about a mile through a ravine between the mountains, crossing a valley & small stream at right angles, then ascended a second very steep & long hill, or rather mountain, descent extremely bad — very abrupt — rocky and rough — far the worst that we have had on the whole route! Struck the river again & camped on a stream emptying into it. Dr. talks of leaving the train about 25 miles ahead — by which it is said we can save 140 miles.

∞∞∞∞

You can see the emigrants' trail, the bad descent Dodge talks about, clearly from the highway, the route carved into the hill and S-curving down sharply. Many emigrants agreed it was the worst of the downhill runs until that point. It's another place where ropes had to be used to slow wagons when the angle of the descent proved too much for the rudimentary brakes.

It's an empty place, the cars whooshing by unstopping — and when we're back on the road, it's dust-bowl yellow-ochre followed by the bright green of crops under the crop-circling irrigation racks.

We're travelling from spring to spring, like Dodge: Rock Springs, Wyoming, to Soda Springs, Idaho, 191 miles in all along the shortest, straightest route. But we're following a more tangled route, back and forth between the two states, with a tiny section of Utah as well. Wyoming roads are better, but the road signs are more shot up. But everywhere, the same thing — sage and sage and cows and sage.

The soil is getting worse, the water harder to find, the habitable spots stretched further apart, white salt crusting the hardpan. The houses — when you see them — are more decrepit with every mile of road.

After Thomas Fork, the highway is a straight line while the river twists crazily up against the highway and away again. The river valley is lush and treed, mostly poplar and willow, but the trees stop as soon as the land rises away from the water, leaving bare, dry ground and sage.

Today, as well as the usual run of stockpiled campers, trucks, and broken-backed mobile homes, I saw an army front-end loader in full camouflage paint, as well as a full-sized American LaFrance aerial ladder fire truck, near a single-wide trailer home park tucked into a Route 89 cliff face. The fire truck was parked in front of someone's house high on a treeless swale as if it was a second car.

I have tried all day to come up with a particular word to suit the failed dream of the abandoned American homestead, something that would capture the whole personal world of loss and surrender and perhaps even a thread of hope for something new — I have not been successful.

∞∞∞∞∞∞

August 1, 1849

Nothing of note occurred today — continued along the river, leaving it & passing over slight hills occasionally to avoid the <u>canyons</u>. Very dusty disagreeable travelling — crossed a great many streams in the forenoon — fine cold water — saw considerable timber & some snow on the mountain tops & sides. On the western side, the mountains are not near as barren as on the eastern — here they are covered with short grass clear to their summits.

Passed 2 graves & some spots on the right where the hillside looks nearly as white as snow — distance 23 — grass
good, willow bushes for fuel.

◇◇◇◇◇◇◇

Chapter 10

The Stories of Soda Springs

O n the long straight sweep into Montpelier, we're in a rich valley bottom framed by mountains, one of them bearing a huge white "M" that curiously marks the town from the air. It's hard to tell how much of the valley's farming prosperity springs from irrigation, but there's plenty of farmland and more green than we've seen for days.

We pass signs for the Caribou National Forest, though woodland caribou have long since been pushed to the northernmost edge of their range, well back into Canada. But that doesn't stop the animal from turning up in everything from hotel names to nicknames.

Near Soda Springs, a high, fast-moving rainstorm flies down the valley behind us, glowering.

If we stop even for a moment for every small town's requisite single traffic light, it catches us, and the windshield specks over and then fills with rain. Pull ahead at highway speed, and we pull out of it, the wipers squeaking on dry glass, the cloud piled up and blue-bruised in the rear-view mirror.

We rush into Soda Springs with the storm running in tight behind us.

The Enders Hotel is where we should have stayed in Soda Springs, despite the higher price. It's in the same family as the Hotel Pawnee in North Platte or the Park Hotel in Rock Springs. Another big, square old-school hotel, but this one hasn't closed. Well, it has, but it's also been reopened, refurbished in 1997 with over $1 million from a heritage foundation. The building includes a museum, the front lobby complete with a stuffed badger and other taxidermied creatures, a plethora of history including the legend of Caribou Jack, and a main-floor 50s-style diner. But we balked at the cost.

Instead, we find the worst hotel we've stayed at yet, the Caribou Lodge and Motel, and I only hope we pass a reasonable night here. The décor is all varnished wood in the halls — walls and ceiling — and it looks a lot like it belongs in the original Twin Peaks.

All I can think is that the owner's parents ran it as a family business — trying to keep up with needed maintenance with a dwindling clientele — and that the son has stayed on, taken it over, and has even less means to keep propping the place up. So little seems to have changed, so much feels like it is on an inevitable downhill slide, though there is Wi-Fi.

The hallway is narrow, the walls thin, the bathrooms aging. We have a chipped enamel sheet-steel shower stall that rings like a bell if you touch it anywhere, fuzzed with mildew in the bottom corners, and a sink where the taps turn backwards. The faucets in the deep, old sink, are billed as Crane Dial-ese, but the automatic drain closure has lost its plug plate, so while you can see the drain lever move across the hole, the water continues down, unabated. No-ese. The faucets are a minimum of 50 years old and might be called vintage if they worked.

Our neighbours are surly or sport the wide-eyed stare of the exhausted road worker, and the sign out front is so faded that soon it will say nothing at all. I thought the Glenview in Dubuque was the lowest point — but at least the owners there sparkled. I now have a new and lower level. We leave the luggage in the trunk of the car, bring in only the essentials, toiletries, laptops, liquor.

There's a man outside the motel leaning deliberately into the hood of his black Yukon, all of him thrown backwards, T-shirt and belly and belt and holstered multi-tool. And he's leaning there like his heart or his spirit or both are completely broken.

August 2, 1849

Travelled 8 miles and came to the famous Beer or Soda
Springs, the greatest curiosity on the whole route. There
are two hills that may be seen 3 or 4 miles off — the largest about 41 ft. high and 25 to 30 rods long, composed
entirely of soda deposited by the water which bubbles
up through a dozen apertures — the places where the
water issues are elevated, some 2 & some 4 ft., forming
a cone inside of which the water boils exactly like a kettle, caused by the escape of gas — it is cool and tastes
very strong of soda — many like it — I do not — with
syrup it might be good. The main spring is a few rods to
the right or east of the hills — it boils like a cauldron —
basin 5 or 6 ft. deep, 3 to 4 ft. diameter — very strong of
soda — many of the mouths are dry — it stands close the
banks of a stream 4 ft. above its bed! Two miles farther . . .
is another large spring . . . it boils extremely hard. Just a
little farther down the hill on the bank of the river is the
Steamboat Spring, which excels all the rest — the water
tastes like the others though not quite so strong, and it
is about milk warm — it boils up through a hole 6 or 8
inches in diameter, with the utmost fury, emitting large
quantities of gas — throwing the water 2 or 3 feet above
the mouth which is through a solid rock — making a
loud blubbering, rumbling noise that may be heard several rods! . . . But little water escapes from them, most of
it falling back into the kettle.

We camped a mile below the Steamboat Spring &
remained for the third division to come up from which we
were to get our provisions — they arrived at dark. Grass
poor — fine fire of a broken-down wagon.

We came looking for the town's namesake spring but were disappointed. There was a geyser instead.

Well, a facsimile of a geyser.

This incarnation of the Soda Springs geyser was created when the town fathers drilled a deep well to get warm water for a municipal pool and launched an hourly attraction instead (every half-hour during tourist season). It's billed as the world's largest artificial geyser.

It's sulphurous, 70 degrees F, and erupts on schedule due to a timing device and an electric motor that opens a valve. (For years, before it was timed, the geyser was set off by request, a task delegated to someone from the police department.)

When they drilled the well in 1937, the drill hit a chamber of heated, carbonated water 317 feet down, and the resulting blowout shot water 100 feet into the air and covered the town in mist for days. The town was close to being flooded before the geyser's casing pipe was capped.

The spray from the eruptions falls across the surrounding boardwalk and coats the wood railings, boardwalk, and nearby tree branches with an acre of yellow-orange, rough-surfaced soda, calcium, and other minerals. It has the smell of brimstone to it and the rough look of flat coral growing on the surface of mussel shells.

We wait, alone with the backside of the main street buildings, for the top of the clock. The water-filled vent gurgles excitedly for a moment, then with a rumble and a chuff, the water shoots up and out and then patters down around us. Wind direction is key; with the wrong wind, one that would throw the mist and water onto streets and buildings, the geyser won't fire. After a few minutes, it shrinks to a burble and disappears again. There is no one else on the boardwalk to see it, no one else in the municipal park at all.

The geyser is right behind the Enders Hotel, where we have come back from our sad-sack lodgings to eat at the diner, listening to three teenaged girls grouse about their parents. They talk brightly about boys, scrolling through their phones, firing off messages and picking their way through plates of French fries.

‹‹‹›‹››‹››‹›

August 4, 1849

Another mountain to go over this morning — ascent smooth — descent pretty rough some of the way. Travelled 11 miles & stopped by a fine stream, on which there is a little cascade & plenty of bushes close to the road — about 11 A.M.

The mountains here are lofty and close peak upon peak. Plenty of Snake Indians in camp at noon — fine ponies — won't trade or sell them. Moved on over another long hill & camped on a small stream by the side of a marsh — grass good, sage for fuel — extremely dusty — it is ankle deep, & being very little wind in the valley it is terrible. Got into camp with Pioneer Line at sunset. Tired & hungry — not well.

‹‹‹›‹››‹›

After it has taken us three tries to find the Soda Springs tourism office, we discover it's sharing space with the U.S. Forestry Service office — you can walk in the unlocked front door, wander around looking at brochures, peer into empty offices, use the office washroom, but never actually see a living person.

We collect brochures from the slatted wooden wall racks, looking for historic sites.

In the *Soda Springs and Vicinity Points of Interest Guidebook*, Leslie points to Attraction #10: we can only shake our heads, but we can't help ourselves.

We have to go.

At twilight, as recommended, we head out to watch Attraction #10: the "Monsanto Slag Pour — Soda Springs' man-made lava flow. View from Hooper Spring Park."

The Monsanto plant just outside Soda Springs covers 800 acres and has been making elemental phosphorus since 1952: the radioactive slag heap is a great grey rock pile that stretches right up to the edge of the company road around it, a massive berm of waste rock from the facility's blast furnaces.

It's not just a tourist attraction, it's a monumental Environmental Protection Agency Superfund site as well: the radioactive slag is part of the problem, but there's groundwater contamination too. The phosphorus is for glyphosate, the active agent in the chemical herbicide Roundup, and also, apparently, popping up now in things as ubiquitous as breakfast cereals.

While we wait in the darkened picnic park, leaning on the hood of the car, our feet on the boggy grass, a police car drifts by, slows, and turns wide into Hooper Springs Park.

An officer has come to check us out, slowing behind our car in the near-darkness and shining a light on our Wisconsin licence plate. The officer behind the wheel waves, and the police car pulls out. We watch his lights shrink and fade, headed back towards the foot of the massive slag pile, and then watch as a purple-white glow flares for a moment atop the darkening rock.

"Was that it?" Leslie asks.

"I'm not sure."

So we keep waiting. At night, the plant looks like something out of a dystopian movie: even more so when the reddish-purple light came creeping toward the top edge of the slag pile.

We stay until the molten, glowing calcium silicate rock slag finally does lip up over the artificial horizon of rock and sky and begins its glowing rush down the hill from its truck-towed cauldron. It's more like visiting Mordor from *The Lord of the Rings* than anything else.

At least one magazine article says that, if you're close enough, you can feel the heat from each downwards-rushing tongue of hot rock poured from the 600 cubic foot cauldrons and hear the slag crackle explosively as it hardens.

We weren't that close.

Two completely man-made "natural attractions" — a geyser and a "lava" pour — in just one small town of around 3,000 people.

It's as arbitrary and artificially designed as Cozad's cherished spot directly on the 100th meridian. Like the statue of Chuck the Channel Catfish in Selkirk, Manitoba, or Petersfield, Manitoba's giant mallard — making a mark to prove we count, to prove that we measure up somehow. Fixing our place in the firmament.

∞∞∞∞∞

August 5, Sunday, 1849

Started a little after sunrise & crossed the creek — passed on W.S.W. toward another mountain over which the road passes — warm and very dusty. Seeing a gape through the ridge 2 or 3 miles to the right of the road, & hoping to find game, I rode over to it. After passing over a succession of hills & ravines & seeing one solitary bird & a few service berries, I reached the gape — but could not pass through. It is one of the greatest natural curiosities on the route. It resembles the Devils Gate — being like that forced open by a stream that passes through, but is much more extensive, the sides being from 600 to 800 ft. high — though not so nearly perpendicular. The sides are very rough — a mere wall of huge broken masses of rocks — the bottom of the ravine is filled with trees & bushes. Nor being able to get through I was compelled to climb over the mountain, the sides of which were so steep that it was with great difficulty that I could lead my mule up it sidewise. When I reached the summit I found the other side equally steep & very rocky, & instead of seeing the camp in the valley below as I expected, I discovered it about 6 miles off to my left, the road having taken an angle in that direction as it crossed the mountain! I saw plenty signs of mountain sheep, & at the base of ledge on the very summit I found a bear's nest, but saw no occupant. At length I reached camp tired and hungry, but only to see new troubles. In crossing a little creek just at camp, Bob upset the

carriage — throwing Jeff into the mud under it & breaking the wood in the fore axletree & the top! None were
injured. To complete our chapter of accidents both baggage teams gave out coming up the hill, & consequently
were behind, giving us no chance to obtain anything to
eat! They came in, in about 2 hours, & the carriage having been repaired, we moved on 8 or 10 miles & camped
at dusk on another little stream, good grass — plenty of
bushes. The load being so heavy we threw away the Dr.'s
tent and gave them ours, we sleeping on the ground in the
open air!

∞∞∞∞∞∞

In Soda Springs, there's the Caribou Lodge and Motel, Caribou
Mountain, Caribou County, the Caribou County Fair, and, on the
outskirts of town, the Caribou National Forest. Not named after
caribou, but after Caribou Jack. Or the legend of Caribou Jack. Or
Cariboo Jack. The hardware store is Caribou Jack's Trading Post
Co. and BBQ: a banner on their website screams "WE'RE NOW
TAKING ORDERS FOR BEES!"

Caribou Jack was a Canadian who found gold near Soda Springs
and founded the now-abandoned mining town of Caribou City. There,
Jesse "Caribou Jack" Fairchild started a gold rush 20 years after
Dodge would have passed right by the same ground. In a short biog-
raphy by the U.S. Forest Service, he's quoted as saying, "I was born in
a blizzard snowdrift in the worst damn storm to ever hit Canada. I was
bathed in a gold pan, suckled by a caribou, wrapped in a buffalo rug,
and could whip any grizzly going before I was thirteen. That's when I
left home." Proof that you can be the author of your own story.

Caribou Jack came to an untimely but probably predictable end:
hearing news of a bear in the vicinity, he rushed out of a Soda Springs
saloon with several drinks already in, heading down to the edge of the
Bear River, where he charged into a willow patch where another Soda
Springs resident had been attacked by a grizzly bear.

Caribou Jack's first shot missed the angry and wounded bear, and as it turned out, Jack couldn't whip any grizzly going.

Severely mauled before someone else managed to shoot the bear, Caribou Jack died a week later of blood poisoning.

But maybe that's what you need to make a lasting name for yourself: a larger-than-life story and an early, dramatic end to it. Caribou Jack, the slag pour, the "geyser" — the story's more important than anything else.

◇◇◇◇◇◇◇

August 6, 1849

Started in good season — morning cool and cloudy & few drops of rain — road leads down the valley of this stream & then passes over another mountain — due south this morning — plenty of fine grass all along — several ox trains from Missouri, Iowa & Wisconsin. I remained until the teams had got some distance ahead — covering a canteen & in hurrying to overtake them I passed about 20 ox teams of the drivers of which I inquired separately how far our train was ahead. The first few said "2 miles" — hurrying on others said "3 miles" — & the last that I asked said "4". About a half mile from there, I overtook them. Following down the valley from camp in the morning about 8 miles we crossed another stream, passed over a gentle ascent & turning to the right, entered a gorge in the mountains. Along this I kept on — it continually turning & winding along between peaks on either side — at each turn appearing as if I could see to the top — which appearance vanished as often as I turned around the foot of a hill — another presenting itself at every turn. The bottom was barely wide enough for a wagon to pass, though smooth, with occasionally a little patch of poplar bushes, but no water. Up, up this I continued, hoping soon to come up with the train, and at the same time fearing

that I had passed them camped off the road, but seeing
their passage marked on a poplar tree I pressed on &
overtook them just at the summit. There is a peak on the
left at the top of the hill, from which it is said the Salt Lake
may be seen — I ascended it, but the atmosphere was so
filled with smoke that I could not distinguish anything,
though I could see mountain tops in every direction and
at a great distance. The descent from the summit is rough
& precipitous — the dust 1 to 2 ft. deep, filled with loose
stones — the path crooked, and in the bottom of the hollow — barely wide enough to twist the wagons along! We
got safely down though 4 of the ox teams just behind us
got upset. Passing out of the ravine to the left we came out
into a large valley, where much to our disappointment we
found no water — though we had travelled near 20 miles.
I had some in my canteen but passing a man who was suffering from thirst going up the hill, I gave it to him and
thus deprived myself of that greatest of earthly luxuries.

There we met a man returning, who informed us that
it was still 13 miles to water. We stopped there till sunset
to rest our teams, intending to proceed again by "de light
ob de moon." Started moon an hour high and passed 4 or
5 miles down the valley then turned to the right & passed
up through a canyon — down into a little valley — over
another hill and after travelling till midnight we reached
the springs in a little hollow — a mean dusty place — 6
days before there were 1000 teams there.

In coming up the canyon several of the mules gave
out, and while I stood at the top the moon just rising
from behind a dark cloud, & listening to the cursing &
efforts of the drivers to urge the tired mules up the ascent,
I could not help strongly contrasting my situation there
with what it would have been at home. Some of the passengers built a fire of sage on the hill and waited for the

carriages to come up — jesting merrily. The Dr. like some others thinks that mules can do anything & loads them accordingly — carrying an immense sight of baggage — the consequence is, the mules are breaking down — the buggy mules gave out & also 2 in one of the wagons — found several Co.'s camped at the spring — distance from water to water 27 miles. Came 33 today — no fuel but sage — grass middling.

<><><><><>

Night comes to the Caribou Lodge, and, strangely, the place is so full that the manager puts a smudged cardboard sign out that reads, "Sorry, the 'No Vacancy' sign is broken, but the motel is fully booked." It's written in magic marker, and only the $42-a-night price tag explains why it would be full.

In the middle of the night, it's hard not to listen as a neighbour on our right-hand side loudly chastises a woman (wife? girlfriend?) on his smartphone as she squeaks back plaintively through the speaker. Bass answered by treble, bass answered by treble. They're both angry by the end — it's hard to tell who hangs up first.

Later, his snoring rings clearly through the walls — along with coughing and occasional stertorous flatulence — while the neighbour above us has stepped on the same squeaking board repeatedly. It must be exactly next to a bed or a chair. His alarm goes off at six, a chirpy melody that screams random cell phone choice, and moments later, the right-hand-side neighbour's phone barks awake with a repeated guitar chord. He is out the door — to warm up his truck for long, long minutes, the scent of diesel making its way into the room. A steadily beeping alarm filters in from the left-hand side. Leslie is in no mood for frivolity — her attempt to charge her computer the night before has somehow overtaxed the electrical system, tripping the breaker on the mysterious GFI plug under the desk. I lean down to take a look: there is a gentle whiff of hot wires wafting from the plug, a smell far too reminiscent of the Soda Springs geyser for safety.

A message from the management: "Dear Guest; For your convenience and for the preservation of our washcloths and towels, we have provided some extra cloths to be used for the following purposes: removal of eye makeup, mascara, foundation, lipstick, etc. (This includes hunting makeup as well) . . ."

My thoughts wander absently: in its own way, isn't all makeup a kind of hunting makeup?

The neighbour on our other side also heads out to his truck, starting the huge, loud engine. He leaves first, mercifully, and I wonder if truck size is a requirement for this hotel, or maybe for this town. Then the utility company truck parked across the lot backs up, backup alarm beeping, and all hope of sleeping later than 6:00 a.m. flees.

I leave our room key — complete with the old-style faded diamond-shaped red plastic tag that says it can just be dropped in a mailbox if we've forgotten to return it — on the front desk and hope to escape without being seen.

We get to a gas station two blocks away, picking up beef jerky and giving up completely on breakfast, and head tiredly out of town. Leslie has found massive cups of coffee, I've filled the gas tank and brought the front tire back up to enough pressure to wink out the low pressure light on the dash.

Despite the "natural beauty" of the slag pour, we're at pretty much the lowest ebb of the trip so far. Dodge's regular notes about missing family and friends ring true every now and then, especially when the day's tinged with exhaustion.

August 8, 1849

Started early & passing 3 miles up through the gorge came to another fine spring, after which we began to descend, & in 6 miles farther we struck a spring & followed the stream flowing from it 3 miles & camped in a very pretty little place. Our road lies through a gorge which appears to have been made on purpose. Several trains are travelling and camped near us — among which are the Milwaukee, the Wisconsin Star Co., one from Tennesse, & one from Ohio. On the south side of the road there rises a high peak — about 3 or 4 miles to the summit — elevated near 2000 ft. Myself & another person toiled up to the summit from which we had a view of the Salt Lake — distant 40 or 50 miles — it was so smoky we could not distinguish clearly anything. The ascent was tedious & we were glad indeed to get back again. Leaving noon camp we proceeded a couple of miles & left the gorge, coming out into a valley eight or ten miles wide — running north & south. We followed the creek about 5 miles out into the valley — where it loses itself in the earth.

⟨∞∞∞∞⟩

This is a strange land, full of contrasts. I can't believe how good the roads are or how empty. Somewhere up ahead of us, there must be one car that specializes in running down antelope and possums and raccoons and deer and pavement-pressed rabbits. We haven't hit any yet, and often, we are the only car on this four-lane, divided, concrete colossus.

Leaving Soda Springs, we curve down into a broad, flat valley of rich-looking soil with the sky heavy and grey above us. There's one small farmhouse in the middle of the valley, a barn collapsed down to one broken storey behind it, but the ground has been tilled on all sides of the buildings, so the old homestead sits like an abandoned island in a sea of turned soil, connected to the highway by a thin thread of gravel.

We drive by, stop, pull a tight U-turn and drive by again, pull over to take photographs. It's like walking into a book cover, the high ground in the back, the sweep of the valley, the lean of the house. It's a novel about hard-scrabble desperation, fighting endlessly against encroaching nature — and losing.

Later, we wind our way down through mountains suddenly awash in deciduous trees, high enough up that some have already been frost-nipped and are maple-scarlet. There's intermittent rain.

We're following a rail line that cuts in and out of sight: at one point, we're high above a long freight train that's bending its way around a hillside, the rail line a single, even line like a belt drawn tight around a mountain's middle. Shortly afterwards, we're on the same level, and the train joins us in the narrow valley gap between two tightly nestled hills.

We're tired, too short of sleep and too short with each other, and we're headed for a town called Lava Hot Springs and the hope that we can find a halfway reasonable breakfast there.

The California Trail has been right underneath the highway as we move through the valley, the highway builders following the same line the 49ers had. Near Lund, Idaho — a crossroads, a handful of houses — Dodge leaves the only route we can take, as he follows a branch of the trail up into the hills to the west and onto the Hudspeth Cutoff.

◇◇◇◇◇◇◇◇

August 9, 1849

Laid over until afternoon, expecting to make a drive of 19 to find water — unloaded & repacked — threw away a few tools, ropes, etc., the loads still weighing between 17 & 1800. After having used the water from the creek all day it was found to contain a dead ox a short distance above, which some villainous emigrant had left there. In the afternoon while busy at the wagon, a man rode up inquiring for me, when lo and behold there was "Low." I was much pleased to see him, & determined at once to pack with him, feeling certain that the Dr. could not get thro' with his teams and loads — & my mules too were being broken down hauling his heavy load. Jack had already nearly given out & was extremely reduced.

Leaving camp we proceeded west straight across the valley & camped by a fine spring and small stream — 14 miles from where we started — grass fine — few bushes for fuel.

◇◇◇◇◇◇◇◇

Chapter 11
Lava Hot Springs

We run out of gas in Lava Hot Springs — not the car, just us. We come into town and stop at the Chuck Wagon Restaurant, have a hearty breakfast with home fries, and decide to stay.

The woman who checks us in at the Alpaca Inn asks about our travels and uses the opening to tell us her family history.

She has a great-grandfather who was brought from Germany as an indentured servant, except the man to whom he owed the debt had no children. Her grandfather wound up working off his debt, going to law school, and founding his own town. It started out as Schell Knob, near Lake of the Ozarks, Missouri, but along the way lost its "c," pretty much the same way Kearney gained its unnecessary second "e."

Shell Knob's town history says Henry and Elizabeth Schell had a trading post there in 1835, and that the "c" disappeared when the post office was established in 1872. By then, the Schells had long since departed and founded a new town: Jacket, Missouri, and there's enough in their family story — building a grist mill, Schell's death by bushwhackers during the Civil War, the destruction of the mill by floodwaters — for the woman on the desk to write her own book.

More and more, I'm convinced that is how we put together our lives, make sense of them, how we connect to the world by finding our own place in a family constellation, with that constellation then fixed among all the rest. But discovering how securely others are set in their orbits hasn't helped me yet. I am still at sea, on the edge of the western desert.

The desk clerk says if it's gold we're after, we should try the mountain behind the hotel — outlaws made off with stolen gold, but were caught with none, and no one's found it yet. We climb the mountain, a narrow path with some long steps on the trail, in Dodge's language "we travelled ½ to ¾, ground rough, long grasses all yellow, plenty of fuel," the brush on both sides changing into fall colours. There are red torches of maples, but at the same time, still green clumps of sage. Tiring before we reach the top, even though the dark windows of two tall caves beckon off to one side of the trail not far above us, we turn to make our way back down, the town spread out comfortably, settled in place across the valley below and in front of us.

Lava Hot Springs in September is an off-season resort town; it's slow and empty, but that suits us fine. We spend virtually the whole day in the hot springs. There's three levels of heat. The only way into the hottest pool, which tips the scales at 112 degrees F, is to start further away from the source where the water's only 102 F and make your way back through the middle pool to the hottest. The water isn't strongly sulphurous, but its payload of minerals makes your skin feel slippery. Twenty-four million gallons of water passes through the pools and out into the Portneuf River every day.

We keep our purple wristbands on and come back for all three seasons of the springs: morning, when it's mostly elderly people soaking out kinks and aches; mid-afternoon, when it's families and children, with no one attempting the hottest spring; and evening, when it's an unlikely crew of night-out teens. It's as if they are obeying attendance rules we haven't been able to read anywhere. They're not posted, because everybody knows them already. The sunset is clipped off sharply by the mountain on the town's west shoulder.

We're still soaking when we see lightning and hear the rumble of distant thunder. We're looking at the aluminum poles sticking up out of the mineral-rich water, thinking about how it makes the perfect lightning rod. We head to the kiosk to ask about whether people have to get out of the springs if there's lightning: the answer is yes, but the woman who checks people into the facility is inside a cinderblock box.

She hasn't heard any thunder.

It's dark now, and the lightning flashes make the sharp edges of the mountains appear and disappear in silhouette.

The mountain we see most in the lightning — and the one we partially climbed — is on the west side of the town and is part of the Portneuf Range. The emigrant trail passes almost directly behind it where we were standing when we decided to turn around, something we didn't know. We're working from rudimentary maps, able to flag locations only from Dodge's descriptions. He's slipped into a land without the usual markers — not even effective maps. After the Hudspeth Cutoff, we'll have detailed trail maps all the way to Sutter's Mill at Hangtown, California (later named Placerville). Dodge will still be following word of mouth, established wagon ruts, and occasionally thoroughly faulty advice.

I believe you can always find the measure of a place when everyone's gone to bed, or else when no one's gotten up yet. Walking the town's empty streets, I'm bird-dogged by slow-moving police cars, part of the cost of an early solo walk.

In the early morning, the gutters on the side streets are filled with windfallen, broken and rotting apples from scattered front-yard trees. As the day warms, small clouds of wasps appear around the fallen fruit, and by early afternoon, they are cider-drunk and sky-staggering, straight-lining toward you low and fast as if ready to pick a fight.

At the Cliff View Liquor Store, a store that manages to look more like a hobby than a business, the proprietor asks us where we're from. When we say Canada, she tells us she was in Canada once, at the home of a Winnipegger who ran a car show, a long explanation that stretches a wire-thin connection between us across thousands of miles. Leslie buys a small tin bottle of vodka that attaches to your belt or knapsack with a caribiner. We're knitting a loose kinship, sharing stories with complete strangers.

We load the car at the Alpaca, which has almost impeccable online reviews: my favourite? "This is hands down the best hotel/motel/private house rental experience I have had in all of Caribou County, Idaho."

How can you not agree?

◇◇◇◇◇◇

August 10, 1849

Started as usual, travelled 5 ½ to a fine stream coming down out of the gape into which we were entering & which follows near the road for some miles, abounding with fine speckled trout — ½ mile from where we crossed it the road from Ft. Hall comes in on our right. From Beer Springs to this point, through the new cut-off is 140 by the Roadometer which is one day ahead of us. At noon I left the Dr.'s Co. and packed with Low & "Bogus." I sold Jack for $80.00 & gave $100.00 for Jenny. From Coxe, whom we passed toward evening I learned that Drury was only 25 ahead, hope to overtake him soon. Crossed 2 or 3 small streams & following along between the lofty hills, the road turns to the S. up a gentle ascent, near the top of which there is a fine spring. . . . Very cold — snow on the mountains on every side of us! We see people travelling in nearly every manner — some with carts & <u>oxen with harness</u>, some <u>packing oxen</u>, others packing with one horse & others still on foot carrying their own packs!

Waited until nearly 8 to fix some of my things — kept down the valley southward crossing a number of small streams and nooned near a fine stream running E.S.E. to the right of which was a spring. Lewis went down to wash his hands, but no sooner had he put them in than he jerked them out again — the water being too hot to hold them in. At this point the road leading from the Salt Lake comes into ours. Since taking the cut off a very errone- ous opinion that existed among the emigrants — many think they must be near the head of Humboldt river — others that we strike it 150 from its head, & are near that place. A great variety of opinions exist but nearly all agree in thinking that we are not more than 400 or 500 miles from Sutters [Sutter's Mill, the site of the 1849 gold find]. The Dr. especially, thinks the distance not more than 400. Nobody appears to know where we are, & look anxiously for the appearance of the river.

A lengthy train of stock cars rumbles past at eight in the morning as we are leaving town. There have been rumblings of trains — and thunder — almost all night.

We drive through occasional mountains, long, steep-sided grass-covered almost-mountains, and one particularly memorable part where the road winds through hills with random black cows and steers appearing along the road on the wrong side of the fence.

On Route 15, heading south, a badger noses out on the road, changes his mind, disappears back into the sagebrush. The trees dis- appear, except in the deep valleys that occasionally cut down from the hills. The sage multiplies, thick short forests of it, knit together across the flatlands. Road and power lines, sage and desert grass. The road here is good — smooth, new, the yellow line crisp.

We take a turn off the highway onto a dirt road, looking for the City of Rocks, 27 miles away. The weather has turned grey and wet, and the sign at the turnoff doesn't look quite right. It's handmade with carved letters, the whole sign leaning, and the route doesn't seem to correspond with anything on the map.

Still, if it's accurate, it will be a radically shorter distance, a "cut- off" of our own, and closer to the route the emigrants would have taken. So we go that way.

It turns out to be 27 long sliding miles of wet, loose sand and mud, the rental car streaked with it, the car always inches from sliding into the verge. There are occasional houses far, far apart and one lone yellow grader working the battered road flat again, turning the gravel and occasionally throwing up short clouds of white rock dust when it strikes a boulder or outcrop. The grader's trail is even softer once we pass it, the hardpack of the gravel road broken up, so the car is sluggish in all ways: hard to stop, hard to get going again, and turning feels like slaloming through snow.

We cross the Raft River, no ferry, scrub grass and sage on both sides. Cattle and hawks, deer and antelope.

We meet up with Dodge's route again just south of the town of Almo and share it with him up into the City of Rocks, which he knew as Steeple Rocks.

∞∞∞∞∞

August 10, 1849 (con't)

Falling into the road running off west from the Salt Lake we turned westward through a gorge, where we saw some of the most interesting looking rocks on the whole route, very high, broken and rough in the form of pyramids and almost all kinds of buildings, called "Steeple Rocks." On top of a high mountain at the entrance of the gorge, some wag had built a fire, evidently intending to make the "Greenies" believe it a volcano! Passing over a rough hilly road we came to a valley at sundown, but found no water. At a place where there had been some once, we found an honest looking German very industriously engaged in digging a well, apparently hoping to coax the water back! Low gave him a dollar for a plug of tobacco when he informed us that water was three miles off the road, & that there was none ahead short of eight miles — we determined to go the 8, but had proceeded only a couple of miles when we found a good spring close to the road. Just before reaching it we passed a grave on the right, & a dead ox on the left, both man & beast having perished in the toil for gold. Camped near the foot of the mountain on the Salt Lake side of the valley — plenty of grass and fuel. A few days since an Indian was found dead in Reed's Creek having undoubtedly been murdered for his pony by some villain — either an emigrant or a deserter.

∞∞∞∞∞

Idaho is often flat, except where it very suddenly isn't, and then it's magnificent. The City of Rocks — a passing point for the emigrants — is amazing: worn spires and boulders jumbled together, and the higher up you go into the back of the valley, the higher the spires reach, until finally the cliffs are the goal of rock climbers from around the world.

Some of the rocks have emigrant names carved into them. Lizards spring around the base of the stones, and eagles hang still above us. Leslie stands under the great open sky, arms outstretched, ecstatic, the twin eagles watching her, curious. We climb one finger of rock, its sides smooth and granular and grey, noticing how potholes have been cut into the solid stone by erosion. When we're high enough, the eagles circle down close. Their wingspan is massive, and, after having a good look, they pull back into the thermals and rise until they are only specks against the sky. As they rise, a sudden blackening front is rolling in from the west of us, and a flash of lightning makes us reconsider our elevation.

It's hot and still, and it's easy to feel close to the time of the emigrants. Everything here seems untouched, except for one small tangle of rusting farm equipment and wire fencing at the mouth of the narrow valley leading into the rocks. We find our first Trails West marker there, a "T" made of cut-up railway tracks that connects to that group's intricate mapping of the emigrant trails to California. Our feet firmly in their footprints, it all feels completely worthwhile, just right then.

Back in the car, we're driving up the road, heading up into the angry clouds of the looming thunderstorm when we meet four teams of Hotshot forest firefighters in crew trucks, winding their way down the road from a blaze that's been reduced to little more than a smoulder. They're in big, purpose-built green trucks designed to seat them all and carry their equipment, and you can only imagine where they've been and what they've seen, but still they've got their cell phones out the windows, taking pictures of the same City of Rocks that drew the pioneers' attention — and ours.

After they pass, we continue up into the hills. It's starting to spit rain and two rock climbers in bright helmets and spandex are urgently bundling coils of brightly coloured rope into the yawning trunk of their car. Fat raindrops spatter down, raising dust as they strike the ground.

The maps for this area are incomplete, and you couldn't find a cell phone signal if you tried. A ranger standing next to a battered green forest service pickup truck tells us that the firefighters had been working an isolated lightning strike fire higher up, even though we're now high above the plains, looking down the gorge across the City of Rocks. From any vantage point, it seems incomprehensible that the stones could be a natural occurrence.

Then we're heading (hopefully) for Oakley, on a long, sliding downhill dirt and mud road run toward pavement, oh please god towards pavement. The rain is starting to pound down on the Birch Creek Road, which is where it turns out we are.

Oakley is full of rain.

There's a dearth of highway signs, and as the rain pummels down in sheets, we accidentally dead-end into the overpowering stench of shit-filled stockyards.

Cattle steaming in the rain, "No Trespassing" signs in three different directions. The stockyards are gluey grey mud and disconsolate-looking steers, the drum-hard dry ground vanishing into soup. The road has standing water everywhere and the ditches are overflowing.

⌒⌒⌒⌒⌒

August 12, Sunday, 1849
This morning we came through another gape down a hill
across a little stream & then descend into a large and most

singular appearing basin. It is filled with abrupt & broken hills — the sides of which are alternately white, yellow, red & green, & are thinly covered with patches of cedar & sage bushes. The road lies over very steep hills — through ravines, until it reaches Goose Creek, where we nooned. Some Mormons are said to be digging gold with great success a few miles up this creek. Some of the Mormons from the Salt Lake camped near us & from their guide books we learn that we are yet 115 miles from the head of Humboldt River, & 170 from their settlement. By some who have just come from Ft. Hall the distance to where they strike the cut-off road is represented at 65, others 85 & still others 100 — others yet 110!

In the afternoon we followed up Goose Creek about 15 miles & camped by the side of it among some willow bushes. . . . Road been good — grass fine — bushes plenty. A great many ox teams are camped in this valley.

August 13, 1849

After following up the creek a couple of miles it suddenly enters a gorge through a mountain — narrow & rough — barely room for the road & creek — for 2 miles this ravine was completely filled with ox teams & after leaving the creek passing a spring at the foot of a rock the road takes over a gentle hill covered with rock and sage — travelled 14 without seeing a blade of grass or drop of water — the dust so thick as almost to suffocate us & the sun fairly scorching us. Descending into a valley we passed a splendid spring at the foot of a rock on the right, but much to our disappointment found no grass. After passing the spring 2 or 3 miles we stopped for a couple of hours, no fuel — no water — no grass — nothing but dust, dust. Having rested our mules we started again & in 2 or 3 came to a fine spring in the center of a little open bare-spot, where the water which sank into the ground some 5 above, appeared to burst out again. The spring was elevated above the surrounding plain, & the water after running off in different directions a short distance, sinks into the parched earth again. Leaving this we travelled on, the road resembling a bed of ground plaster — 5 or 6 farther & descended into another valley where we found some very coarse grass — a little poor water in holes which had been dug & large numbers of ox teams camped. The country along has been thickly covered with sage. Distance 35 miles. Low is unwell — dysentery.

∞∞∞∞

We turn around at the stockyard and make our way into downtown Oakley — well, as downtown as it gets. Only three streets cross the town core's South Center Avenue.

We've hit town just as the school buses are fanning out and dropping children off from school, all traffic slowed. We run through the rain into a gas station on Oakley's main drag, Searle's Gas Grub and Goodies, only to be told we're on the right road, already and finally. And then we're on the interstate, the wide trail with trucks roaring all around us, until it's Twin Falls and the Snake River Canyon.

As we head west, the ground dries out even more, as if the rain we'd just experienced had never happened. The soil and sand is baked hard, the only signs of water the swirls it has left behind in the dust and alkali as it dried. Sage's dry blue-green is the only colour that isn't brown or yellow. Our skin and hair are different, skin drier, hair reedy and flat. Water seems to disappear from its bottles. We're not stopping for bathroom breaks. We don't need to.

∞∞∞∞

August 14, 1849
On account of Low being unwell, we concluded to lay over. Larkin having bought Leeche's saddle, I was obliged

to give up Perry's, & Low lent me one of his trees, & I
spent the forenoon fixing it, & after I had got it all fixed I
traded with Larkin for his. About 3 P.M. we started & went
about 9 miles where we found the same kind of water &
grass, with a few bushes. Low got some medecine from a
physician in an emigrant train.

◇◇◇◇◇◇◇

We stand near the visitor centre in Twin Falls and stare down into the
Snake River gorge, standing out on a cantilevered platform that shakes
gently when we walk. But it's not only our footsteps: the platform also
trembles in the wind, an updraft that comes up and under us from the
gorge. On the side opposite, a golf course has been cut into the hill,
incongruously bright irrigated greens and fairways filling the dips in the
peaked rocks. It even has a small lake, a broad water hazard where no
lake should rightly be. At the edge of each fairway, the terrain returns
to greyed and eroding rock and the bright yellow of dried grass.

The river is far, far below us, winding through the deep cut it has
eroded for itself, while off on the right, the rust-red web of girders
under the Perrine Memorial Bridge curve up to grip the roadbed, the
bridge's metal feet set squarely into the cliff face.

Snake River's been part of my memory since Evel Knievel set out to
jump the gorge on a steam-rocket-powered motorcycle on September
17, 1974. The tourist signs still show his take-off ramp. A different
stuntman was planning the same jump for September 17, 2016, three
days after we passed through. The more things change, the more people hurl themselves off cliffs.

Later, we slide into Nevada at Jackpot, a border town that shows
up first as a row of green trees on green grass, standing out against the
sedge and yellow of the rest of the desert. We never get used to it. The
first store is Stateline Liquor: "Cheap Vodka $9.98." Then, it's Barton's
Club 93 casino (24-hour restaurant), Cactus Pete's Resort and Casino,
the HorseShu Hotel and Casino, the Four Jacks Casino, the West Star
— you get the picture.

And even more clearly from the street names: Dice Road, Roulette Drive, Slot Drive, Ace Drive, Casino Way, Keno Drive, Poker Street, and Lady Luck Loop, off Lady Luck Drive. The town — now of roughly 1,000 — was founded by casino owners forced south from Idaho after that state banned gambling in 1953. It's so connected to its Idaho gambling customers that it keeps its clocks on Mountain Time, despite actually being in the Pacific zone. It's the largest employer in southern Idaho, despite being in Nevada; scores of workers are bussed the 40 miles from Twin Falls every day, because housing's limited here. Even the trash goes back to Idaho.

The sky is starting to fade as we leave the brightening pool of lights and neon green grass that is Jackpot; it's back to desert sedge and the incipient darkness as we leave a town whose success is as arbitrary as where the line of a state border happens to fall.

In Elko County on the Great Basin Highway, Route 93 (but not the old, now nearly abandoned Route 93, which is still haphazarding its way alongside, next-to, and across our path), we cruise through the wreckage of the abandoned Mineral Hot Springs, with just one tin-awninged, cinder-block-and-pale-blue building left that hasn't tumbled down. It's the only thing that's salvageable, according to the seller.

It used to be quite the place, apparently, and was the original Cactus Pete's casino. There used to be big-name bands, a dance floor. The lure for this location was its highway-side hot springs. The hotel spring at Mineral Hot Springs produces 20 gallons a minute, maybe more, at 135 degrees Fahrenheit. It's 240 acres in all, and it's all yours for the low, low price of $500,000. I know this because, having seen the "For Sale" sign, I go online in our next hotel room and look up the listing. Leslie and I are smitten with the idea of the place, of negotiating the price down, going into debt to it, building it into a desert writing retreat and business. It would only have to be the smallest of goldmines, turning out enough ore to pay our way.

No one else appears interested in buying this crumbling opportunity, just past Contact, on the two-lane heading south. Five years later, it's still for sale — "This is truly an Oasis in the High Desert and should be a great RV Park or similar use," the realty ad says.

Contact is little more than a highway depot and a handful of houses for the employees, out of sight from the highway. It's another gold mining ghost town, dating to a gold discovery in 1897. Again, gold found only a handful of miles from Dodge's track. Beyond that, Salmon Falls Creek has enough water to open up basin lands into pasturage, but there's precious little high ground to let you see where the water runs.

Buildings flash by occasionally — this road is wide and empty, the shoulders pushed well back by heavy equipment, the sightlines good except for the spots where hills rise and fall.

There are dots on the map that indicate towns, though it's only to keep up the appearance of habitation, of inhabitants. Sometimes, a road sign tells you that you're entering a town, and that road sign is the only thing there.

It's into evening now: headlights coming toward us show up more, and the sun's almost down to the horizon. As it gets dark, the evening doesn't just cool: the temperature drops 10 or more degrees as the sun vanishes, the heat wicking away into so much open sky.

◇◇◇◇◇◇◇◇

August 15, 1849

This morning Low is unable to travel again & Randall went on to find grass & water. Low, when the Dr. came up, got into his wagon and rode through the day. Travelled 15 miles up the dry valley with poor coarse grass & no water but that found in the wells or holes dug by the emigrants, which is a very inferior quality. Travelled S.S.W. Road is extremely dusty & the earth in many places is covered with a white alkaline encrustacion. Toward noon we struck a creek running N.N.E. & followed it several miles. The water was very warm even in the evenings though the nights are very cold, especially just before day. Ice and frost are frequently to be seen at morning. Already many of the packers are short of provisions & cannot buy at any price scarcely. Flour sells at from 15 to 25 cts. per pound and no bacon to be had.

If Low should not be able to travel tomorrow I think of returning to Dr. White's Co. I shot a sage hen which made us a fine supper. A large number of trains are camped along the valley which we think to be but a few miles from a branch of the Humboldt River.

August 16, 1849

Low continued with the Dr. After they had been gone sometime, Bogus & myself started on after them. After proceeding a few rods up the stream, we came to a large collection of boiling springs — covering at least ½ an acre. The water was so hot that I could not hold my hand in it for a moment, which I found to be the cause of the stream being so warm below there. After leaving camp we travelled some six miles along the valley without water or grass — nothing but sage, & then left it, turning to the left into a gorge where we soon found water. Leaving the road, we went a short distance up a hollow to the left, where we found a little grass & water, plenty for noon. The fore part of the day was cool & looked like rain. A few drops of rain fell yesterday afternoon, but not sufficient to lay the dust. While we were feeding off the road, the Dr.'s team with L. passed us. We proceeded up the ravine over a hill and came into a valley where the road forked, the right hand one striking the branch in the valley below, & the other or main one leading to the left of a high range of abrupt hills, the tops of which were spotted with snow. Supposing the wagons to have taken the right one we followed that and soon entered one of the most broken, rocky, and forbidding looking canyons that I ever saw. The road frequently crossed and recrossed the stream to avoid the rocks, were loosely hanging far above us looking each moment as though they would tumble headlong into the ravine below. A great many lay loose in the road & by the side of it, & there were several very bad crossings & slough holes. After travelling 6 or 8 miles through this we emerged into a large valley covered with coarse grass & a very few bushes along the stream. While passing through the canyon I observed two or three places where the water boiled out in large quantities from under the rocks & emptied into the stream. I did not stop to examine it, but a man camped a short distance below informed me they were boiling or hot springs. Passed on a couple of miles & camped near a camp of mule teams close to the branch. I ate a piece of bread which was given me by an emigrant, he refusing to sell it, and for the first time in a month slept warm.

We were satisfied that the wagons had taken the other road, & nobody could tell us anything about how far it was before they united again. For the last few days we have passed several graves & a large number of dead cattle.

<><><><><>

Chapter 12

The Road to
Wells, Nevada

The emigrant trail crosses our route again below Mineral Hot Springs near Wilkins: the light is really fading now, so we don't see exactly which cut over the hills is the trail.

We're heading for Wells, once called Humboldt Wells after the deep springs that mark the start of the Humboldt River. The springs are fenced off now and modified for agricultural use — water isn't just a lifesaver, it's a commercial commodity.

Many of the springs that the emigrants depended on en route are fenced in tightly, the fences encompassing every inch of ground where non-desert plants give away the secret of hidden water.

"No Trespassing" signs bloom like their own foliage, making spring-to-spring travel like Dodge's impossible.

Dodge's route is at this point underneath another reservoir, the Bishop Creek Reservoir, which edges down Bishop Canyon and bypasses Humboldt Wells completely. When he passed through here, Dodge had already believed that he was close to the source of the Humboldt for weeks.

Until now, he's been wrong every time . . .

◇◇◇◇◇◇

August 17, 1849
This morning we rode 6 or 8 miles & came to the junction

of the roads about 20 miles from where they separated. Here I was informed that the other road was a very good road, & from inquiry was satisfied that the wagons were behind. Passing on a few miles a most furious storm appeared in front, which proved to be nothing but wind and dust. When it came up the wind blew a hurricane & the dust flew so thick that we could scarcely see our mules. I stopped near a couple of mule teams, but "Bogus" determined to be as contrary as usual, went ahead. After feeding I packed up, put on, intending to overtake him & lay by for Low. Overtook "Bogus" camped where the road crosses the stream about 3 miles ahead. By some men I heard of Ebon ahead, & leaving my pack animal I rode on several miles, in hopes of overtaking him, but without success. My mule being weary I returned, much disheartened. I kept up a continual inquiry of the passing teams for Low & the Dr., but could hear nothing of them, except one man told me he thought they were on ahead, but that I knew to be impossible. What to do I scarcely knew. I went to the creek and washed, then sat down under a shade I had made & began to reflect on my situation. I should have had provisions sufficient to have lasted me, but supposing I was going to continue with Low I had cooked for him and "Bog" out of mine, which had reduced them to about 15 lbs. hard bread, 8 lbs. meal, 1 ½ sugar, & 2 lbs. coffee. To augment my troubles Low was hanging back & refusing to lend me the pack saddle I used which belonged to him, but which he had promised me to go through with, so that I could go on, nor would he sell it except at a price which he knew would exhaust all the money I had, although he had no animal to use it on. Thus I sat meditating and thinking, when up rode a couple of packers. I invited them to alight, when one of them remarked that he thought he knew me. Upon telling him who I was he recognized me & then informed me that they formerly belonged to Capt. White's Co.; all of whom packed from Salt Lake. They concluded to camp with us, especially as there were some suspicious looking characters — apparently deserters — camped near by, who looked as though they might take, if they did not need animals, having but one apiece. Upon telling them of my fix they urged me to go on with them, but I had no saddle. A portion of Dr. Brown's Co. were camped near us, and as good luck would have it I got an old pack saddle frame from one of them — Johnson — who was so kind as to give it to me. We built a fire, and by their help we had it rigged by 10 P.M., ready for a start in the morning. By another train that came up I learned that the Dr.'s train with Low would be along before noon of the next day. Plenty of grass and bushes at that place and a few miles below was splendid grass.

◇✕◇✕◇✕◇✕◇

Rolling fast along the dark highway, the last light a bright fingernail on the western horizon, we see Wells first as the swell of a highway bridge against the light: the highway rises up over the transcontinental railway line. The first sign we see? A red-letter sign, Bella's Hacienda Ranch. The next, Donna's Ranch. Both open 24 hours. Bella's has the bigger sign, Donna's the longer reputation.

Donna's has been in business for over 140 years, a legal brothel that traces its roots to 1869, just 20 years after Dodge was spending cold nights in the empty desert. Sometimes, seeking comfort is a commodity. "Donna's offers complimentary showers, coffee, shuttle rides to and from the brothel, truck parking, a fully stocked bar, and of course, beautiful ladies. It is our duty to satisfy and fulfill your every fantasy and desire." It's the other side of the tracks, literally and figuratively. Both brothels are on 8th Street, which runs right along the rail line. Even Google Street View simply decides to see nothing where the brothels are, though you can find them on satellite imagery. (And even though the street numbers are on 8th, the two brothels nestle safely down a side road off 10th, well tucked away and out of sight from town.)

∞∞∞∞∞

August 18, 1849

This morning got under way with Dunn and Norman & left "Bog" to wait for Low. Our road lay along down the river, passing through a wide bottom covered with the finest grass we have seen in a long time. Stopped at noon & caught one fine trout. Continued down the river, as we supposed, passing a great many ox trains, & toward night crossed a branch which we supposed to be Martin's fork, but which proved to be the North branch, the one we had followed being S. branch of the river instead of the main river itself. The bottom grew narrower & grass poor, when we left the river and took over the hill, and descending into the valley again about sunset, & crossing to the S. side camped in one of the prettiest places imaginable. It was on a little island surrounded entirely with willows and covered with fine grass. It was shut out from the road by the river banks which were everywhere lined with willow bushes. Being again with <u>moral men</u> we decided to spend the Sabbath there.

∞∞∞∞∞

We check in at the Motel 6 in Wells. ("Simple budget lodging with seasonal pool," which could be the title of a poetry collection.) A room on the second floor, strangely bright colours, and geometric patterns like the hotel company had hired a random Danish designer and never revisited his now-dated creation.

Wells used to be a destination: performers, casinos, bars. But one by one, the casinos closed; people were looking for something else, something bigger, something with more flash.

"The casinos went out of business and the earthquake of '08 knocked them down flat," the desk clerk tells me in between coughing fits. During that week in 2008, the rest of the world was caught up with the Wall Street financial collapse, so the quake news didn't make the cut.

Outside the big sheet-glass front window, Leslie's trying to get my attention, but I fail to notice, waiting for the room key and hoping that every rasping breath the clerk hauls into her lungs isn't going to be her last.

Leslie's met another real cowboy, an aged, more leathery version of the Marlboro Man who has come across from the phalanx of parked-running-and-still-lit-up semis, all lined up side by side. He's looking for a light or a cigarette, and she's trying to get my attention so I will at least see her making time with a genuine cowboy. I don't — she's crestfallen.

The next day, on foot, it's easy to see the results of the earthquake in old Wells. News reports from the time say the town's historic downtown took the brunt of the damage. We can see it plainly: there's a bulldozed chunk of main street, buildings with brick walls that are split or hang away from their buildings.

The core of downtown Wells is mostly gone, with damaged and tarped buildings like the battered El Rancho Hotel just waiting, it seems, for some small shake or tremble to finish their fall. The people seem equally battered.

There's also the other economic wreckage that's still standing: the usual string of faded, abandoned strip motels, all just that little bit too far from the highway junction where the Great Basin Highway T-bones into the I-80 and the cookie-cutter modern motels grab up the business before it has a chance to get to town.

The Lone Star Motel boasts "LOW RATES" on a sign encircled by 60 incandescent light bulbs — most still intact — but the horseshoe of rooms around the gravel parking lot are boarded up. The Shell Crest's standing sign, old-school neon, is freckled with peeling paint. The Wild West Inn is a battered streetfront, the most notable feature

of its crumbling stuccoed second floor the holes where the individual air conditioners have been harvested for other uses. Every empty
room once full of life and life's stories — all gone.

We find a hand-painted sign, red letters on white, standing on
the ground: "WANTED YOUR OLD HISTORY – PICTURES
– STORIES – ANTIQUES 18-1900 DONATE THEM TO THE
WELLS MUSEUM."

The museum is what you might expect, a collection of random
artefacts from Humboldt Wells, with a heavy tilt toward the illicit:
one of the guides points us to a wooden box, used to collect tips for
a brothel's collection of prostitutes. There's something almost seedy
about how his hands caress the worn box as he tells us about it. Not
one of Dodge's "moral men," it seems.

But the stop at the museum — sorry, the Trail of the 49ers
Interpretive Center — tips us off about the story of Metropolis.

◇×◇×◇×◇◇

August 19, Sunday, 1849
This was a fine morning, & while cooking breakfast,
myself feeling unwell was lying by the fire, Dunn &
Norman standing. In front of me, a rifle ball came whis-
tling between them and me, <u>passing within a foot of my</u>
<u>head!</u> It was fired by a passing emigrant on the opposite
side of the bushes who did not know that anyone was in
them. After giving him a "Candle" lecture upon carelessness, we ate and having taken a good bathing, once more
assumed the appearance in part of a white man. I built a
bower and laid down in the shade! What a fine time to
think! And I improved it too. It was just about time for
the people of our village to be gathering at church, and
in my imagination I could see them gathering there with
their happy faces and tidy apparel and could see too the
Sabbath School — the class, the vacant seat — all as plain
and vivid as I ever saw it in my life — & oh, how could I

help contrasting my situation here with what it had been there! Here I was with provisions only for a few days — 550 miles from the nearest settlement — out of funds almost — no provisions to be had at any price, and if my mules should give out my last and only dependence would be entirely gone. Such were my thoughts that day — still I did not despair. Providence had provided well for me this far and I trusted that the same power would still.

August 20, 1849

Started early & passed a large number of ox trains. Fine grass all along before noon. At noon found no grass & we kept on till night & camped on a dry branch 2 or 3 miles from the road. During the afternoon we came to where the road forked, one heading over the hill to the right, the other following the stream. We took the latter and found it very crooked & passed through some deep canyons with high broken rocks. Crossed the stream several times and came out again into the valley. All through this valley the soil like that of Warm Spring Valley is of a light yellow color, & has the appearance of never having been wet by rain. It is just like ground plaster wherever there is a path having no sod — nothing but sage on it. In many places the wagons have worn 2 ft. into the earth, producing a thick bed of fine dust, which almost smothers man and beast. The bottom is narrow & hemmed entirely in by lofty mountains on every side. The River is very crooked, & indeed, is nothing but a little brook at best, with now and then a pool of stagnant water.

<hr />

We drive toward the Humboldt River, close to the deep springs that gave Wells its name. The pools are out of sight on our right behind a row of ranch houses. Then we turn to the north onto dirt roads, the town ending and the desert beginning in an instant, like the second hand ticking past on a clock.

Just before Metropolis, we cross Bishop Creek, Dodge's "little brook at best." Dodge came down the route that ran through Bishop Canyon, which is kicking out here with Trout Creek in a flat meadow. We meet his trail as we roll down a small hummock to the brook. There's a farmhouse and barn, and a fortress of rolled hay bales. Incongruously, parked in the yard, a faded and battered antique fire truck.

Metropolis was a grand plan that failed to take into account the most basic necessities of life. The Pacific Reclamation Company devised a city of 7,500 at the centre of the 40,000 acres of farmland it had purchased. The New York–based firm attracted more than 700 people by 1912, two-thirds of them Mormons eager to take the company up on its promise of cheap farmland.

On its empty grid of streets, there are shotgun shells all around, and anything made of metal is punched full of pellet holes. There are decaying concrete foundations, and everywhere the sage has moved back in. Down 15 miles of dirt road from the river, far into the dry sage country with no water source — who thought that would work? Manufacturing an ersatz but completely planned community by diligently pounding a square peg into a round hole.

In front of the arch that was the entrance to the school for the town — the only part of any structure standing higher than foundations — there is a hole in the ground with a nest of small snakes. The arch is pocked with bullet holes.

In its heydey, the town had 2,000 residents, a school, hotel, and lumberyard. After that, it was like a combination of good intentions, slapstick, and a test from God.

The town's residents killed off nearby packs of coyotes — a move that resulted in a plague of hungry jackrabbits. After that, there was typhoid, huge swarms of ravenous Mormon crickets (the brown wingless ones Dodge found overrunning part of Wyoming) devouring crops, and the never-ending drought. The town had Biblical trials in spades. But it was the most easily predictable one that actually did them in.

Metropolis had expected to get the water it needed for the city and for farm irrigation from Bishop Creek, dammed with 6.5 million pieces of brick left from the 1906 San Francisco earthquake, but even Dodge would have told them it was folly — remember, "The River is very crooked, & indeed, is nothing but a little brook at best, with now and then a pool of stagnant water." The creek was too small — and downstream, the town of Lovelock had the legal rights to all the water anyway.

A lawsuit took the dam down.

And Metropolis finally, unequivocally, died of thirst.

◇◇◇◇◇◇

August 21, 1849

Started early & soon came to a branch which we thought must be Martin's fork, but we soon learned our mistake, & that Martin's fork came in on the opposite side, & miles back, where we did see it. Leaving the river we took over a long steep & very stony hill, descending into the valley again through a long & deep canyon, 20 miles from where we started. Finding no grass we stopped only a sufficient time to get something to eat & rest our mules, & then we proceeded again through the dust, passing numerous trains. For two days I have been trying to purchase a few pounds of bacon, but could not, even at 30 cts. per pound. The whole valley of the river is filled with ox trains, but few of them have more than sufficient provisions to get through with, & many wish to buy. As usual a great variety of opinions exist as to the distance, nearly all thinking it to be from 100 to 175 less than it is, and no two scarcely thinking alike.

Toward evening we passed a notice stuck up by the roadside, stating that the day previous a band of Snake Indians stole 40 cattle from a party of emigrants, entirely depriving several of them of their teams. They were pursued into the mountains, with an attempt to capture them. Three of the Indians were killed, & one of the white men wounded. We camped on the river bank by Waldo's train, who, though he would not sell me any bacon, very kindly gave me a few pounds. Grass exceedingly short — rather gone in this vicinity.

⬦⬦⬦⬦⬦⬦

We travel through the Emigrant Pass, uncomfortably high for the travellers coming west, with its cold nights and fast-changing weather. Then on the descent we pass through the small hamlet of Emigrant, the highway signs reading "Emigrant — No Services."

Truer words were never spoken; it sums up Dodge's crossing in three words.

There is sage on the flat white plains, the alkali broken up into plates by the shrinkage of its drying.

And then we're in Battle Mountain, supposedly named in 1866 for a battle in 1857 between 24 townspeople (led by a Capt. Pierson), and a group of attacking Native Americans.

Battle Mountain suffered the indignity of being voted the Armpit of America in a 2001 *Washington Post* competition, where it was given this description: "Take a small town, remove any trace of history, character, or charm. Allow nothing with any redeeming qualities within city limits — this includes food, motel beds, service personnel. Then place this pathetic assemblage of ghastly buildings and nasty people on a freeway in the midst of a harsh, uninviting wilderness, far enough from the nearest city to be inconvenient, but not so far for it to develop a character of its own. You now have created Battle Mountain, Nevada."

Harsh indeed. But this is America, where any fame, any story, even infamy, has value. Battle Mountain parlayed its armpit reputation into a summer festival (The Festival in the Pit, with the slogan "Only Inches from Your Heart" — sponsored by Old Spice deodorant.)

Oddities abound. Battle Mountain is holding the World Human Powered Speed Championship when we get there, featuring bicycle-powered teardrops of carbon fiber. We peer into the workroom, watching as crews, huddled together and murmuring quietly, shrink heat-sensitive plastic with a hair dryer over the spokes of bicycle wheels to reduce drag. The vehicles compete on a highway they close for 20 minutes at a time to let the race go ahead unimpeded. A woman from the chamber of commerce can't tell us how many teams there are, but says they speak at least seven languages. They are all young, the drivers lean and whippet-y, like the rodeo cowboys we'll see later in Winnemucca. One of them, Todd Reichart, will set a world record of 89.59 mph at this particular competition. It's not just the bikes that are designed to break records, or the riders themselves. Even the road is designed to make record-breaking possible.

"Highway SR 305 just south of Battle Mountain possesses the unique traits necessary for these highly engineered bicycles to achieve top speeds. The high altitude and arrow straight section of pavement has drawn athletes worldwide to test their speed bike designs and sprinting abilities since 2000," the International Human Powered Vehicle Association writes. "The remote section of road used for this event was repaved in 2009 with an exceptionally smooth surface specially prepared for human powered cycle racing by way of an economic development grant for rural Nevada from the U.S. government and with the assistance of Lander County Department of Tourism."

Anything to make a mark.

We're just looking for old-school bathrooms and the unusual arte-fact of a payphone. Leslie wants to let her mother know where we are, that we're safe.

We head out along route 305 to have a look at the race site. The road's empty when we get to the special pavement. The time trials happen in the light winds of evening when the bicyclists, sealed lying-down inside their kidney-bean-shaped craft, can get the best speeds with the least risk of crosswinds. It's hard to take world records seriously when everything, every possible variable, is designed and managed to be in your favour.

We turn right, up Copper Basin Road, near the giant Newmont Phoenix Mine that, in 2016 alone, produced 209,000 ounces of gold and 42 million pounds of copper. There's believed to be another 4.3 million ounces of gold reserves still in the ground. All of it a hop, skip, and jump away from the emigrant trail — barely a day's travel for Dodge away from his route.

We get out to wander: the hard-pack alkali ground is strewn with small pebbles near the dirt road heading to the mine. There's a tall fence. After a while, a white crew-cab pickup truck trundles down the road from above us, pulls to one side and sits with all its windows rolled up. Its driver is wearing a white hardhat. The truck sits there until we get in the car and pull away.

Then it turns around and heads back up the hill.

Somewhere, in all this broad, open country, there must be cameras.

It seems, by the way, that the "battle" in Battle Mountain didn't even happen. As the Lander County Convention and Tourism Authority says on its website, there's no evidence the battles described by a prospector, George Tannihill, even took place. There were two possible skirmishes that he might have inflated, but, "The third possibility is that Mr. Tannihill was lying. He knew something happened here in 1857 and just tried to make himself sound important. This one seems the mostly likely of the three possibilities."

If you don't have a story, you can make a convincing one up, and it just may stick. Caribou Jack is proof of that.

Battle Mountain it became, and Battle Mountain, it remains.

~~~~~~~

August 22, 1849

> All night we had the wolves howling close around us, &
> we felt very uneasy about our mules, but morning found
> them safely there. Started just after sunrise & kept along
> down the valley, travelling sometimes S.W. at others S.E.,

the road being very crooked. After continuing down the river the travelling became much cooler and less dusty, for 20 miles, we came to a beautiful valley where we found some fine grass. At this point the river makes a bend to the north causing the road to pass over the foot of a hill a few rods where it is very stony, & then opens upon a large bottom covered with sage. Plenty of alkali among the sage. At this place we saw another notice that the Indians had stolen 7 oxen the night but one before, & were pursued but not overtaken. For nearly 10 miles we proceeded over this bottom of sage, though the distance did not seem more than 3 — striking the river again — found no grass scarcely at all. Camped near an ox train from Illinois and tied our mules to the bushes close by us. The night previous, the Indians had unsuccessfully tried to steal the animals belonging to 3 packers camped close by the same train. Passed over 125 ox trains & 3 graves today. I bought 8 pounds of bacon for $1.66.

Chapter 13

Winnemucca and the Start of Real Desert

Outside Winners Casino Bar and Restaurant in Winnemucca, there is a white car that sits low to the ground, packed with clothes and boasting housewares in every seat except the driver's. That seat is dented and empty, a knitted quilt thrown toward the buried passenger seat. The back window is obscured with coils of clothes. There's a silver sun shield inside. Someone is living in their car.

I like table games: cards. Particularly three-card poker, even though it generally separates you from your money quickly. We're in the casino, me playing, Leslie writing.

The rodeo cowboys, long and lanky, are rolling into the casino. They started making their way into town earlier in the day, and they've already been practicing roping and riding. The table's dealer says when the rodeo's in town, the casino stocks up on Coors Light and smokeless tobacco, and sometimes it's three-deep with people waiting to play the tables. The dealer has two jobs — dealer at night, gold and silver miner by day. He likes them both. When the dealers switch, every time someone gives him a tip after winning, the new dealer says, "Another dollar for the ex-wife and her boyfriend."

He's funny, but hard-edged too.

The manager at the Winners casino is a large man with soft, soft hands, a big diamond earring and the kind of jewellery that lets you know he's both well off and knows his business. A deep, rich laugh that he readily throws into the conversation when he greets new customers. He's comfortable, you're comfortable, and everyone else is too. Drinks are free while you're at the table — two Modelo Negras, and you feel welcome. But it's only a veneer: managers and pit bosses are tough as nails when they have to be. Our pleasant welcomer is brutal with a dealer who mishandles a deal. In Henderson, Nevada, at the Skyline, I watch a pit boss named Joe go from comfortably jocular to dead serious as he kicks a banned player from the blackjack table. When I ask why, he turned the sudden stone face on me too, all pleasantness washed away: "He's banned." It was clear no further questions were welcome.

Losing at three-card poker is like erosion: steady, and it only goes the one way, barring a sudden lift from a tectonic event. The odds are the same, no matter what. Over time, your chips will vanish, with no sign they had ever been.

Dollar chips are large, heavy silver metal coins. Once a trademark with the Winners name all over them, they are now battered, worn and scratched so that you can hardly read the name on them. I wish I'd slipped one into my pocket. (I do at the Skyline.) Winners is worn too, but the food in the steak house restaurant is good, the portions huge. The mixed drinks? You have to be careful to avoid what we're now calling "the American pour." Leslie, who doesn't gamble on cards, has to be poured out of the casino after just a few drinks. A vodka and soda is easily three drinks in one. None of the ounce-and-a-half, carefully measured servings we're used to.

The next morning, when the construction crew is tearing up the concrete in front of the building, their saws screeching as they cut, I see that there is indeed someone living in that car, or at least sleeping there until they start work. Sleeping rough, in plain view of strangers, might seem like a foreign concept now: Dodge was doing the desert equivalent every night.

Face up in the front passenger seat is a stuffed bear in a white T-shirt, red lettering on the front. I want to know what it says, but I am too embarrassed to get that close, nervous that the sleeper might wake up.

◇◇◇◇◇◇

August 23, 1849

Started without getting breakfast, before sunrise, and went 10 or 12 miles, when by crossing the river we found pretty good grass. I saw plenty of sage hens, but could not succeed in killing any.

Cranes, ducks, blackbird, larks, etc. are seen. During the afternoon we had a very strong storm of wind and dust with a few drops of rain; dark and cloudy, could not see 10 rods from us in any direction. Crossed the river and camped. Grass better, but so much alkali that my mules did not like it. Just as we were about lying down a rattlesnake took lodging with us by crawling among our baggage, after giving us notice of his intentions by rattling. We did not like his company quite so close — just at the foot of my bed — and accordingly moved the packs, when to our pleasure we found he had taken the hint and left. I have seen more snakes within this valley than on all the rest of the route. Caught a fine mess of fish for supper.

August 24, 1849

Travelled along the river & then over a hill 6 or 7 miles — then struck it again, bottom narrow — grass coarse & all eaten off, worst that we have had for some time. My mule Fanny is very tired and much reduced. Crossed the river and looked for grass but found nothing but a few packers, bare ground, bushes, boughs, and plenty of snakes. Last night we slept very uneasy, waking frequently for fear the Indians would steal our mules. A slight drizzling of rain during the night with plenty of wind. Afternoon went about 8 miles and came to a spot of good grass. Camped early on account of our mules. There was a perfect meadow of grass near, but we could not get at it for a stream that lay between us and it. Started early — shot a duck with my rifle — 60 yards — fat and fine. At this point the road looks as if it ran straight against the mountain to the west, but bends to the left & after following the river for a short distance takes over a sandy bluff. Heavy winds and disagreable travelling. The old road keeps along the right bank of the river in the sand, but the emigrants have made a new one through the bottom which crosses the river frequently.

During the afternoon we met a Mormon train of wagons, direct from California, having left there the 10 of July. They had passed 1,500 teams besides many packers. None had arrived from the States when they left. They showed us some of the gold and represented business as brisk and provisions cheap. Flour at about 15 dollars a barrel. They had a lot of fine horses and were on their way to the S. Lake. Grass and water was good they said all of which news did much to revive our wearied spirits.

∞∞∞∞∞

The Scotsman Motel in Winnemucca has surprisingly large rooms, the walls painted a glossy squash-orange. Our unit is near-windowless and quite dark, but has a bathroom you could land an airplane in. The bathroom window is clouded glass, but not so opaque you wouldn't notice that there are security bars outside of the window.

The weeds between the street and sidewalk fill the soles of your shoes with cactus barbs and burrs — they draw blood from your fingers when you pull them out. The Scotsman's office is redolent with the smell of curry. I'd love to be asked to dinner.

Instead, it's a quick impression of my credit card.

We have two queen-sized beds in the room, each with an identical picture above them — a mauzy print of three spruce trees in front of a lake, a mountain range behind, all in pastel pink, orange, and grey. The shower has oceans of hot water, but when you touch the faucet, a fine trickle of electricity courses up your arm. A faulty ground somewhere.

Awake at two, I'm afraid that the door will be kicked in again. The doorframe shows that has already happened once, patchy repairs, and given how long it would take to get 911 on a non-activated cell phone, I lie there and think about prospective weapons instead. I decide on a beer bottle because the scotch bottle and the big vodka bottle are plastic. I worry about sounds outside, about the fact that we're the end unit, our door sheltered under the overhang so someone could come in and simply throw themselves against the door in the dark, no one the wiser.

I slip into a happier dream, eventually. Awakened by Leslie shifting in her restless sleep and me wondering why I have to lose the happy spot.

The Scotsman is another all-in family business: the next day, we're asked several times about when we're going to be checking out. The limited number of family members have several rooms to make up, and the sooner we're on our way, the sooner they can get in and clean ours.

The Griddle restaurant is just down East Winnemucca Boulevard from the Scotsman. The diner is fast-paced and full — we find a spot for two at the counter, where the customer beside me never once puts down his smartphone, texting all through his serving of French toast, sticky fingers leaving marks on the touchscreen. Behind me, another customer is explaining to his girlfriend all the reasons why no one in the U.S. presidential election can be trusted. We haven't heard much about the election, but when we do, that's the sort of talk that sets the tone. Two bad choices. People seem to be reluctant to talk about the election at all, as if it's so divisive that it's all better left unsaid.

At the Town House motel, the neon "No Vacancy" sign is failing, and sends out a single strident bright-pink word: "NO."

In the laundromat on Fourth Street, the clocks are all on different times, but within 10 or 12 minutes of each other. More of the washing machines are out of order than are working, and I'm warned not to use Dryer P, that it sometimes decides to keep its door locked at full heat and spontaneously burn things. No one has been able to figure out why.

There's plenty of talk about politics here, but it's not the presidential election. No, this is small "L" local politics — how hard it is to get permits, the problems with balky septic systems, the ins and outs of parking tickets. No one in government is doing a good job; everyone is just in it for themselves.

Then the talk shifts to the weather.

They're hoping for snow this winter — it used to be feet of snow, now they're likely to get one dusting through the whole winter.

Water's always short, and getting shorter: used to be, it got cold enough in the winter "for the kids to skate on the Humboldt River," the attendant says.

"Now, by the end of the summer, there's no water left."

And that lasts on into the colder season. She says she knows the weather's changing, knows that eventually there won't be enough water left.

We're interrupted by a small crisis. While we've been talking, someone has fired up Dryer P with a full load and a fistful of quarters, and there's about to be trouble.

~~~~

August 26, 1849

Have been informed by the Mormons that the grass was better but 12 miles ahead — we went on there and laid over. Nothing worthy of note occurred there.

~~~~

I wonder if, when they find they don't fit in, people sometimes end up trying to create that space instead: in a way, trying to force themselves in somewhere.

Past Winnemucca and before Imlay, there's an odd and ragged patch of fencing held up by broken tree trunks and scrap wood, structures of metal posts and bedsprings and leftover metal of indeterminate origin. There's also a remarkable three-storey folk art tower, surrounded by carved wood figures, a windshield pressed into service as a window here, a rippled piece of shower stall glass serving the same purpose over there.

This patch of dry ground was the home of Chief Rolling Mountain Thunder, its largest feature now only the tower and its surrounding smaller buildings, all haunting and haunted.

The buildings are made of mountain rock that's been hauled here from miles away: concrete and glass bottles poke through and into hand-mixed cement, along with rustic statuary and rusting, repurposed cars and farm equipment. It sounds like a mess, and in some ways it is, but it's also a remarkable monument to one man's particular vision and backbreakingly hard work.

The ground is dusty and trackless, the whole place silent except for the tires on cars whipping by on the nearby freeway and the soft whistle of the wind over the exposed mouths of bottles cemented into the walls.

The structures are topped with arches; Chief Rolling Mountain Thunder reportedly told his son Dan that the loops were a kind of handhold: "In the last days, the Great Spirit's going to swoop down and grab this place by the handle."

It's also a tangle of contradictions.

Chief Rolling Mountain Thunder was really Frank Van Zant, a Second World War veteran who came to Imlay to build a monument to the one-quarter Native American heritage he believed he had. He also wanted to start a different sort of society: the site flourished, grew for a while until it reached 40 people striving for "a pure and radiant heart," but after everyone — including his wife and kids — left the five-acre homestead, Van Zant shot and killed himself.

Now a Nevada State Historic Site, the place is slowly returning to nature. Pieces of Rolling Mountain Thunder's work have been stolen, glass has been broken, both in the buildings and haphazardly on the ground, and at one point, large sections of the compound were burned down. You can build something, even a place for yourself, with hard work: you can't make it last.

In less than a day, we've passed a town named for a battle that wasn't a battle, and a state monument named for a chief who wasn't a chief. Shapes shift.

◇◇◇◇◇◇

August 27, 1849

Being unable to sleep on account of the cold, I arose very early, woke D. & M. got breakfast, and got under way before sunrise. . . . We soon overtook some packers who were anxious to have us join them in taking a new route which turned off a few miles below & instead of going over passed through the Nevada, striking the head of Feather River a week sooner than the other route — we concluded to try it. On arriving at the turn off 75 miles above the Sink, about noon, we found several pieces of board standing covered with cards from the Co.'s that had taken the different routes — most appeared to have gone the new one, about which there seemed to be considerable doubt on account of grass & water. Turning to the right we struck for a hollow in the mountains, which appeared to be about five miles distant, but which proved to be fully 12 before we reached it. Not a spear of grass nor drop of water did we see & the sun pouring down upon our weary animals which had not stopped since daylight made it extremely hard for them & us, especially as one of mine was quite tender-footed — having lost both her fore shoes, & the other was lame, I having slightly pricked her in shoeing her a day or two previously, my only tool for which was a very poor hand axe. After toiling 12 miles in this way we came to a spot where there were some 30 wagons camped. Here we had expected to find plenty of water but instead of that we found a little damp spot on the hillside & about 200 cattle trying to get enough to cool their parched mouths. We unpacked our mules and set about getting our supper. Our mules could get no water, though we got barely enough of the muddy stuff to make some coffee. Not a spear of grass could be seen — nothing but sage and grease-wood. Remaining there between 2 & 3 hours we left just before sunset, for another spring, distant 20 miles. As we passed through the sage our mules found a few scattering spears of dead bush grass, which they devoured instantly roots and all. We passed a number of ox teams, travelling by night to reach the spring. We travelled rapidly and after exhausting every conceivable method which our ingenuity could furnish to keep ourselves awake, we saw about midnight, away off to the right from the road, a faint glimmering light. Putting spurs and whip both to my tired mules I rode up and found a party of packers who had just arrived before us. We found no spring, but someone who had previously stopped there had dug a hole from which could be obtained a little muddy moisture. Returning to the boys we drove up, and after giving our animals some of the water, turned them loose and laid down to rest, having travelled about 45 miles that day. There was not a particle of grass, but plenty of dead cattle, the scent from which was not very agreeable. The ox teams cut grass at the river and brought it with them, but in spite of this precaution we found them lying dead all along the road. Many of the teams were so exhausted as to be obliged to stop by the way to rest.

<><><><><><>

Chapter 14

The Western Desert

Dodge's new route was to be along the Applegate Trail — away from the river, deep into the dry country, and hopscotching between springs and seeps, but supposedly shorter than the alternative. For us, it's a dirt road out of the Humboldt Sink with no signs of any kind that looks like it is going in the wrong direction, heading back the way we came, the riverbed just a distant and ghostly outline.

We had tried to find a way into and across the desert at Imlay, a battered small town on the edge of the I-80. We were looking for the Lake Road, which would take us across the top of the Humboldt Sink reservoir. We are low on gas, driving on rough roads with wrecked cars sprouting on both sides, and the only road we can find in the right direction is jagged stone, and is labelled Dump Road.

We gas up and cross below the reservoir on the Humboldt, the much-diminished reservoir behind the New Deal Rye Patch Dam, where the stone hoodoos stand white and carved into curves by water that now barely pools at their feet. We sign our way into the Rye Patch State Recreation Area, the process involving taking an envelope from a brown metal box that sits by a small, empty registration building, slipping the money inside, and dropping it into a mail slot after tearing off a tongue of receipt to put in your windshield.

We get "User Permit #1601295," even though it turns out we'll be in the park for only a handful of minutes. Maybe it will be important, that scrap of a record of our travels locked in a roadside metal box — name, address — especially if we disappear somewhere in the desert in the next few days. We follow the paved road down to where there's the small recreation area with a dip of navigable water cupped deep down into the lake bottom, a covey of motorboats and recreational craft. Route 40 ends even though it's just begun.

Heading back, we take a right turn onto a rough, narrow road, too small to be a state road. We peer at the map we picked off a visitor centre carousel miles ago. This is what the highways department calls a bladed road, carved clear once or twice a season by a grader: on the map, bladed roads are thin black lines, hardly visible.

We decide to try it — Leslie braver than I am — and then we're heading into sage and dust on a dirt road mined with potholes. Anywhere else, these would be water-filled potholes. But here, instead of water, they are filled with dust like flour, dry and fine. Ahead of us, they are almost invisible, and when the car thumps through them, dust billows like an explosion in the rear-view mirror, bursting out in all directions. It's impossible to tell how deep the potholes are — the baby-powder dust is the perfect cover. Moments in, I can taste that dust on my tongue inside the car.

It highlights every fingerprint on the outside of the car as if it were a crime scene. It seeps into the doors, streaking the insides of the windows when you roll them up, making the door hinges creak, and it finds its way into the trunk and coats the luggage. I'm sure we're lost, but the map makes sense as we make the first crossroads and turn toward what could be Rosebud Mountain. That's the problem now, like it's been since Nebraska, since St. Joseph really. Once across the Missouri, the only fixed geographic descriptions Dodge offers have been the handful of forts and the big natural features like Independence Rock and Devil's Gate. The smaller ones are only descriptions: a pair of mountains in a certain place that look like volcanic cones, a spot on the route where you can see the Great Salt Lake. Find one, and it feels like treasure.

We head along the road, still not sure if we're on the right route: it seems too small and battered. We stop to look at the sage and stones next to us, watch as the rooster tail of dust we've left behind slowly starts to fall out of the still air. To the east of us, the East Humboldt Range looms out of reach.

Every movie ever made seems to have added a touch of menace to the desert: it's where murders happen, where people have their horses and water taken and are then left to die. Open ground and no escape, no matter how hard you scrabble and run and fall. Hollywood has not been kind to the great still cathedral of the sage desert. Because of that, it's hard not to be vaguely alarmed on an empty desert road, watching the plume of another vehicle coming in the other direction, the dust high and white and getting closer. Then a four-wheel drive pickup with two T-shirted young men, all the windows down, hoots by, and dust rains down on the car so thick that you can turn the wipers on and brush tablespoons of it away.

We're looking for a crossroads and, with it, a trail marker: if either one — well, both, really — don't turn up, we'll have to turn around, head back and regroup. Roads lip away to the right-hand side heading toward the low grey hills to the east, but there isn't a full crossroads. The roads that do head out to the left are barely more than trails, and if one of them is actually the route we have to take, I know our Hyundai Sonata won't make it.

When we finally come to a full crossroads, there are no signs, though there is still a lump of hill to the west that could be Rosebud Mountain.

There's the remains of a stuffed animal hanging from a fencepost: it's Wile E. Coyote from the Roadrunner cartoons, its stuffing sprayed out behind it from where it's been shot apart. The ground is littered with broken glass, flattened cans with bullet holes, empty cartridge casings: small-gauge plastic shotgun shell sleeves, slender .22 casings, fat, short 9 mm brass sleeves.

There are signposts facedown in the dust, but, while they mark the distances to towns, there's no clear way to figure out which way the signs were originally facing. Nearby though, we find another one of the official emigrant trail markers — a T-shape of solid railway track. When we first saw these, it seemed a ridiculously overweight and overengineered design for a sign, but now we see how much abuse signage takes in the desert when no one else is around. It's the Haystack Butte mark, so we know to take the left fork of the road. This road is not as potholed and dusty, it's recently bladed gravel but far narrower than the one we left — adding to my concern that we might find ourselves on a route that meanders away to nothing.

We cut uphill on black and grey gravel and see a bright green patch of land against the duller blue-green of the sage. It's our first desert experience of what a spring looks like from a distance: a dash of sharp colour like a flag against the hillside.

This one has a fetid, algae-filled pool, a dry creekbed heading up to the source of the spring, and piping cut into the hill so that the water can be directed into a tank for watering livestock. Straggly, tired willows with battered bark grow around the edges of the creekbed, but only within the immediate root-reach of water. There's no one in sight, and the lack of sound is oppressive. The ground around the spring pool is stomped with cattle hoof-prints, fat heavy pats of manure dotted around its edges. But no cattle in sight.

This is yet another Willow Spring — but the trail is no sooner found than lost again: our road turns right toward the Imlay Summit, the emigrant trail went left and uphill more gradually towards, eventually, the Painted Canyon. It will be this way for most of the driest parts of the desert.

Hide and seek, touch and go.

❧

August 28, 1849
The fear of Indian, bad smells nor nothing else could prevent us all from sleeping soundly until sunrise, when

I awoke & looked for the mules — not one of which I could see. I was somewhat alarmed for fear that we might not find them among the hills. Leaving the boys I set out in search of them & soon found them up a ravine where they had gone to find grass, but got none. Besides us there were several companies of packers — among whom were three — one old man and two young ones from Ohio, packing on foot. Without waiting to get breakfast we left that dismal-looking hole and proceeded down hill a short distance where we found several trains camped near a poor apology for a spring. Dead oxen lay in every direction — five in one heap. We travelled till 9 A.M. hoping to find some bunch grass, but did not — then stopped to breakfast — which consisted of a little fried bacon & hard bread. Packed up and travelled again — our mules showing strong signs of the want of food & rest. The country grew more and more barren — the only thing to be seen being grease-wood — sand hills — & dead cattle becoming still more numerous, with small elevations of very curious looking rocks, which ran in ranges & appeared to have been the mouths of former numerous little volcanoes. The earth was just an ash heap that had been rained on — filled with gravel stones — very bad for our mules' feet. The wind and dust blew strong, & the day was cool, cloudy & dismal enough. As we advanced the stunted bushes grew more sparse & stunted & the dead cattle more plenty. At length we were in the midst of a perfectly barren plain, across which we could not see in any direction, for the dust & smoke. Not a shrub nor plant of any kind showed itself anywhere. The earth was covered with a crust of salty formation, in many places hard enough to bear up a mule — in other places they would sink up to their knees in the ashy earth. We passed several trains — some toiling on — others stopped to rest their weary & exhausted cattle. Frequently we would pass a yoke & chair, the remaining portion of the team being too much exhausted even to draw this tackling of their perished mates. Occasionally we're overtaken by a horseman from some train hurrying on in advance to solve the awful mystery that seemed to hang over all & see if they could possibly find grass and water for their animals before they all should perish. We passed several wagons — the teams having been driven on to grass to recruit to enable them to get the wagons through. Towards night we met a train of 11 wagons with a guard & some beef cattle from Oregon, which had come this route expecting to meet the Gov. train on its way from Ft. Hall, but they had taken the northern route. One of them had killed an Indian a few days before. From them we learned there was grass and springs at the foot of the mountains across the valley, we having by this time got pretty much across the desert & into the sage.

∞∞∞∞

After the latest Willow Spring there's a long pull uphill, switchbacked in tight against the hill, the turns sharp, the grade almost impossible, the engine temperature rising while the sun belts down. The hillside is as steep as friction will allow: any steeper, and the hills themselves would be tumbling into the valley. Sometimes, they do. Turn a corner, and there can be a sharp-cornered rock perched in the middle of the road, a piece of the hillside that's come unstuck and rolled until it met the flat of the narrow road.

The car climbs higher, and there's a point at which your eyes shift from the roadway ahead to the shoulder beside the car: a height at which the beauty of the view — out over the dust-bowl belly of the Humboldt River valley — is suddenly overtaken by the hazard of the slope. Lose your focus on this stretch of road, and you can imagine the car barrel-rolling sideways down the steep embankment just like the rolling rocks, coming to rest only when the car loses enough sideways energy that the next roll is impossible.

And then we're over the bow of the Imlay Summit, little more than a fold between two peaks, and we're alone among the steepled and mineralized mountains on both sides, cruising down into a long valley with short blind hills, the trail stretched out ahead of us, a thin beige line against the sage. We're on an emigrant trail still, but a different one than the one we're tracking — this one, a route used after 1857.

We stay on it until we reach the Knight Stamping Mill, a place that is neither expected nor even marked on maps.

It's a former mine site where we find shot-up old cars and shards of smashed quartz everywhere, along with the powdery-flour dust that's filled with the swimming tracks left by travelling snakes. Travelling snakes: that alone is disquieting.

The stamping mill is still making noise, though it has been closed for a lifetime. The corrugated metal pings and rattles in the windless heat. Every noise seems bigger in a place so still you can hear your heartbeat in the shells of your ears.

A historical sign, uprooted, tilted backwards and now safely inside the chain link fence that guards the route into the adit, says the mill operated for years, crushing stone in the hunt for gold, splintering quartz veins harvested from different mines, though there is hardly even a one-lane road left into the site.

The bird droppings and the coyote scat and the whispers of what sounds like shifting bats from inside the steel building tells me more, tells me that you don't really win out here. You succeed merely by surviving, by taking advantage of whatever place or thing you can find for shelter. And nothing human is really surviving: the rangeland fence is drooping groundwards, tire marks vanish, and the road is filling in with sage. Despite the helpful route number on the map, there are no guarantees of passage. A sign warns of the complete absence of emergency services. There's nothing even close to cell coverage.

The mine works across the road from the stamping mill are concrete waste now and the piles of tailings are being subsumed by the flour-dust and animal tracks. Dig into them and there is startling bone-white quartz, like you are exhuming the skeleton of the hill. Spit, and the spit coalesces into a knot for a moment, but then untangles, dries, flattens, and disappears.

The concrete that is still standing crumbles along its edges, shoulders braced but wilting under the heat. And hot it is, around 100 Fahrenheit, bringing the smell of the sage, the smell of the desert, into your brain with a bite like wasabi.

The hills in the distance speak of waiting permanence. There is the red of iron, black sulfide knobs that promise metal finds, spears of magma-grown volcanic rock still hard and sharp as if laid down yesterday. Pumice, light and easily broken, but always with an edge. Rocks in reds and blacks and greens and yellows; a few miles ahead, and it is the impossible pastels of the Painted Canyon. Emigrant miner Alonzo Delano wrote in August 1849 that "descending a couple of miles through a defile, we passed the most beautiful hills of colored earth I ever saw, with the shades of pink, white, yellow and green brightly blended." (He was there just a few weeks before Dodge crossed through the same canyon.)

The flat hardpack of the desert floor stretches out, unchanging.

Things man-made seem both strangely permanent and inexplicably transitory: that crushed steel can, rust-red but still intact, could be 100 years old, the air too dry to oxidize the metal into flakes of rust. Even here, where it seems like there's nothing worth owning, the lines of fencepost march around perimeters, their strands of barbed wire fencing things in, and fencing things out.

We begin to think we may not find our way to Gerlach, the only town for 100 miles, before sunset. Or at all. That night might close in, making it impossible to find that small dot in a big, big map. We're geared up to overnight in the desert, jugs of water in the trunk, but it would not be our first choice.

We're looking for what's supposed to be another significant mine site, the sprawling Hycroft Mine, a 61,000-acre open-pit quarry and heap-leach operation that produced over one million ounces of gold between 1987 and 1998 — the map shows we're close, but there are only empty signposts. Since the crossroads below the Willow Spring, we've seen only one other vehicle, a pickup truck that never gets close enough to even see how many people are in the cab. We're heading down through a crease between long runs of black, jagged volcanic rubble, watching as occasional smaller roads peter away into the emptiness. While it looks as if the pickup has to pass by us, it doesn't. A quick turn down one of the threadlike side roads and it disappears, leaving only the settling dust.

There's little to say which road to take: every route is shrinking, like an artery devolving into a tangle of threadlike capillaries, and the only option seems to be to stay on the most travelled. We pass the marker for the end of the Painted Canyon, where Dodge's trail comes back and meets with ours, but it's no help. The road we are on weakens and narrows, the sage brushing in on both sides and then springing up in the rise in the middle of the road underneath us, and when it's almost in to the sides of the car and we can hear it whispering as it brushes the exhaust system, we're forced to admit that it's not going to suddenly widen out again, that this road has become nothing more than a trail.

We are lost in the desert, and very close to stuck, the Sonata sedan at the outer edge of its abilities.

We can't even open the doors, an automotive cork in the bottle, and yet we don't want to stay stopped for long. It's an oven outside, and we don't want to leave the exhaust brushing against the tinder-dry sage beneath us.

Then, on both sides of the car, rising out of the sage, a herd of horses appears, nosing in towards the windows, tilting their heads down, looking in as if marvelling at our stupidity.

We slowly back up the path, hoping that at least one of the wheels will get enough grip, the slipping tires throwing up clouds of dust. The horses stand, watching. Finally the tires grip enough to pull us off the tangle beneath us, the car leaping backwards in a sudden buck. We stop once we're back on even ground, but panic's close: as we head back, going into a deep dip, I stomp the gas instead of the brake, and the car leaps over a bump and crashes down. Things are going sideways fast.

Settling down and regrouping at the last crossroad we went through before getting lost, we're caught fast between maps both macro and micro: we have our road atlas of major routes across the United States, marked in ink with the route we've taken, but it's such a big picture that it won't get us out of this tangle of small roads. It doesn't even admit that they exist. We also have the trail guide for this section of the emigrant trail, but it's a point-to-point route map with detailed photos and maps — all of which is fine until that spot where you lose the thread between its here-to-there-to-there instructions. Which is the point we're at now.

We roll the dice and head back towards the chalk-painted hills we can see along the back of the Painted Canyon, pink and green and yellow and unworldly like huge poster-painted kindergarten water-colours, and turn left on the only other significant road we can find, riding up through a series of old gold works, mines, and mining sheds and barred-over holes in the sagebrush-littered and mounded hills. The hills are pockmarked with the workings that came well after the long march to California. And this is far from the first place on the trip that the gold-hungry emigrants walked and rolled and rode past millions of ounces of gold. It seems a cruel joke.

We have no idea if we're going the right way but then we're heading down a huge incline, a covey of sage hens bursting out across in front of us, and through the dry sage again until the playa of the Black Rock Desert appears.

We reach a crossroads that has the markers we need: the long line of the railway, clearly marked on the map, the road to the now-obvious Hycroft Mine tucked back into low mountains, its tailings spilling out in orderly huge wedges of white-and-orange striped stone, and the abandoned town of Sulphur, only holes for basements and collapsed roofs and splintered beams. There's a road sign, finally, for Gerlach, shot through with the requisite bullet holes. We've been travelling along the emigrant trail since the Painted Canyon, but it cuts across the playa now, away from us towards the low mound of Black Rock and the water sources at Rabbit Springs and the Black Rock Spring itself.

We're on the Jungo Road. Finally, again, a road that's large enough to have a name. And how glad we are for that.

∞∞∞∞

August 28, 1849 (Con't)

Oh how gladly did we hail the first glimpse of the dark outline of the rough mountains as we descried it far off through the dull heavy smoky atmosphere, while crossing that weary desert. Soon after we reached a wet spot covered with about 20 dead cattle & many more left to die, above which to the right near the foot of some very curious looking mountains we spied a large spring or basin 50 to 100 ft. across. We hastened to it but much to our disappointment we found it so hot that we could not hold our hand in it much less drink it. It was a very singular looking spring and place. One of the holes where the water boiled up was about 10 ft. across & so deep that we could not see any bottom, though the water was perfectly clear. It tasted very brackish & strong of sulphur & other mineral substances. Our mules would drink but very little of it though nearly choked. From there we took across a perfectly smooth & barren plain about 9 miles to the foot of the mountains on the opposite side of the valley. D. & M. had a mule which they called Milligan from a fancied resemblance to a man formerly of their company — he was a very singular mule — he would generally take the lead & with his long ears flapping time with his feet, would walk off with all the dignity of a Broadway exquisite. We had been expecting him to give out for some time, having been obliged to help him up when down several times.

> After going a short distance he began to lag, and leaving
> them I hastened on to get grass.

∞∞∞∞∞∞

We've reached the Black Rock Desert, the huge flat plain Dodge had faced.

It's ominously empty, sitting below and to one side of the endless graded gravel road, the ruler-flat surface of the playa a heat-shimmering pool of hot mercury. It is the 200-square-mile remains of the 500-foot-deep Lake Lahontan that disappeared 15,000 years ago.

Huge alkali dust devils rise up and spin along the flatland, easily a hundred feet in the air. We haven't seen anyone for hours, and I'm wondering how far we have to go, and just how much more the car will take. We've nicknamed it Milligan.

I stop when I think I see a snake on the road: it turns out to be a snapped bicycle chain. Later, we find a bicycle tire. Then, a torn inner tube. We joke that eventually we'll find a parched and desperate rider stranded in the oppressive heat. We joke, but we watch carefully anyway.

The shores are exactly as Dodge wrote: sharp black gravel leading down to hard dusty alkali lakebed, strung with tracks — elk and coyote and snake and rabbit, all of it an unknown amount of time ago in soft mud that the sun has hardened nearly to rock. Behind us, the big hills with their poking-up broken volcanic rock loom menacingly, but the lakebed is the most startling thing. So flat, so solid, so far across — it's hard to imagine the heat of the sun, the reflected heat off its iodine-white lakebed crust, the crunch of its thick surface giving way.

I now regularly pick cactus spines out of my socks, my feet.

I am stuffed full of huge sights, of vistas so massive that I can't even soak them in anymore. Can't take photos that do them justice in any way.

A train rolls along the rail line that travels through the salt desert, small against the scale of its surroundings, looking like a model train when we spot it first.

We reach Gerlach, which claims to be "The Center of the Known Universe."

The sign at the edge of town advertises "Population wanted" and asks people to clear the brush around homes to reduce fire risk. Nailed beneath the official town sign are a row of white wooden slats with black paint: "Gerlach — more than just a pretty name. Where the pavement ends and the West begins. Five, 4, 3 bars, no churches, no wars. . . . The time that town forgot."

We stop at Bruno's Country Club — its sign says, "Motel • Café • Casino • Saloon." Bruno has his own parking space with its own sign, "This Space Reserved for Bruno." I picture him as a tousle-haired Greek, in charge of the whole town. A sign at the motel units, just a sheet of loose-leaf paper, scribbled with ballpoint pen and pinned to the wall, says to see the bartender down the road to rent a room.

Lacey's the bartender. She slides the key to #65 across to me, hands me the bill. She came from Colorado, stopped in Gerlach years ago, and never managed to leave. She has found a place where she seems to fit seamlessly.

At the table next to us in the restaurant, they're talking rockets. Yes, rockets. Two different groups have come here this weekend to launch rockets — up to 12 inches in diameter — as far up as they can go. The rocketeers like the salt flats just fine — especially "12 miles out and six miles north." It's loose math directions to the launch site, and they will be firing rockets all weekend. "You're driving a rental car, right?" they ask.

Yes.

"Of course. You wouldn't drive something you owned out here, you'd never get the dust out of it."

For many people, the Black Rock Desert is ground zero for Black Rock City and the annual Burning Man festival. Gerlach is the closest town — we arrive short weeks after the madness has ended.

"It's insane," Lacey says of Burning Man. "There's 100 people here and 75 are retired and never come out of their houses. And every year, 80,000 people drop in."

One resident makes stickers saying, "Is it October yet?" celebrating the end of the massive festival.

We now apparently have a dog — a black-and-brown shepherd mix who, when I turned around, was standing close and staring at me. Now he's lying on the floor at my feet, eyes cycling around the bar.

Eventually, he tires of us, and lopes away to another part of the bar.

I meet Bruno Selmi. He is not what I expected — an old, tired, lost man. Rheumy eyes. A personal assistant helps him to his chair. I go to introduce myself, though Lacey is shaking her head at me as I go over. I persevere. I shouldn't have. I'm only an intrusion. Selmi came to America from Italy after the Second World War, washing up in Gerlach, where he opened a restaurant. After it burned down, he launched the Country Club in 1953. At one point, in 2013, the hotel was up for sale for $1.5 million, along with all of Bruno's myriad holdings. A year after this night — which will turn out to be just our first visit to Gerlach — and Bruno Selmi will have died. But his parking space is still there, still marked. And his name is still on everything.

The passing train shakes Bruno's Motel so hard that the whole building creaks in the night. I listen to a man snoring on the other side of our thin wall, the motel as simple as a bed, a side table, a clock, a heater, a bathroom.

Outside, the next morning, the rocket men are up early and whispering about the prospects for the day's wind: "They say you're not even supposed to say the word." Wind speeds are important for rockets going up 100,000 feet. A New York plate on one of the trailers reads, "RKT DOC."

I ask at the former Shell station — now an unbranded gas supplier but still with the same colours — whether I can get a cup of coffee in town. I'm told I can get one at Bruno's. Everything's at Bruno's, "if Lacey's awake." She is, and though the front door's still locked, she lets us in and pours two cups for the road.

Out front, two truckloads of bees, all packed in their hives, sit on parked flatbeds, the trucks rumbling in the morning light.

On the edge of the Black Rock Desert, the wind-blown sand works over the broken bottles, misting the glass, leaving them opaque.

>∞∞∞∞<

August 28, 1849 (con't)

Hour after hour we toiled on driving our mules before us, the mountains appearing far off as when we first began. The plain was hard and perfectly smooth having the appearance of once having been the bed of some lake, whose waters had dried up leaving the mud to bake in the sun. It was about 9 miles across & as much as 30 long. The desert out of sight among the mountains on our left reaching as I suppose to the Sink, & is part of the same which emigrants who go that way are obliged to travel 75 across. As I neared the foot of the mountains I was much Perplexed to decide whether the light spot which we had so fondly hoped was grass, was indeed grass, or only weeds. Looking back I could see M. with Milligan far behind — a mere speck on the plain, & leaving D. to come on I hastened forward with my two and one of his mules. Just at dark I entered the sage which everywhere borders this vast plain & after travelling about a mile I reached the long sought for spot, & much to my joy found both grass and water. I hastily unpacked & started a fire that the others might see where to direct their weary steps, by which time D. arrived. We set about getting some supper, but when we had got our bread ready to bake, we found that the frying pan, our only hope, was behind on Milligan. Not liking to fast longer we determined not to be hindered by that, so managed to bake it on a plate before the fire. After waiting some time M. made his appearance, but alone, having left poor Milligan 2 miles back, being unable to get him further, though he had left his load some time before. So tired were we that night that we slept soundly in spite of our fear of the Indians & everything else. We had travelled over 80 miles without any grass and with nothing fit to be called water.

∞∞∞∞

Another way into Gerlach is east on the I-80 out of Reno and Sparks, following the Truckee River, and then north into the sad town of Wadsworth before a left onto the 447 toward Pyramid Lake. The whole way, the Truckee winding with us, wending its way first between the jagged shelves of volcanic rock and then a softer, smooth-shouldered gorge, complete with rounded standing stones like hoodoos, grouped together in disconcerting, evenly spaced clusters, a small company of beige giants.

The Truckee is deep down in its own valley by then, settled into its course, shouldered in on both sides by hills. A roadside historical marker about a battle between troops and a Native American tribe is covered with Plexiglas for its protection, but it's been shot through several times, and someone has taken the time and effort to scratch "LIES LIES LIES" into the surface.

The road's straight line is either framed in with wire fences, or you're rumbling over cattle grates and seeing yellow signs warning that it's open range, that the cattle may appear out of the sage, uncaring. For a handful of miles, a sign warns of drifting sand. A long, flat climb, and then the unexpected blue of Pyramid Lake, even some meadowed flatland near Nixon, a town with no obvious means of support.

There's a big rock column of dolomite or limestone, stuck straight up like a fist atop an arm in the middle of flat gravel desert, and people have stopped to write on it with spray paint. Up close, it is sharp at times, and pillowed at others, and sometimes it is laid down in crystalline lines at chemistry's deliberate instruction. There's broken glass where bottles have been thrown at it, and a small lizard like a gecko that darts. Leslie is on the side of the highway behind the car, the back open, getting her long snakeboots on, when a double-trailer gravel truck crests the hill, blowing its horn and sliding into the opposing lane at high speed like it is afraid of her and has jumped almost out of its streaked and metallic skin.

I climb high enough to see a hole where a rodent of some kind has built a tufted nest of grass. Parts have slid down through the warren of limestone and blown out below, like a two-level apartment where the top level has collapsed.

Across from us is the dry clay bottom of Lake Winnemucca, a lake until the water was stolen in 1903 for the Pyramid Lake reservoir, a project that stopped the Truckee in its tracks. There's water on it now, in October, at least, enough water to darken the alkali, but no reeds grow, nor are there any waterfowl. The lake was a National Wildlife Refuge, a status that went away with the water. Like Metropolis, the presence or absence of water changes everything.

The sky over the Nevada wildlands is full of aircraft, and the sound of them rumbles through the quiet. Even at dark, contrail lines light up with the last of the sun.

It's six miles to Empire, a town that U.S. Gypsum closed and walked away from, its homes and amenities featured in many photo collections of the abandoned: hardhats and coveralls left hanging in lockers, coffee cups left on breakroom tables. U.S. Gypsum owned everything — the electrical grid, the water and sewer system, even the golf course.

Families uprooted, services shut down, houses abandoned.

The town was started in 1923 and taken over by U.S. Gypsum in 1948, closing in 2011 as a result of a housing construction slump. The town turned off like someone had thrown a switch, and, at the company's electrical utility, somebody did just that. Sometimes, you leave town — sometimes the town leaves you.

In 2016, the mine and town were purchased by a new company, just starting up again, and when we pass through, the grounds are full of camping trailers and recreational vehicles. Maybe empty Empire houses will become homes again. Boom and bust and boom again.

◇◇◇◇◇◇◇

August 29, 1849

So tired and exhausted were we that "Old Sol" had already poked his glowing countenance from behind the mountain on the opposite side of the valley ere we were awake. On arising and looking for our animals we found Milligan dead. Poor Milligan! He had stood it much longer than any of us expected, and then died at last just as the goal was reached.

We concluded to spend the day there to fix our packs and rest our tired animals, although the little patch of grass was nearly eaten off. About 2 P.M. we travelled on 2 or 3 miles along the foot of the mountains where finding another patch of good grass we stopped & soon found some water by digging a little hole among some bushes. It was clear but brackish and salty. Leaving there at 5 P.M. we made for a point of the Mountain apparently distant about 3 miles, beyond which we expected from appearances to get into the road directly. But after travelling through the sage often as high as our shoulders, & over ground sometimes covered with hard crust — at others so soft as to let our animals in half way to their knees, for five miles instead of three, we reached the point & instead of the road we saw another point farther off still than the first — beyond which we knew the road must run. Making for the next point through the sage — across ravines — we passed some men camped in the sage, and reached the second point sometime after dark, pretty well tired. Beyond this we expected to find the road certain, but again we were doomed to disappointment.

◇◇◇◇◇◇◇

Nighttime at the Miner's Club, Gerlach's other bar: the bartender's from Alaska and boasts blue spear earrings. Alaska's gotten to be too much, he says, so, like Lacey, he's washed up here. The four guys at the bar are from Empire, well into the night's drinking, and talking about working the trains, both drunk and stoned. The dusty Hamm's Beer clock on the wall has stopped at 5:03 and looks like it has been that way for years.

In the morning, it's a coffee and breakfast place, and down at the end of the bar, there's a man who looks to be in his seventies propped against the wall. His glasses were stylish in 1970. A huge stock truck rattles up, the driver comes in: grey moustache, patterned shirt, black cowboy hat, pipe stem jeans. "I'll have a vanilla latte, please." Day or night, everyone clearly knows everyone else.

Down at the former Shell station, half the gas pumps are out of commission. Someone's driven away from the station with the gas nozzle still in their tank, pulling the hose right off the pump.

"A rocket scientist," the garage guy says, pointing out it will be weeks before a new hose arrives, and then another long wait until a state inspector comes to check the installation. I love the fact that it really was one of the rocket scientists who damaged the pump — at least, it was one of the rocketeers, here to launch their big-bored and calculated cannonades into the desert sky. Maybe the big picture is the stratosphere, not a lowly gas pump — too many large things to think about to be focusing on anything small like taking the nozzle out of the tank before driving away.

In the evening, the rolling hills across from the motel are magic, even though the foreground is a camper-trailer, a pump shack, and a long line of truck trailers that seem to have been forgotten there. The setting of the sun is making the hills' shadows recline. That sounds wrong, but it isn't; the sun sets, and the back edges of the hills, the parts in shadow, stretch out and fill in and dip lower. The rail line is a straight and level line, its telephone poles, cross tees, and wires either cruciform or the stuff of musical staves. And above it all, the round-topped hills slouch and lean like a tired audience in the high cheap seats. And now the sun is low enough to light all of the reflective triangles on the backs of the trailers and heavy equipment, so there are red and orange eyes scattered out in front of us, all at the same level.

Inside Bruno's restaurant, there are four deer heads on the wall, one turned quizzically towards the room. Neon Pabst sign, neon "OPEN" sign, a six-foot-long rocket on the wall, the mountains outside looking in. Camo is the basic wardrobe.

The hills shift through yellow, beige, sand, ochre, grey-blue to the flat black stencil of silhouette. Nevada's music hasn't left the 1980s; now, it's Tracy Chapman's "Give Me One Reason." Earlier today, in a Mexican restaurant, it was Billy Idol's "Eyes Without a Face."

Scattered conversation: hunters look out at their truck, "No dogs in the front seat, so we're good."

"Chili cheese fries and the pork chop on special."

"Don't want the bullshit, don't want to go to meetings. Just want to get things done."

At the bar, they're talking business about next year's Burning Man, about bumping up the numbers to the top of their permit, 99,000 people. It's $12 million on the table, a rough estimate of the new money that would come in before costs. There are people who go every year, who find some semblance of kinship there. My younger brother went once, years ago, in a tired Jeep that overheated regularly. I wonder if he found what he was looking for: I realize I don't know adult George well enough to know for certain if he was actually looking. Could it just be me?

Above Gerlach, it's another 50 miles — mostly on dirt road — to the Fly Canyon and Mud Lake, little more than a marsh now but once a lake. Also, eventually, the mouth of the High Rock Canyon. The canyon's likely inaccessible to our rental, but we hope to overnight at the mouth if we can reach it.

~~~~~~~

August 29, 1849 (con't)
Feeling certain that the road ran along the opposite side
of the valley we struck across, although the distance was

twice as far as we supposed. For some time we toiled
through the tall sage & over sand hills, the earth becoming more soft and loose, our mules often sinking nearly
to their knees until D. began to decline going further
— thinking that the road must have crossed and gone
behind the ridge on our right. M. and myself felt certain
that the road was ahead of us, & to settle the matter I rode
ahead supposing myself to be near the foot of the mountains whose dark form we could faintly see through the
dim moonlight, which scarcely pierced the dense smoke
that filled the valley. I had proceeded some distance
out of sight of the rest when I was compelled to stop
— my mule completely miring in the light ashy soil. By
the time I had got her out, M. came up and went ahead
certain that the road could not be far off. After waiting
some time with great anxiety he returned stating that he
had been a mile & could see nothing of the road yet. D.
was for turning off to our right without further delay —
while M. and myself felt certain that the road was at the
foot of the mountain. Again we started making straight
for the foot of the mountain & after travelling till half
past 9 over sand hills, through sage, across ravines & had
proceeded but a short distance when one of the mules
in going down the side of a sand hill made a misstep &
pitched headlong, pack and all down the hill, falling in a
position from which he could not rise again. In spite of
our alarming situation, I could not refrain from laughing right heartily at the efforts of the poor mule to regain
his perpendicular & more especially at the ludicrous
appearance of my friend M. who stood with both hands
raised in astonishment, without making a single effort
to relieve him! Getting him up we proceeded across a
ravine — through the light earth over another sand hill
& much to our joy reached the road! After getting into it

we soon began to descend gradually a very stony piece of road — the mules stretching out into a line, marching slowly along, picking their steps among the stones by the dim moonlight — strongly reminded me of the pictures I had seen in the old geography of travellers crossing the Andes. The mules having become reduced & scarcely able to carry their loads they loaded their saddle mules & travelled on foot except as we would take turns in riding my mule — which yet stood it very well. In this manner we proceeded until after midnight constantly passing dead cattle & horses, each of us growing more tired and sleepy. The wind blew from the north extremely chilly, & I was compelled to exert myself to the utmost to keep myself and my companions awake! At last we descended into a valley & discovered a patch of dry grass, but no water. Just at this eventful moment their unfortunate mule stumbled over a rock in the road and fell again. This time we were compelled to unpack him before he could get up. We determined to stop there, let the consequences be what they might, & after setting fire to some bunches of grease wood, which ignite like tinder, warmed myself tho' the boys objected to the fire, fearing it might betray us to the Indians, I rolled myself in my blanket and was soon lost to all sense of danger, except that of freezing — for in spite of my precautions I soon became so chilly as to prevent me from getting much sound rest.

∞◇◇◇◇∞

Heading north from Gerlach, you pass Great Boiling Springs and cross another branch of the emigrant trail, the Nobles Trail. It curves under the road, unremarkable. It took much of the traffic away from the Applegate route when it was set up in 1852. The Nobles wends its way west along its own line of water sources — when we find it, it's another thread of unremarkable dirt trail, significant only to those who know its reputation.

The Great Boiling Springs is fenced, like most water sources, but this one is closed off by private owners not to hoard water, but after trespassers were scalded to death diving into the wrong pools. Dive in and, unlike Dodge, you can't simply jerk your burned hand away.

Route 34 heads east along the base of sage-specked mountains to the north, the mountains spilling rock falls that look loose and dangerous and unclimbable. Above the rock falls are abrupt grey stone cliffs. The road is new asphalt, a sharp black against the beige and brown of the desert, at least it is until the pavement reaches the exits onto the desert playa that spill late summer traffic onto the plateau for Burning Man. After that, the road falters, loses purpose. Route 34 becomes pothole-patched and rough, and then abruptly becomes gravel.

In the cold air of evening, random hot springs reveal themselves with telltale wisps of steam: stop, and the steam and the thick sulphur surround you and reach down your throat. The source of the water is a single spontaneous point, and often you can hear the sound of it percolating up from the depths, gurgling and muttering under its breath from the sinkhole that marks the start of the spring. At one spot, near a crumbling homestead, the source is further up the hillside, a hole where you can hear the ground rumbling and groaning like an overfilled stomach, the heat wafting up from gaps and crevices, the water still deep and out of sight. When it does appear, it starts a stream spontaneously from nothing, and is making the sound of water in a pot at full boil.

With the cool air, the water shifts from boiling hot to a temperature you can touch after a run of 50 yards or so, and the watercourse leaves a white crusted alkali edge along its banks. But every hot spring is different — in temperature, in temperament, in drinkability.

The playa is yellow today and flat — we drive out on it, and you can see every cut turn and route taken by every vehicle since water last covered the now-hard surface. A white van is barrelling towards us — it's impossible not to have a Mad Max–like sliver of fear, the glass-windshield-bright anonymous sparkle of it, the way it always seems to be heading directly for you, the occupants invisible, intentions unknown. The long, straight, rising rooster tail of dust. Behind, the lumpen mountains shoulder up purple and bruise. We are into the car and away before they can reach us.

We park near the fork in the road — Route 34 goes straight, while the road to Soldier Meadows is random stone, dust, and gravel heading east. We climb a dust path cut into the sage so we can look out, and we see a different flat-surfaced alkali lake, and still more mountains. Leslie wants to take a picture, but there's a car on the curving road that bends down around the hill we're standing on. She waits and waits and waits for the car, even though it is travelling fast, to exit the picture. That's just how large the scale of everything is.

You reset your compass, reset your eyes, reset everything. Travel here is still along the path of least resistance, not the straightest line — you wind through low and flat and unblocked, just as it has always been, because mountains win.

A fat-bodied horned lizard, small and awkward and reminiscent of a drunk businessman in its gait, stumbles across our path. There have been horses here, leaving fresh prints in the fine, fine dust, a pile of dried droppings. There's a spot where there was a fire, made with wood that had to be carried in, three pieces left next to the rock hearth.

Everywhere, there are signs of humans: cartridge casings, footprints in the dust, broken glass, unexplained rock cairns, flattened scraps of metal cans and other unknowable things. Signs of people, but no people, and no real way of knowing how long anything has been there. The sage is yellowing and dry now, but the smell is strong. There's a feeling, not really a smell, not really a taste, something that's different from both of those things, from the dust that rises up all around you when you walk.

We take a short run along the road that heads to Mud Lake and Soldier Meadows. It's advertised as a bladed road without services, without regular maintenance. It's washboarded and full of potholes, the surface shifting between regular gravel and sharp large stones.

Some places, it's bare rock. We travel around the first run of curves, bending along the edge of a low hill, just far enough to be worried about tires and stone and wrecking the car. We plan for the next day.

It's all something new to worry about through the night in Gerlach, not sleeping in the dark of the long row of motel units. One orange streetlight holds back the darkness as, just across the highway from the motel, a train horn picks at the silence and the diesel engine's light leads dozens of track-clacking railcars through the desert night.

<><><><><><>

August 30, 1849

Rising early we concluded to start on, hoping soon to reach water, from which we knew we could not be far distant, as we had been informed that Mud Lake was but 30 miles from Black Rock spring. In getting up our animals I found that during the night, in coming through the sage & sand my mules saddle had worked loose & hurt her back — the consequence of which was that I put my pack on my saddle mule & went on foot. We had gone but a short distance down the hollow before we saw water & plenty of grass — the former covered with ice and the latter pretty well dried up. Proceeding around the point of the hill to our left & coming out into full view of the valley we found ourselves in a large basin entirely surrounded by mountains, the bottom of the valley being a kind of swamp covered with grass — this we knew to be Mud Lake. Several companies of packers & about 100 wagons were camped there recruiting their stock. We concluded to do the same & soon set about preparing some breakfast.

We remained there till 3 P.M. during which time we learned from some of the ox trains that instead of being in a cut-off we were on the southern road to Oregon, that Myers was intended to make a cut-off from a point 30 mi. further on & had started it the day before. When we left

Mary's River we saw notices stuck up purporting to have
been done by men who had been through the cut-off stating plainly that it was but 146 miles to the Sacramento
Valley & leading not only us but hundreds of others to
take that road supposing it to be the cut-off itself. But we
here learned that the cut-off was yet to be made, if at all,
& we were satisfied that we were going far out of our way
as a good part of the time our course lay north and northwest. To make the matter worse, instead of being in the
diggings at the end of 146, we had travelled nearly that
and were then told that we had yet 350 to go!

∞∞∞∞∞

We're below Fly Canyon, above the Marsh Meadow on Soldier
Marsh Road, paralleling the trail as it curves up the playa after leaving Black Rock.

We're now 50 miles off the grid, no electricity, and we were planning to sleep in the car, much further up the trail, but the route went
awry. We have a snake bite kit, first aid supplies, emergency blankets.

We end up at a Bureau of Land Management cabin we stumble
upon, set into the flat of a silent valley surrounded by hulking grey
mountains — with an outhouse, a bunk room, a wood stove. We spotted it across the plain, thought at first it was an abandoned truck, drove
over to look and found, instead, an unlocked door and a cabin open for
anyone's use, first come, first served.

It is so incredibly quiet.

Earlier, we were up on the 60-foot chasm of the Fly, where Dodge
passed through the canyon below.

Now, all around us, it's again yellow grass, the smell of sage, the
sound of your own blood in your ears, and the stillness disturbed only
by passing nature and the occasional high-routed aircraft. The shadows are stretching out of the hills, and I think that tonight will be the
darkest night I have ever known, miles from electricity, only a sliver
of new moon, and big sky opened up above us for miles. We arrived

here to a mule deer fawn — or maybe an elk, and then six or seven more, and a male with a rack of antlers who guarded the back of the herd when they started to move. I cannot believe we found this place — there's a logbook, full of just-as-surprised others. The logbook has people scoping for big game, hunting chukars, or simply looking for time alone, for respite from the world.

It is a singular treasure.

The road was wash-boarded and dust-pit-pillowed, and when we got here, we first headed for the canyon, for this is where the emigrants came off the flat of the playa and headed up and over a low ridge of mountains, through the stone gap of a narrow canyon. We couldn't make the road: the car couldn't manage the sharp tilting boulders and the narrow gap through the sage, so we found our way to the route and then ditched the car, heading up for an hour into the wilderness with water and determination.

Fly Canyon starts as little more than a wrinkle in the desert, an unprepossessing opening out into the bottomlands. Looking west, it's almost indistinguishable from every other terrestrial fold and heave. You can't even see how it funnels everything into itself unless you're looking backwards, having already made your way up the hillside. Starting in, it's shallow and flat and sage, then rising almost absent-mindedly on both sides, the change almost insignificant. It's less a canyon than a swale, then it's a valley, until suddenly, the sides are so steep that there aren't any options for escape beyond turning back.

We walk up the northern side, climbing fast: soon, the roof of the car, white in the sun, winks in and out, one moment there, the next, not.

An hour and 10 minutes in, we could see the stone fissure of the canyon carving through the scrub, and we cut across to look down into the huge drop and the stone-bottomed canyon that the emigrants dragged their wagons and carts through. We were easily 60 feet up above the floor, sitting on big slabs of broken rock that balance almost at the canyon's sharp and sudden edge. The difference between the bright sunlight of the valley and the cool dark of the fissure is remarkable: you can't take a picture into the canyon if any of the canyon's top is in the shot, because the ground is too bright, and the gap becomes just a black mark on the photo.

Later, when the air is cooling, and the light is cutting down with more yellow in its tone, we'll be boiling someone else's left-behind potatoes in the coffee pot, and then we will look at the wide open stars.

And this is just part of the day — I haven't mentioned the welded grave marker at Wagner Springs, "Harold E Sims, 10-9-29 12-1-99" worked across its surface in round welding-rod writing.

There were flint-knapped sharps from working stone into weapons all around the fence blocking trespassers from reaching the spring itself. I haven't mentioned the pastel of the Calico Mountains, haven't mentioned the hot spring that we mark as our own or the pickups ranging fast past us on Soldier Marsh Road.

I haven't mentioned the short length of the existing Applegate Trail that we walked when we were beside the Wheeler Reservoir, the stacked basaltic sticks of stone making up hills we had to wend through on the dirt road, slow, to try and keep our tires intact. Haven't even mentioned today's small fast lizards, like anoles, or the endless explosive hares that burst from the sage. Or the side roads that we'll head for tomorrow, access roads that reach into the expanse of this reserve, before we head south to head north again and reach, hopefully, Cedarville by tomorrow night.

Broken bottles and crushed cans and shotgun shells: 4-10s and larger, the rifle bullets through signs, the trio of 9 mm brass Luger cartridges I gathered up from the gravel in a space the size of my right hand.

The sage or the mouse holes or snake holes or rabbit holes, the huge variety of plants with spines and attitude. There's a car going by in the distance, and I hope it just keeps going. I can't see it, not even its lights, because the road is a dip cut down into the earth so you're always driving in a gully, but I can hear its tires on the gravel in the fading light. Early on, there was a wrecked green Ford van with the completely rock-shredded driver's side rear tire and the sliding door broken off and tied to its roof. Inside, it's full of spilled beer bottles, some of them smashed from the crash. It's a clear warning about speed and sharp rocks. The miles of road and sand and dust and gravel, punctuated by small tufts of deciduous trees where the springs are.

This whole place is full of discrete sounds, things you hardly catch.

Two crows just flew over us, croaking. Then, an instant later, you could hear the sound of their wings. Feathers, working through air: it is like the sound of the slip of rope around a pulley, like the sound of poplar leaves, except stretched out long. In the absence of all other sound, you can hear each feather paired with another.

The sun is just approaching the horizon, and coyotes are howling to the south of us. I hope they are back later, that they howl and howl and lonesome howl. Meanwhile, the sun falls behind the mountain range and you can watch the shadow step across the valley toward the other mountains to the east. The temperature keeps dropping, and though it was near 70 today, it will be barely above freezing when we retreat to bed.

And the cabin: no bedding, just a wooden bed frame, but a small wood stove with a brick wall behind it, two tables, odds and ends in its inventory ranging from paper towels to peanuts to canned pinto beans — large can, 1.13 kg SunVista pinto beans with a pull-tab top, best before August 5, 2018.

There's olive oil and balsamic vinegar, a 3.75 oz Chicken of the Sea pull-tab can of sardines, "In Oil — Lightly Smoked," "NEW AND IMPROVED QUALITY," good until June 19, 2022, and one — just one — yellow-packaged Trojan condom, lubricated, expiring Nov. 1, 2019. A safe sex cabin, it seems, but only for that one attempt.

Cleaning supplies. Bleach. Soap, dish detergent. Two coffee pots, one large, one small. Board games. Books. Magazines. A pattern, written on the floor in brass shell casings, pounded straight into the floorboards: "WESTOLN" it appears to say, the first four letters clear, the next three, sloppy, like someone had a plan, and then lost the true thread of it as the liquor kicked in.

Darkness falls, like a curtain, like a weight on the end of a rope, unstoppable like a moving crate when you lose your grip. Like a case of something breakable that you cannot afford to drop but feel slipping away anyway.

There is a raft of tea light candles, waiting to fight the darkness. A fire extinguisher. Two brooms.

The bunkhouse diary, full of notes. October 11 has no name, but reads, in total, "Left a couple of night's worth of wood." Big round logs. Maybe we'll put one in, just for the light and sound of it. The cabin diary is both record and confessional: some have come upon the cabin by accident, like we have. Others picked it out as an escape — sometimes alone, other times for respite with children or lovers. Some have come back, looking for what they had when they were there before. It's plaintive and yet uniting: every word seems familiar to us, new members of this cabin family. They are grounded here. You know exactly what they mean when they talk about the light or the rabbits: you share in the familiar as you read each set of words. We don't know any of the authors by anything more than the variety of handwriting on a page. Yet, somehow, we do.

A pink contrail streaking by. The tin roof is singing, shrinking, pinging, ringing.

The building is cedar on the outside, repaired recently with new and uneven shakes, tin roof, tin chimney. A horse corral on the side with its own corrugated tin rope-latched door, a vault toilet off to the north across the gravel pan. The eastern mountains are all dark grey now, the last red/pink tip fading away, and the wind has jumped up cold from the east and suddenly stronger. And the moon is a high and bright sliver, the western sky light blue running down to yellow along the mountain-edge, and the jackrabbits are creeping up close, working on the grass, stray mosquitoes. Crows in the distance, calling back and forth. The eastern sky pink now, a glow above the mountains.

Mountains after the sunset dress in black felt.

The car that was going by is not going by anymore. It's a white van with no headlights, and it's heading toward the cabin, rising up out of the valley of the roadway.

Heading closer, side on, and I can see the shape of each window. I tell Leslie, and we both watch as it heads by us, up toward the Hot Springs campground where, earlier, we had to stop to ask directions to the Fly from three guys, parked there with their pickup truck, beer, and a pile of firewood.

Our relief at the van continuing on up the road is astounding.

◇◇◇◇◇◇◇

August 30, 1849 (Con't)

Much doubt and uncertainty existed among all in regard to the distance. Worse than all else was the startling fact that we were almost out of provisions and could not buy a single pound at any price. Most were already short & the rest would not sell for fear they soon would be. In this dilemma, with our mules so much reduced by their late travelling without feed that we were all obliged to walk — we left Mud Lake about 3 & started over a very stony & for a mile or so, very steep ascent.

◇◇◇◇◇◇◇

Chapter 15

Night Falls

L ater, I am in a corner of the cabin, drinking Maker's Mark bourbon while the fire sputters, and outside the sky is a riot of stars. I have my shoes and socks off, there's a crosswind through the cabin to clear the smoke, and we're already planning for morning, for coffee and a better fire when I might actually use kindling. And I wonder, as I have before: was there any point at which the toiling settlers looked up at the sky and the mountains and the great, broad light, and wondered about how amazing it actually was to be there? To be here? We have a few tea lights lit. A failing Coleman battery lamp. Everything else is darkness.

Outside, the sky is so huge that we both go out to see it at the same time, there are so many stars that it is almost oppressive, Big Dipper, Little Dipper, Cassiopeia, Milky Way. To go out alone is to be made tiny. I know them all, only not like this, not so insistent and bright and reaching for you. There is only one electric light anywhere, across the valley at a small ranch, where they must have a generator. Planes are nipping by, satellites bending their arcs across the sky, and when we go back in, I am in the northwest corner of a one-room cabin in the only lighted space that exists, kitty-corner with the failing wood stove while Leslie reads a book and the last tea light winks out.

Once, when she was upcountry in Newfoundland and I was on the road, she phoned me, because she was outside smoking and looked up and the stars were too much, too frightening. And tonight, just tonight, I know exactly what she means.

The moon is angling down toward the horizon, and I have my feet stretched out, my legs crossed at the ankles, and there is a rough board floor and I can't explain how much I love it.

∞∞∞∞∞

August 30, 1849 (con't)

Four miles carried us to the summit, after which we found the descent equally stony & bad. Crossing a small deep valley of this light earth covered thickly with sage we travelled about 4 & entered a most singular canyon — the bottom being perfectly smooth & from 4 to 8 rods wide, with walls of perpendicular rocks rising on both sides to near 400 ft. in height. It was a strange sight & to me a solemn looking place as our mules one by one passed wearily along — looking like some funeral train — now stalking from behind some jutting point into the faint glow of the moon — & then hidden away again by the deep shadow of some tall rock. Along this natural opening we passed for nearly 3 miles, when we came to one of the grandest and most magnificent sights that I ever beheld. The canyon was about 6 or 8 rods wide at the bottom, & the rocks on both sides, but more particularly on the right, ran perpendicularly for about 500 ft. & in the middle of the road was a bunch of willows around a little pool of fresh water, at which was camped a Co. of four footmen.

∞∞∞∞∞

Up at the Fly Canyon, you could look down into the rock gut of it and imagine the settlers trying to push their wagons and carts up the narrow enfilade. Dodge described it as four rods wide. Broken rock, ledges and wedges, balanced and teetering, stacked unevenly just before the cliff. If you threw a stone, you would hear the sharp retort of it hitting bottom, then the repeating echo. You can imagine the echo of the remnants of Dodge's company, too, trying to force their way up a throat of stone, over ledges, through pools of stagnant and silty water, around the few sprightly trees that seem to find every single watercourse here, no matter how small. High Rock Canyon is supposed to be even more impressive, but I can't imagine travelling the cart path to get there, even though the cabin's diary talks about people coming the other way in Toyota 4Runners, showing up here for a little rest for their bruised behinds and kidneys.

By now I know the heat of the sun and the gritty dust, the spikes of cactus in your feet and the vibrating, trembling heat of the playa, and I can't imagine that a story — even about riches — could be strong enough to drag me all the way across an entire raw and wild land, trusting completely in what I was being told about the trip and the gold, especially when the story changed so often, sometimes in as little as a day.

And Dodge's route? A mere five years after he passed that way, the Fly Canyon route itself was a thing of the past. By 1854, it was already being written about as history: "June 27. — It was 4.76 miles to the south end of Round valley, where we came upon an old emigrant road (Lassen's) which is said to leave the Humboldt river above the point at which we crossed it, and to cross the Sierra Nevada near the southern line of Oregon, in the vicinity of Goose lake. This part of the road has also been used in travelling from Oregon to California. Its trail is well worn, but at present seldom used." (*Report of Explorations for a Route for the Pacific Railroad* by Capt. J.W. Gunnison, Topographical Engineers.)

∞∞∞∞∞

August 30, 1849 (con't)

The rocks were not smooth but broken into the form of
huge pillars & recesses — rising in the dim moonlight
like some gigantic piles of architecture, far exceeding anything that man ever conceived. At the foot of one of these

pillars was an opening about 4 ft. high which lead into a cave having an arched roof 15 ft. high — 25 ft. broad & 35 long. At the further end was a hole in the roof, opening upward & having the appearance of another room above. I did not visit this but got the description from a man who did. Passing this we soon merged into a little hollow or bowl entirely surrounded by high rocks, except where we had entered, so far as we could see. Finding grass & water we camped, turning our animals loose as usual, & soon had our blankets spread in the deep shadow of a tall cliff which rose before us like the dome of some Feudal castle. Before going to sleep however, we discovered a light at the farther side of the basin which was not more than half or three-quarters of a mile wide, which we knew to be a camp, & concluded that our road must pass in that direction.

∞∞∞∞∞∞

We were cold as the night dropped to freezing — by then, we were in the car, me under a thin foil emergency blanket, Leslie in four layers of clothes, bulky like an astronaut. We had to start the car at 4:30 a.m. to stop shivering. At that point in the night, the stars were as hard as cut glass, far more stars than I have ever seen, but I was shaking too hard to enjoy them.

Some carnivore left the right wing of a bird — a sage hen? — on the concrete pad around the outhouse: I imagine the pad stayed warm late into the night.

In the morning, around 6:30 with a heavy frost, I got up to gather kindling, including fistfuls of thorny brush, and finally got a fire going. Coffee in a blue enamel pot, thick greasy smoke pouring out the chimney. In the first light, I could see long lines of steam coming up from a series of hot springs, running down the valley under Soldier Meadows like the Earth had left a zipper open down to hot magma. Inside the cabin, on the walls and in the diary, people have written about hunting chukar, about mice found dead in the cabin. I don't know what a chukar is. Oh, and I found new left things: a plastic coffee filter, one cup, and a box with leftover bullets: two soft grey lead tipped .22 long rifles, three brassy 9 mms.

Outside, a small concert erupts from a whole group of coyotes over near the ranch, and then there's a single answering warble from high up near the mouth of the Fly Canyon. Then it's a third group's turn, yodeling their place and presence, all of them, just after the sun runs full into the valley. There may be plenty of reasons to hate coyote, from what they do to livestock to their hunting of pets. But hearing three packs howling back and forth, the liquid of their calls, in the desert, lit by morning sunlight, is beautiful beyond compare. They stop as quickly as they started and melt away. We know that they are all around us, all the time: we don't ever see one alive.

All around the sagebrush, the surface of the ground is hard and rigid, made up of an inset crust of pumice, hard black flinty ash, and other granules. Nearby, among the bright yellow meadow grasses, and between, the solid ground is made up of plates of hardening alkali. In both places, you come across scattered metal: crushed and flattened tin cans, plates of indeterminate origin, all of it not breaking down and flaking the way it would in a moister climate, but somehow annealed instead with a coat of rust-brown surface metal.

We head south again with many stops, leaving the emergency blanket and paper towels behind in the cabin, along with a book Leslie's finished: the cabin is full of things left to make the place better, left by people who don't claim credit for what they leave.

We pass the Wheeler Reservoir and make several stops, including to climb well up into a notch between a cone of rock that looks as if it was formed from broken iron, and two other very different rock formations, each bleeding white alkali. A metal post reads "Route End." Then, down to Gerlach and back up the other side toward Eagleville and Cedarville, the shrubbery of the sage finally giving way to high-ground cedars.

All manner of cacti — ones with long, sharp spines, designed to wound the unfortunate, others built to latch on to clothing or hair — break away from their stalks and get carried to the next possible planting site. So many and diverse solutions for a harsh and unforgiving environment.

Leslie, driving, keeps having to dodge coveys of quail; the birds, with their ball-like headpieces, are easily the stupidest wildlife we've seen so far, regularly bursting from cover straight out in front of the car.

We land at a motel in Surprise Valley outside Cedarville, California, and tomorrow morning we're going to backtrack into Nevada and into the back end of the High Rock Canyon from Steven's Camp. Susie, who owns the Sunrise Motel, has left a note in the window of the office: "If you need someone, please call . . ." Underneath, in different, shakier handwriting, is another note: "High — John. Will not be staying tonight."

The only other guests at the Sunrise were three couples driving restored cars from the 1940s. One of the women had to lend me her flip phone to call Susie when we checked in. Smartphones don't pick up a signal in Surprise Valley: the older flip models pack a more powerful punch.

Susie turns up after we've waited for her to get back from branding calves with her husband. She asks us why we're in town off-season, and we tell her about the diary. She knows Fly Canyon, knows the back end, the wagon slide, where the pulleys that were used to lower wagons down the steep incline stayed in place for years, but were finally stolen. Her family and another one once bounced ownership and use of Massacre Ranch and the High Rock Canyon area back and forth between them, before both became historic sites.

She tells us the best access for Steven's Camp, tells us that the road has recently been graded and that we'll "just have to watch out for the big sharp rocks." Another day, another person with an interlocking story.

She tells us that there's no safe way through the High Rock in a vehicle right now anyway — not that we were planning to try with our low ground clearance — that the weather has taken a heavy toll, flooding and tearing up the trail this year, and some people who have tried to pass through, even in four-wheel drives, have wound up having to be rescued.

Rescue. That's at least a possibility now. It certainly wasn't always.

∞∞∞∞∞

August 31, 1849

Rising early we hastily prepared our breakfast consisting of coffee — hard bread, & a very little jerked beef; & made for the point where we had seen the light. There we found several wagons belonging to different persons camped by a kind of spring or hole where there was plenty of grass and water. Passing them we entered the deep canyon to our right & proceeded through a place similar to that we, had previously passed although not near so imposing & grand. Some portions of the road were very rocky & there was plenty of grass — water & bushes by the side of it. In this we continued most of the forenoon — occasionally entering a place where the bottom was wider & the walls not quite so high — frequently passing holes where the water had not all soaked beneath the soil — & many small elevations which were very stony. Toward noon we passed a water hole close by a large rock which had the appearance of being a very small puddle, but which we found to be 8 ft. deep & very dangerous for animals to approach. Proceeding a short distance we stopped for noon — plenty of grass but no water. Afternoon started & had gone but a little way when the mules stopped to drink at a hole & one of them slipped in — when we found it to be 6 ft. deep, though it did not look to be 2. Took off her pack & finally got her out. Struck & followed up a small stream — fine bottom — open. Many trains camped there — passed on and entered a very rough rocky canyon — creek ran in the road — rock & bushes — broken down wagon — high rocks on each side — look as though they had been placed there while in a fused state — twisted — bent, & broken like candy — up hill through there — came out of it onto large hill covered with sage — passed a fine little camp on the left & passed over a rough stony hilly road till 10 P.M. & camped in a deep — though narrow valley where we found 100 wagons that had been waiting for Myers to make his cut-off. Learned there was to be no cut-off — was told that 30 miles would take us to the mountains and 30 more into the valley. All this time we had been expecting that Myers had made a cut-off which would take us into the Feather River diggings in 2 or 3 days — yet we were much dissatisfied to find that our road still continued to go N. and N.W.

∞∞∞∞∞

In the morning, after a delightfully heavy chicken-fried steak break-fast in Cedarville, it's out across the route that bisects the Middle Alkali Lake and tips quickly back into Nevada, where it becomes the 8A: the pavement stops at the California state line, the numbers change, and we're back onto the trail.

We head across the ridge where 49 Rock sits on the roadside, the numbers painted and overpainted with grease so many times that they stand out by almost an inch against the rest of the stone. Then we angle up toward the Vya townsite and follow 8A toward Steven's Camp — it's another Bureau of Land Management property, this one a bunkhouse, another wilderness site at the end of a long dirt road, and I wish we had enough time to overnight there, even though it's much larger than the Soldier Meadows cabin. (On the way, the road is littered with volcanic glass rocks that break open along edges so

sharp they cut and draw blood. Leslie is applying pressure to a gash
on her finger as we climb back into the car.)

The ground is chocolate brown and sometimes sandy, looks rich
enough, but all that grows is miles upon miles of more sage brush —
wherever it grows, whether it's two feet high or four feet high, all of
it in that area is the same height. Maybe it's the weather or the soil
or other environmental causes, but it has a manicured look: gnarled,
dusty, old, but even. Here, it's the tallest we've yet seen, right on the
line between shrub and tree.

We finally take a long downhill curve to the right to Steven's
Camp, which has existed since the 1870s. The bunkhouse lies on a
crease in the hill, just below where the spring surfaces, enough room
to sleep eight, another squat wood stove, and the collection of random
supplies, from soap to bullets.

The bunkhouse wasn't there when Dodge was, but the spring and
small meadow was — he mentions it, just before writing about heading into the Upper High Rock Canyon, in the section of the diary just
before this.

While the bunkhouse now belongs to the Bureau of Land
Management, it was built by country and western singer Tennessee
Ernie Ford, who ranched most of the surrounding land for 20 years.

There's plenty of water, running out of a black plastic pipe into a
reservoir by the bunkhouse camp. The water runs down through the
meadow and joins the slight brook that must have originally created
the High Rock Canyon. You can follow the deciduous trees back to the
spring's source, and I think autumn is the best time to find the springs
of the western desert: the leaves on the poplars and willows are changing, and the trees flag where the water is, as much as any divining rod
could. If the sage stops and there are leafed trees, there's water.

Above the bunkhouse, you can look out for miles over the valley:
the Upper High Rock Canyon towers next to us on the right, but its
big brother, out in front and with walls in places hundreds of feet high,
lies hidden.

We walk the trail backwards, heading toward the Fly Canyon, trying again for access to the High Rock. It's two hours in, two back out again in the autumn sun, still hot but luckily not August, and the trail is one wagon wide, constant dust and jackrabbits and snake trails and holes. And sage. At one point, we stop and can see a clear imprint in the dust of a hawk's wingtips and tail: another hawk spins on the thermals over us, comes down close for a look, soars up again. Plenty of life here and all of it better equipped for the desert than we are.

What is there to say? Four hours of walking, cut only by a brief lunch and rest. Another hawk circles above us, comes in to look, shows us the pattern like a face on the bottom of its wings. We ration our water, though we had started out with plenty.

Turning to look back over our shoulders, we watch the bunkhouse shrink to a dollhouse, then to a dot, and then disappear. Dodge liked to mark the distance each day: today, my phone will clock us in at 24 kilometres, or just a hair under 15 miles. There is an optical illusion in the desert — you look out over so much of it at once that it looks flat and smooth and even. That's deceptive: the uneven and difficult is hidden until you're upon it, or in it over your head.

Later, an owl bursts from cover next to me and follows the trail back the way we came, not bothering to rise above the high cobbled shoulders of the canyon. There are all kinds of small life: ants and spiders and beetles, strange shiny bugs. The sides of the canyon look armoured, like a dragon's scales, red-brown and pouring into the valley. Stinking willows make their unpleasant presence known, and there is low grass and even, fleetingly, marsh. All in all, an exhausting hike, under hot sun. Unimaginable, day after day after day.

We settle into what little shade there is, dappled with light and dark by willow leaves, the sun high, and eat tuna salad on crackers, fruit. It's another of the moments when I know he was exactly here, in this spot. The bottom of the canyon is completely torn up: there's been big water through there, and the trail is eroded in some places and covered in drifts of loose and sliding stone in others. The water's long gone — only its footprint remains.

We climb out of the canyon and back toward the bunkhouse: Leslie picks up two spent 9 mm bullets below Steven's Camp, and we walk through rafts of casings. Other camp users have hung targets from the hitching posts, and there are lead circles from flattened .22 bullets hitting flat metal head-on.

The diary in the Steven's bunkhouse is a little less cheerful than the Soldier Meadows camp: in one entry, a set of past users is chastised for leaving the wood stove full of empty, crumpled beer cans. There are plenty of hunting parties talking about their successes, everything from scoping animals and birds they would hunt later, to talking about the game they'd brought back.

And then there's the Jeep driver who, with friends, drove the length of the canyon and wrote in the diary that "if you heard guns firing, it was us." These are scattered pieces, lacking the unity of Soldier Meadows.

There's also the heartfelt: a message from people who had scattered the ashes of a cremated family member near the site, out into the meadow below the rough-hewn building, and I'm not surprised how easy that choice of location was for them. I wouldn't mind a final resting place along the trail. Given Dodge's experience, I wouldn't be alone.

∞∞∞∞∞

September 1, 1849

Went 18 miles through heavy dust & sage with very hot sun — no grass or water — to an alkali lake 5 or 6 miles wide & 25 or 30 long — four miles beyond in a canyon or pass over the little mountain we found a good spring and bunch grass. Afternoon went into a small fine valley 4 miles further stopped — Fine grass & water and for the first time in a long while began to see cedars on the mountains, & up the ravines occasionally a pine — signs of game abundant, but can find none.

∞∞∞∞∞

We come around a wide corner on the way back to Cedarville and there's a black cow and her calf on the road, the fence keeping them hemmed onto the pavement instead of away from it.

Here, just across the California line, there are signs warning that the ranchlands are private property, and to stay off them. On one side of the road, the cedars, which have a way of not standing in copses but instead all separate and apart like grade seven students at their first school dance, are all being cut down over a wide swathe of the hill, presumably to make better grazing land. The air is full of their scent, the trees drying out in huge piles that I suppose will eventually be burned: there's no sign of any attempt to harvest any part of them. Nearby cedars that haven't been cut look like an integral piece of the landscape. Cut down, the landscape has moved on, and it feels like a very different place.

We use the trail guide to try to find a hot spring at the side of Middle Alkali Lake — it's still hard to believe that you can be working your way up a dirt road with sand and dust as fine as flour, no sign of water anywhere, then all at once find a stream following a fold in the ground, a stream where no stream should be, framed by opportunistic plant life, itself the result of the chance fall of the luckiest of scattered seeds.

Deer with big antlers nod up out of the knee-high plant cover and stare. We watch huge eagles circling on the mountain-slope thermals near a place actually called Eagleville.

We pass a fenced-in enclosure with half a dozen well-fed mules. Flies circle, but they are otherwise healthy and, I think, lucky not to be heading in traces for the American River at Placerville. They wander up to the fenced edge of their enclosure to stare blankly at us, as if we're an incomprehensible roadside attraction.

The variety of wildlife in such a sere place: sage hen, jackrabbit, dead coyote, western burrowing owl, desert rat, red-tailed hawk, eagle, quail, horned lizard, striped snake, Canada geese, elk, mule deer, skinks, and the strange otherworld colour scheme of the Jerusalem cricket. I have the luxury of fleshing out my notes in the relative comfort of our string of motel rooms, while, tired and flagging, Dodge's entries are thinning down, his words as depleted as his mules and himself.

⟨⟨⟩⟩⟨⟩⟨⟩

September 2, 1849

Passed several ox trains & for 5 miles had a very stony road down the stream — then over stony hills & through the dust and sage to the hot spring 12 miles from camp — nooned there and bought <u>5 lbs. of hard bread for $2.50</u> of the Ashland train from Ohio — Capt. Darland. D. & M. got him to carry 60 lbs. of pills for 10¢ per lb. to the diggings.

It was so cold on the morning of the 2nd that coffee froze in our cups after breakfast; water freezes nearly every night.

Went on 6 miles through sage and across a dried up lake to the foot of the mountains & found splendid grass & plenty of water in holes. Trains camped ahead.

⟨⟨⟩⟩⟨⟩⟨⟩

On the edge of Dodge's dried-up lake, we find a stream that flows from a source called Chicken Springs. We also meet a loner who would clearly be a hippy if hippies were still a thing.

We were looking for yet another trail marker, following the guide and looking for unmarked roads, trying to divine if we were on the right one from photographs in the guide, and from directions like "drive 1.23 miles and look for a dirt road opposite a field with a cattle grate at the entrance." Hide and seek, but when you do it right and find the marker, the feeling of achievement is visceral.

The man is set up near the spring we're looking for in a big white square-fronted Chevy camper (10 miles per gallon, he tells us). We don't see him as we approach the camper on foot. We're trying diligently not to surprise. We've left the car below so it won't get stuck in the soupy sand. Walking up, leaving blurred footprints, counting more cartridge casings and hoping that we're on the right path and not trespassing.

He appears in the doorway all at once, just as I imagine we must have appeared to him. But he is welcoming enough. I think if we had said that we were staying, he would have simply unfolded two more lawn chairs to join his own. There's a faint smell of weed. He's in his socks, dark blue socks, and he goes back into the trailer for his shoes, as if shoes are a necessary formality when meeting strangers.

He's got solar panels set up to listen to music, the panels spread out on the dusty ground, wires running back into the camper. Solar array, solar arrayed. He hadn't heard us coming.

He says the spring used to be called Chicken Spring because you could — and people did — cook a sage chicken in it. He has built up a small dam, lower down on the spring-generated brook, where it was cool enough to sit in, making a sort of homemade and constant hot tub. From that pool, you could rest your back against the bank and look out across the great flat hot plain of Middle Alkali Lake, across the bottom of the Surprise Valley, and see the line of the Warner Range, one more mountain range for the emigrants to cross, this time through Fandango Pass. (Dodge believes, erroneously, that this next crumpled-upwards piece of the Earth's surface is part of the Sierra Nevada Range — it's actually part of the Great Basin Range.)

At the very source of the spring, you can see sand grains roiling up in the flow, a tiny granular storm that never ends.

The man with the camper is there for two weeks of holidays, he says, and only sees someone about once a day. He's been other years and likes the solitude of the place. Once, he says, his visitors were two dragonfly photographers. That's all they did — dragonflies.

Now it's us.

I step in the hot spring accidentally, expecting a patch of alkali to hold my weight where it looks caked and solid. Boiling water floods my sneaker. Leslie burns her hand. It's hard to accept that there's so much heat in what looks like a brook, hard to accept that in the midst of this great parched dryness, there's constantly running water, even if it does smell like brimstone. Between Leslie and me, Chicken Springs becomes its own touch-point — defined by our shared experience. Later, even telling the story will be like spreading our own glue.

◇◇◇◇◇◇◇

September 3, 1849

Started early feeling pretty well, expecting to cross the long looked for Sierra Nevada in 12 miles. Had proceeded but 2 miles when one of mine & one of their mules got mired in crossing a little run. Unpacked and finally got his out. Worked at mine a long time & about gave her up — she would not even make an effort — & was almost covered. We got a larriette around her & by the greatest efforts at length succeeded in drawing her out — but she could not get up for half an hour. Passing some ox teams hitching up we kept along the foot of the mountains north & soon came to a beautiful stream of clear cold water, by the side of which stood half a dozen or more tall pines — 4 or 5 feet in diameter. This was the most welcome and cheering sight we had seen — not having seen such a thing since leaving the States. Went 12 miles & nooned under the shade of a pine a short distance up the mountain. Started & went up the first ascent — very steep but smooth — crossed a fine little stream & started up the 2nd ascent — so steep that we could scarcely climb it — ox teams has 12 pr. to a wagon & it scarcely moved — it took 2 hours to go up the 2 miles. When we reached the top of a fine valley stretched below us, with heavily timbered hills on both sides & Goose Lake 10 miles ahead. Behind spread out the dry lake we had crossed looking like a vast plain. We started down the steep & stony descent with hearts elated. The fine valley — the tall pines & 3 deer which just then crossed our path beyond rifle shot all conspired to make us think we were near our journey's end. I had procured a copy of a guide given to an emigrant by Palmer of the Oregon train, which had proved correct thus far, leading us to hope that it still would — by which it was 90 miles to Sacramento. Many large trains camped in this valley — all appeared cheerful & happy, thinking their journey nearly finished — the previous night we were very cold — several spots of snow on the mountain top — tonight the sun set very pleasantly — & the evening warm. I took a turn up the side of the mountain among the tall pines & rocks hoping to find game, but saw nothing but the smallest kind of ground squirrel. There I saw two brothers — Dills from 7 Mile Creek, Wisconsin.

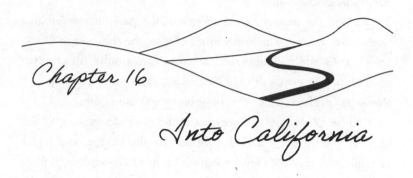

Chapter 16

Into California

We take the road from Goose Lake, travelling briefly in the opposite direction Dodge did, east up County Road 9 towards a gap in the cedar-mounded hills. Route 9 becomes Route 4, skirting the edge of the hills as we look for the gap.

As the rise starts from the valley floor, we're suddenly surrounded by huge pines with heavy, crevassed bark, the inside of the car full of the smell of hot needles and pine pitch. It's so thick, so intense, and everything is so dry that you can imagine that the air itself could burn. We pass a woodland fire station, forest firefighters washing and reloading gear, and start to climb. We cross a cattle grate and the pavement disappears, leaving us on brown dirt and gravel, with huge plumes of dust once again arising behind us.

Big pines give way to pasture, the road curving along topographical lines — and, occasionally, with sudden turns and angles around property lines. As we start to climb again, the pines reappear, interrupting the sun so that the light strobes through the car as we drive.

I stop on the side of the road because the car suddenly smells so hot, the smell of hot brakes, hot engine, and dust, and standing behind it, listening to it click and ping, I wonder if the car's about to overheat. There is no wind, the trees ramrod still, every needle motionless. We're on the trail here, the route overlapping our own, but we're continuing on to the Fandango Pass, the high point where the emigrants stopped climbing one side of the Warner Range and started back downhill.

We find the marker at the apogee of the pass, and everything Dodge saw, we see. The heavy forest of pine, the shimmer of Goose Lake in the western distance, and, when we turn around, the great flat plain of the Upper Alkali Lake. Same spot, same view. The impact is almost physical, yet it's just two-line highway, under pines.

Gnarled plum trees are growing in the roadside ditch, with soft pink-red plums, sweet and sharply acid on the tongue, and I pick handfuls, wondering if they were the result of a long-ago castoff plum pit, the way so many roadside apple trees spring up from tossed apple cores at home. The pines so big and fragrant that the air feels constantly charged. Beside a short path to the trail marker, we let the car sit and cool.

The Applegate Trail, for Dodge, has now become the Lassen Trail, a route that criss-crosses the Pitt River toward its end point at Lassen's Meadow.

Dodge is hoping to reach a settlement he calls "Lawson's" — it's close to his end goal, the place where his goldfield journey ends, and, he hopes, his fortune begins. But the end of his journey, like ours, keeps skittering out of reach.

September 4, 1849

Started early & travelled west toward Goose Lake — road very stony — struck the lake and passed south down the shore into another valley. Saw plenty of ducks and geese, but all out of reach. The ground was covered with pebble stones from 6 inches down to 1 in diameter, rough outside, & when broken the inside was a fine smooth flint-like jet often variegated with streaks of yellow — for miles the earth was covered with them, making the travelling very bad especially as my best mule has become very tender footed. The grass was all burned off in many places, as we supposed by the Indians, but as we afterwards learned, by a train to spite Myers for delaying them & not being able to make a cut-off as he had pretended he could.

Crossed several fine creeks running N.W. into Goose Lake, & camped on one by some wagons of whom we tried hard to buy a few pounds of any kind of provisions, but could not get a single pound — ground miry — feed poor, and bushes for fuel scarce. Saw a fire up on the side of the mountain — supposed to be the Indians who were shooting & stealing cattle every night, though not a single one had been seen by anyone — feared for the safety of our mules.

Like Dodge, we travel west towards Goose Lake. We're looking out at the water, not down at our feet. And then, we do look down.

The shoulder of the road is strewn with rounded black stones, up to six inches in diameter. Looking closer, we see some are broken, revealing curved wells of smooth volcanic glass. We start gathering them up, smashing them open, cutting our fingers on the sharp edges we've made. The broken stones are a black that seems to swallow light, shot through with bright yellow-gold streaks. Unexpectedly, breathlessly, we are holding Dodge's 160-year-old words in our hands.

Some of the rocks come back with us and nestle in amongst Dodge's collection. A perfect fit. Like they belong.

September 5, 1849

Rose early and found them safe — started & soon found one of my mules was lame — shoulder swelled — could not tell whether she had got mired in the night and sprained it, or whether it was a snake bite. Proceeded 8 or 10 mi. & struck a creek which we found to be Pitt River — main branch of the Sacramento. At that time we felt certain of being within 45 miles of Lawson's settlement. Nooned on the bank & when ready to start I went to get up the animals & found the pony fast in a mire hole — his legs stuck in the mud plumb up to his body. There was a fix sure. <u>We dug him out with our hands</u>, but after trying two or three times he could not get up with all our help. I sat down & looked at him, & as the drops of sweat, one after another, rolled down my face I thought of home & the scenes "I left behind me." After letting him rest and trying several times, we finally got him out — washed him off & started on. Cut across a bend through sand and sage — & struck the river again — followed down it & came to Myers' train, camped just before sunset. I went to him and told him that if he knew anything about the route & distance I should be much obliged if he would tell me. He looked very wise — turned his head on one side — shut his eyes & said that he had been over the route several times — that he ought to know something about it, etc. He then said it was just 100 miles to Lawson's — 40 from where we struck the road from Oregon to California — 30 from there to the top of a mountain and 30 from the top to Lawson's — tried to buy some provisions but could not nor could we kill the least bit of game, not even as much as a hawk! Went on and camped 4 miles below on the river near some ox wagons. Tried for some fish but got none — grass mostly burnt off — bushes plenty. M. went to the wagons and tried to buy something but they had none to spare. Night very cold.

◇◇◇◇◇◇◇

A strange footnote about Dodge meeting with Myers, and the trail guides that we have been using. I found out about the guides late in the planning process for this trip: writing back and forth about our plans,

I shared a small portion of Dodge's diary, about Myers and the unsuccessful cut off. Unknowingly, I had information about Myers that no one else does. The guide planners and their archivist were keen to have the diary: I didn't want to share. Because Dodge's story was something that belonged to me, and somehow, I was something that now belonged to it.

◇◇◇◇◇◇

September 6, 1849

This morning my mule's shoulder and leg so badly swelled as to render it impossible for her to travel with us. I went to the wagons and told the men exactly and plainly my situation & desired them to haul my bag of clothing — 30 pounds. They readily agreed to do it & I left the mule with them to get her through if they could. More than this they gave us 1 ½ lbs. of bacon & 5 or 6 lbs. of hard bread — refusing to take a penny — they said they had none to sell, but they would not see anyone suffer. This was part of the Pike Co., Ill. train, H. Taylor, Capt. Crossed the river — passed over a hill and struck it again — followed down the narrow crooked valley, among the sage & stones — frequently leaving the stream and passing over a hill while the stream ran around. Struck a branch from a spring & nooned — then went on — there I succeeded in shooting a sage chicken which made us a fine supper. Kept on down the river — road very stony. Passed a fine bank of white chalk on the stream and entered a rough rocky canyon. Kept on & camped on a bend of the river as it turned south into a most terrible looking canyon. No grass except on the sides of the mountain — wood plenty — the mountains are all covered with tall pines, firs & cypress. Felt rather fearful about our animals — night cold.

◇◇◇◇◇◇

The road toward Alturas: I walked part of it in the evening, where road crews have been stabilizing the cliffs to stop slides and rock falls. Even though the heavy equipment stopped working only a few hours before, the muddy shoulders of the road are spider-webbed with deer tracks, though I don't see a single deer.

In Alturas itself, we're stuck behind a cowboy driving a pickup truck and towing a huge trailer. On the trailer are three — just three — 20-foot-long pieces of the trunk of a massive tree. The tires on the trailer bulge fatly with the weight.

There was smoke hanging in a long thin line over Cedarville when we were coming in from Nevada. After we climb through the winding mountain valley and then chute down to the other side, we can clearly see the massive Santa Rosa fire, a high purple column of smoke in the sunset, spreading into a pink and purple line.

We head down the 395 for Susanville, hoping for a motel sooner, but passing through towns so small they are almost not there: Brockman, Moran, Termo. Termo is a cluster of sheds and a few small buildings, a closed and crumbling tin-roofed store, a line of three decrepit fuel pumps. And then it's gone.

We remember at that point that we'd done the responsible thing and told the kids that we were traveling on foot in the desert, out there in a space where there's no one to help, where the advice, a little dryly, is that if you're in trouble, to stay with your car so at least your bodies will be found. We'd left a detailed plan about where we were going, one part of it being that we were supposed to let them know that we were out of the desert safely — and we hadn't done that yet. We're suddenly concerned that the cavalry might be getting ready to mobilize, dispatched by our children wondering if they'd waited long enough, or too long, to call for help. It was open plains and pitch black on both sides of us, but I can't hit a cell phone tower anywhere to send my simple two-word text: "We're safe."

I finally find one bar on the phone, my head down close to the dash, the text flying out into the ether, when Leslie jams on the brakes and hauls the car up tight — I'm thrown toward the dashboard, get caught by the seatbelt, and look up just in time to see the beige flash of the side of a deer in the driver's side headlight, and it's once again just pavement stretching out in front of us in the twin cones of the headlights.

The rest of the drive is on edge, both of us snapping at each other. We want to stop, but there's nowhere — so we roll on, exhausted. At one point, we see a huge expanse of orange lights next to the road, and think we're finally approaching a town of some size. It turns out to be the lights of the High Desert State Prison at Leavitt. Prisons: another new goldmine of the American West.

We drive on, tired and out of sorts, looking for a hotel — at this point, any hotel.

◇◇◇◇◇◇

September 7, 1849

Morning found all safe — started & entered the worst & most rocky canyon we had yet seen — across the stream to the right I noticed the mouth of a cave or den — did not go to it. Road crossed the stream & a few rods below, recrossed — bad rocky crossing & deep at the first one — we kept along over the rocks — among the trees & bushes with great difficulty without crossing. Road grew worse & worse — stony — springy — sideling, with frequent crossing — finally the canyon became so narrow & rocky that the road could go no further, but left it & turned over a high hill to the right — came out into a wider bottom & near noon struck the Oregon road. Nooned and after starting soon came out into a beautiful wide valley, which many thought must be the Sacramento. My mule was so lame that I could not ride her at all — walked hard all the afternoon, and struck the river at night — plenty of bushes and grass — everything appeared as though we had actually reached the long looked for valley — I was very tired and my feet were sore — saw plenty of cranes — blackbirds — ducks but could not kill even as much as a crow. Slept very little for fear the Indians would steal our mules — Bivin, foot packer, camped with us & was much frightened — kept talking all night & kept us awake because he dared not go to sleep.

∞∞∞∞

Eagle Lake looks parched, long beaches of dried mud and sand before you can come close to reaching the edge of the water. Boat ramps and docks offer access only to dry lakebed. We arrive in Susanville at the height of the Willard Fire and there are scores of firefighters, the hotshots teams everywhere, Cal Fire forest fire trucks rolling through town in convoys. We've followed two more into town, reinforcements for the crews already on the fire.

Susanville's hotels are all filled with firefighters, so we're at the Knight's Inn Motel — the second worst we've been in. We strip the bed to look for bedbugs, leave all the luggage in the trunk of the car. There's a massive exercise machine in our room, blocking the connecting door. It's built by Human Medextec and there are two pads to stand on, two cushioned handles to hold for balance. Its Korean manufacturer says, "(The) Lipolysis Vibration Exerciser is a new concept that burns off body fat especially around the abdomen and the fat from internal organs. This is achieved by converting the rotary motion of a powerful motor to bilateral symmetrical amplitude energy."

In other words, you stand on it, and it does all the exercise for you. It feels as fake and hollow a come-on as a promise of endless easy riches on the other side of a continent — or an ocean.

We don't even turn it on, but it makes an excellent door stop.

The other door, the front door, is another one that has been kicked in and repaired. The bedspread boasts a massive eagle, wings spread. On both sides of the bed, there's a lamp with a sculpted and chipped cowboy carrying a saddle, with cactuses and a spilled canteen at his feet. The bathroom wall in the shower has an English Leather soap dispenser from another era, its single servings long gone, its corners and edges filled with captured grime.

306

At a breakfast diner, there's a tired Cal Fire firefighter staring into his coffee at the counter.

I ask him how it's going: the Willard fire is winding down, he says. "What's next?"

"I don't know and I don't care," he says, adding that he's starting three weeks of vacation.

Our car is so completely dusted that the hinges creak loudly on all the doors, and dust falls off it whenever they slam or the trunk closes. There's dust inside the door panels, streaking the inside of the windows when you put them up. The burgundy Hyundai Sonata that we've slalomed around lost mountains and flour-dust trails, the one where the satellite radio up and quit two states out of Wisconsin. Our own Milligan, and now that all of the backcountry driving is done, a Milligan that hasn't died under us. We break a couple of five-dollar bills into quarters at the self-serve car wash, and Leslie vacuums the inside before I foam-wash the outside.

It's impossible to clean — muddy water keeps streaming out from under the rocker panels, out from behind the licence plates, even from the sealed spaces around the headlights and taillights. I'm suddenly glad that we'll be turning it in at 4:00 a.m. in Sacramento a few days from now, in the dark, and I hope that no damage is going to turn up.

∞∞∞∞

September 8, 1849

Started early and instead of turning to the right over the mountains as we expected, the road bore to the left running almost due east. I felt stiff & weary. Soon passed a train where I got an old horseshoe nailed on my mule's foot for $0.50 but it did no good — she was as lame as ever. Left the valley and went up a mountain on the left very gradual at first — supposed it was but a few miles over & that we should certainly see the settlement in the valley beyond. But after ascending the first range — another & another & another presented itself — each

more steep than the preceding, until we had crossed 7 or
8 & then began to descend — passed large ox trains but
could not buy even a piece of bread. Two of the trains
had several oxen shot by the Indians the night before —
some had half a dozen arrows sticking in them when they
gathered them in at evening yet not one Indian could be
seen. Went on down ravines — twisting around among
the mountains, over the rockiest road that ever man saw
for 12 m. from where struck the mountains & came to a
splendid brook — but no grass — dense forrest on every
side & in many places the rocks were so large & thick
that the men and animals were obliged to step from one to
another without touching the ground, & that too on steep
side hills. We did not reach there until 2 or 3 P.M. stopping
but a little while, then went on through the tall forrest &
up a very steep hill, when we reached the top we could
see the sun setting far below us, something that we had
not witnessed for many a day — which more than ever
led us to think that we were near the valley. We stopped
under a tall pine which stood alone in the middle of a little patch of bunch grass where the stones lay so thick that
we could not even find a place to lie down until we had
removed them. We made a fire and laid down to rest, ourselves & our mules being nearly exhausted — no water
— saw fires in the mountains in every direction — therefore undertook to watch the mules, but when my watch
was off, feeling no danger, & knowing how tired the rest
were, I did not wake them — we got no supper & rested
but little.

∾∾∾∾∾∾∾

Every now and then, a single image is startling: a roadkill deer that's
been unwrapped from its skin by the force of the impact, leaving a
pile of hide in one spot and, further away, a carcass that manages, in

its nudity, to look almost human. The huge pine trees of the forest conservation area at Modoc massive and motionless, so that any movement we make seems twitchy and frenetic by comparison. Standing under them, you feel like you should be whispering. All the time.

⊲⊳⊲⊳⊲⊳

September 9, 1849

Started without breakfast & going 2 m. crossed a fine little stream & went on 6 or 7 — came to a spring to the right & stopped for breakfast — no grass — mules so tired they lay down and did not try to eat. Leaving there passed along on a ridge through a dense forest of tall pines, cypress, firs & with a good road & soon began to descend gradually. To our right rose two enormous peaks spotted with snow, from which the wind blew chill — making the doubt & gloom which hung over us still more dark. Continued going down gradually — most of the way fine road, for 15 to 20 m. & came to a little open space where we found water and a little grass. At this place we got 10 lbs. flour at 25¢ per lb. Stopped but a short time & went on standing alone in the center of an open space where we found a little grass but no water. Toward morning I got so cold I could not sleep — got up & made a fire. Fires were burning in every direction in the mountains — some of them were supposed to be Indians — others where it had spread from camps.

September 10, 1849

Started without breakfast & went 5 m. — came into an open place — grass & water down to the left away from the road — got breakfast — Capt. Warner's party with pack animals passed — belongs to the Topographical Engineers on an exploring expedition — could not learn where they were going — started with 30 soldiers, all sick but 2. Hiring emigrants to go back — giving $306 per

month. Report it to be very sickly in Cal. — flour & beef
$1.00 per lb. at the diggings — men average from half to
an ounce per day — went on to a small lake on the left .
5 m. learned it was 20 miles to the next water & 100 to
Lawson's; kept on down hill gradually till dark & no water
or grass yet. Road stony — night dark — mules and us too
about tired out & dispirited — kept on — saw a light &
soon heard water roaring over stones — went down a very
steep & stony hill — large loose rocks causing us to stumble & bruise our shins woefully. Came to a creek — got a
light — found no grass at all — stopped — tied our mules
to the trees, built a fire, and got supper — a couple of other
packers arrived & stopped with us — found where there
had been a small spot of grass — let part of the mules run.
About midnight so cold could not sleep — got up — took
my mule to where the rest were — came back built a fire
and laid down by it. Found three other men there who had
come in during the night.

There are specialized Cal Fire firefighting rigs and teams everywhere.
They spill out of hotels, convoy down streets, shoulder up to the counter at every restaurant we're in. California is burning, it's almost the end
of September and it's still burning. Even when you don't see the crews
themselves, there are road detours warning about firefighting operations, aircraft angling overhead, and often, big scars of already-burned
ground where the fires have been put out and the teams have moved on.

There are lines of smoke on the horizon every evening, milky
orange in the sunset, and often the smell of it as well.

September 11, 1849
Started & crossing two fine streams came to a spot of fine
grass in 2 m. — stopped & baited — went on 8 miles &

came to a large valley or basin of fine grass & water — but so miry that the animals could feed only around the edges. Spring several rods across, clear as crystal. Saw great numbers of cranes — plenty of deer & bear away from the road — train camped by us brought in a deer at noon — followed along the western edge of the basin at the foot of the mountain — good road — over a ridge — stony & 8 miles to a large valley in the center of which we crossed Feather River running E. of S. Clearest water I ever saw — although belly-deep it did not look more than a foot — fine grass & several very large & fine springs. River all made by springs — the head being but a few miles above. Several trains were camped there & most of them had killed deer. One of them had killed a beef & we bought 5 lbs. for $1.00 — also 4 lbs. of flour for $2.00. Bought an old horseshoe for $2.00 — blacksmith broke it — bought another one for $2.00 — gave him $2.00 for nailing it on. Said to be 80 miles through. Hedspeth met us here.

September 12, 1849

Started early and continued descending gradually — got a glimpse of 6 or 8 deer through the brush. 8 m. came to a fine little stream running S. of E., followed up, passed its head & struck another running W. & plenty grass. Very high peak on our left — top spotted with snow. Signs of game abundant. Camped at noon in a very pretty grove by a fine spring & stream, where some old trapper had formerly had a hut. Went on and in 3 miles came to a small valley where we found many teams camped, & among them a company of U.S. soldiers lying sick. Crossed Deer Creek several times & finally left the valley, taking up a little creek to the right, which we soon crossed and took up a very steep mountain side, where the trees and bushes stood so thick that we could not see 10 rods from the road in either direction. Kept along the side of the mountain then into a dry branch & about sundown reached a spot where expected to find good grass, but instead found some soldiers sick, a number of packers & one of the worst mire holes I ever saw, & not a bit of grass scarcely.

✕✕✕✕✕✕✕✕

We cross the Feather River, heading south, tucked in between tall pines with almost no underbrush, and everything dry. We stop at Deer Creek Meadows, little more than a wide brook through a small meadow, the next range of mountains looming on the horizon. Two men are fly-fishing in the clear brown water, one of them completely under the bridge. It's still and hot, and the valley looks just the way many of the emigrants described it. There's a broad swampy meadow stretching to the south, coloured for fall, corralled behind barbed wire, and a huge grey log lies toppled, looking as if it has been resting there since the gold rush. Our eyes and Dodge's eyes: seeing the same shape of the valley, little changed.

✕✕✕✕✕✕✕✕

September 13, 1849

In the morning we hunted a long time before we could find our mules — then put out and passed several ox trains — travelling bad — up & down steep & stony hills. A short distance from camp we passed where a mule & it was supposed a man also — had been killed the night before by a Grizzly bear — the tracks of a couple of the monsters led along our road for a mile or more, but we saw nothing of them. Passed along the top of a high dividing ridge running W. — heavily timbered with ravines very deep on both sides. At noon we stopped on top of the ridge & drove our mules down a ravine to the right where we found a very little dirty water near a mile from the road — but no grass. Had expected in the morning to reach Lawson's before night but

that we found to be impossible, although we had only sufficient for two scanty meals left. Passing on we soon came out
of the heavy timber — kept along on top of the ridge among
scrubby oak and a strange kind of very prickly bushes. The
road grew worse and worse — very rough and filled with
large loose stones & rocks. Toward night we came to a very
steep hill, down which we got our mules after much difficulty. At the bottom we found some mule-teams unable to
get up, their mules being exhausted. A mile and a half down
a rough rocky canyon to the left was a little water, but being
told that 4 miles further on was grass and water both, we
concluded to proceed. But upon trying to ascend the steep
hill we found it almost impossible to get our weary mules up
it — mine, although I had not rode her any for several days,
gave out entirely, and would not move an inch for whip or
anything else. By pulling and working I finally got her to
the top, where we camped for the night being unable to get
any further. M. & myself went after water — after going 2
or 3 miles down a steep rocky canyon climbing over rocks
& crawling under bushes we gave up. On our way back
I espied a little green spot on the hillside & going up to it
found a little hole where game drank. Oh how thankful we
were. By digging with our hands and waiting some time
we finally got about 2 ½ qts. of this water & then it tasted so
strongly like soakings of a barnyard, that we could scarcely
use it. With gloomy forebodings we ate a portion of scanty
supply & laid ourselves down among the stones as we hoped
for the last time.

⬦⬦⬦⬦⬦⬦

The highway is switchbacked and narrow and fast, following the right-
hand side of Deer Creek, then crossing over and following the left.
Cars coming the other direction pop into view mere seconds before
they're passing you.

We take a side road, a paved route no bigger than a driveway, and find ourselves at a landing pad for Forest Service helicopters. There are hay bales for spilled fuel, big, loaded heavy tarpaulin drop-bags with handles for the snaphooks of the helicopters' lifting ropes.

Over the side, we can see how high we've climbed, the river valley with Deer Creek hundreds of feet below us, the points of the pines like rows of folding olive-green umbrellas beneath us. Dodge talked about fire in the hills, likely the fires of the Modoc Peoples. Looking down into the valley, we see a standing figure that looks like a woman, facing us, holding something in her arms. We can see enough to almost make out facial features, to see the narrowings of waist and neck, but there's no track, no path to get to her, no sign of whether she's a natural feature or man-made. We check back and forth between us: "Do you see that?" The forest below is still and quiet — across from us, the blackened remains of a huge forest fire climb up over the mountains and disappear. We are unnerved.

Back in the car, we run west along the spine of the same ridge Dodge mentioned, the road suddenly straight, the pines giving way to well-spaced trees with olive-coloured spatulate leaves. The downhill seems even drier as we go, the leaves on the trees withering.

❧❧❧❧❧❧❧

September 14, 1849

Went 3 or 4 miles and came to the watering place — it was down a very steep long & stony hillside in a deep canyon. It was with the greatest difficulty that we could get our mules to it — the hill was so steep that we often had to stop and rest ourselves. It was one-and-a-quarter miles to the water. A short distance on we passed a team from whom I succeeded in buying a small piece of venison. In our road were the fresh tracks of a Grizzly bear for several miles. The road grew rather better after a while & the oaks larger. Passed some wagons — left, the teams having given out & been driven on to grass & water.

Weary & exhausted, a little after noon we descended the
last hill & finally entered the valley, thankful that Heaven
had, after so many trials & sufferings landed us at the
long looked for goal. At a creek at the foot of the hill we
camped & cooked our last meal, which we divided with
a man we found there without any. After noon we proceeded on to Lawson's settlement. It was just dark & we
had nothing to eat except a part of the venison I had got in
the morning. We camped under a large oak & soon after,
a wagon loaded with provisions camped close by. We
built a fire — cooked most of the venison & then inquired
of the gentlemen how they sold their provisions. They
replied 75¢ per lb. for hard bread etc. which perfectly
astonished me, as I had not more than 1.50 in the world.
We ate our meat clear except the gentlemen (Townsend of
St. Louis) gave us a cracker. Not knowing where the next
meal was to come from or what I was to do, we spread our
blankets and went to sleep.

∞∞∞∞∞

We find the last official trail marker on the Lassen Trail, the familiar
crossed pieces of railway track. It's tucked back in the brush on the
edge of a vineyard at the Abbey of New Clairvaux, a Trappist monas-
tery. Wild black walnuts fall out of the tree above us and patter down.
Finding the marker is almost anticlimactic: every step before this has
gotten more and more difficult, each part of the journey more harrowing. But nothing seems harrowing here: nature is pretty and tamed,
except for the weeds growing up towards the trail marker and dap-
pling it with their shade. The marker is like so many official historical
reminders, grown over and slipping toward forgotten.

We take pictures anyway, and a Lexus sweeps by us as we do, its
windows rolled up tight to keep the air conditioning in, and it curves
through the manicured vines toward the winery. In the pictures, we're
both hidden behind branches laden with dead and dry leaves — almost

camouflaged. You wouldn't find that marker unless you knew exactly where to look.

This is where Dodge rested before heading south to Hangtown, later known as Placerville. It's September but it's still perishingly hot, and while the desert is behind us, I'm still picking cactus spikes out of my shoes and out of the floor mats. The predominant colours are still straw and sedge and grey, and it feels like every single drop of water has been sucked out of everything.

The trail marker quotes Pardon Tiffany, who was a month behind Dodge on the trail: "At Lassen's . . . saw many of the emigrants arriving here. They are broke down with the fatigue. Young men made old and stiff. Many are dying with dysentery, fever, scurvy."

‹∞∞∞∞∞∞›

September 15, 1849

In the morning D. who had 7 or 800 dollars in his belt went out to get some flour of some of the emigrant trains. M. and myself set about preparing fire etc. as usual when D. returned with a few cups of flour, which I supposed he had got for the Mess as we had previously been doing.

But while I was busy with the fire he came and laid down the remainder of the venison & remarked in his sneaking tone, "Here is your venison." "My venison" I replied in astonishment. "Yes" said he, "I thought you would want it" I comprehended him in an instant, & replied, "Very well." I broiled the venison and bought a couple of crackers at 10 cts. each, which made me a very good breakfast. Before noon I got a chance to work my way to the city with some of Capt. Briscoe's train who were going after provisions, intending if I could not get a situation there, to return with them to the mines at Reddings, where they intended wintering. Nothing strange happened on the way down.

‹∞∞∞∞∞∞›

We find a roadside restaurant, nearly empty, and plot our next move.

Dodge's diary stops for a month, as his travel to California becomes his life there.

We don't have to wait for venison.

Lassen's Steak House and Sports Bar has plenty of televisions and loud music, but few 2:00 p.m. customers. We order the squid and the zucchini: "A tender calamari steak cut into four strips, hand-dipped in our specialty panko batter and deep-fried to a golden crisp. Served with our Signature Caribbean Sauce;" and "Fresh zucchini cut into strips & hand-dipped in our special beer batter & fried to a golden crunch. Served with your choice of a dippin' sauce."

And water. Lots and lots of cold, clean water.

It was $17.75, all in, which made us a very good lunch.

∞∞∞∞∞∞

October, 1849

The valley was beautifully interspersed with groves of large spreading oaks. There was a ranch about every 20 miles. The grass appeared very dry & dead, and the sun very hot, making the travelling as usual very tiresome. We reached the city on Friday morning the 21st. On the way down I came across a man who was sick & having some pills he took nine boxes of me for $40.00. In addition I sold my mule for $50.00 which made me the owner of about $100.00. This I laid out in company with a young man, Mr. Tulley, in the train in articles to sell at the mines. Here I came across Holcombe, Ingalsbee, & Chapman who were doing a fine business, & I would have stopped with them had it not been for the arrangements I had already made; & nearly everyone thought the chances above were excellent. Two days after leaving the city I was so badly poisoned as to be unable to walk — part of the way I rode a horse belonging to Maj. Reed, who was taken with the fever and died at Cotton Wood creek, and the remainder of the way some of the boys, especially W. Briscoe & Wm. Ewing let me ride when not able to walk. I recovered by the time we reached the mines so as to be able to walk around. Finding things very plenty there we were unable to sell them as we had expected — nor indeed at any price scarcely. I traded part of them for a pretty fine Cayuse horse & having sold out the rest of my share to my partner, Tulley, I concluded to return to the city where the rest of our boys were. In the meantime I settled with the Parson for coming up. He charged me $25.00! The Dr. who was in his mess charged me $45.00 for a bit of Castile soap & a little mercurial ointment. After paying 5 more for a saddle and bridle I had just 5 left!

I left the springs for the city on the 12th & came down 12 miles to Hall's camp, where I found them nearly all sick, 6 out of 7, & wishing to give my horse a chance to recruit a little, I concluded to stop a few days as he desired my help. I had been there but two days before I was myself taken down with the fever! I immediately got some medecine from the Dr. & he assured me that I would be up in a few days. But instead of getting better I grew worse, and the next day he gave me some more which he was sure would do the work. For a little my fever seemed broken, but it soon returned again worse than before! Three times it returned in this way, but at last I got it broken by taking cold baths [in the] mornings. But still I was very weak — no appetite — got some wild grapes of Indians — made a pie — tasted good — began to get better — more appetite. My horse had been lost 5 days — I gave him up for lost. On Wednesday Mac found him. I sold my Bowie knife for $10 & my spur for $1.50. I went to the Dr. & told him just how much I had & told him to take what he thought was right. He acted the man — dividing it — taking $7.25 & leaving me $4.25. That morning we buried a young man by the name of Dixon from Washington, & as his partner Duvall was going to the city I concluded to go with him — we started on Wednesday afternoon the 24th & rode 12 miles — next day we rode 28 & next day about the same. My health continued to improve except that I was much bothered with boils, which made it very hard riding. Next day Saturday 27th we rode 25 to Potter's ranch where we got some milk at 50¢ per quart. Oh how I thought of home then, & how my father's hogs were fattening upon that which here was such a luxury & so hard to obtain!

Scenery in the valley beautiful. Live oak grove — wild oats — grass dead & dry — ranches — filthy Indians naked — huts etc. horses & cattle — game — bear — antelope & elk — birds, crows, ravens, vultures, magpies — quail etc. California dress — pants, drawers, leggings, knife, hat, sash, blanket; riding, throwing the lasso, etc.

<><><><><>

We cross American River on a bridge that's set down into the canyon, having wound our way down to it on a series of hairpin switchbacks. On the other side, back up again, a matching, if reversed, set of switchbacks. It is exhilarating driving — not so good for passengers.

It seems wrong to be moving so quickly through the last ground that came so close to defeating the tired and hungry Dodge. But that's not the worst of it. Below us, on the river that Dodge has come so far to reach and begin the hard work of hunting for gold by hand, the water is full of brightly coloured whitewater rafts and their passengers. We hear the sound of excited voices echoing up from the river canyon as we pass at the point closest to the water. Now that we are here, 1849 is very, very far away.

‹‹◇››‹‹◇››

October 28, 1849

Finding good grass at Potter's we laid over that fore-noon to give our horses rest & afternoon we went on 10 mi. to another creek. Our provisions being about out we bought a few pounds of flour at 50¢ per lb., but found it so full of wevil as to render it unfit for use, nearly. Nothing remarkable happened from that time until we arrived at the city, which place I reached on the evening of the last day of the month. I found Wainwright and "Bogus" with H. & I. Ingalsbee and "Bog" were sick with the fever. W. had been but had recovered. I went over to town next day and there found Drury preparing to go to the mines, although he was then hardly able to be about. He looked very bad and appeared to have lost all his energy, though not so with his pride! I felt satisfied that he would die in less than a month if he should go, and finally succeeded in persuaded him to give it up though we knew of no chance of doing anything there.

I looked around and soon found a situation as 2nd Steward in a hotel, where I was to have had $100.00 a month, but the rascally proprietor would only pay me at the rate of $80.00. I commenced there on the 3rd of November and having found employment for myself I began to try to get D. to arouse and make an effort. But he was completely disheartened, and talked of writing to his brother for means to return home. I said and did everything in my power to arouse him, and finally got him to go with me to call on Dr. White, who very kindly gave him some medecine which helped him.

My own health was far from being recovered, and the hotel having nothing but a cloth roof, the room in which I worked and slept was constantly damp and chilly, as the rain began falling the same morning that I went there, and continued for nearly two weeks with but little intermission, the result of which was that my fever returned again with renewed fury! During this time D. was living in a tent a short distance from me, still quite unwell. I applied to Dr. White, who gave me some medecine and next day thought I was gaining again — but again I was doomed to disappointment. Having no place to lie at the hotel except on the dining room floor, and not even there in the day time, I went to D's tent to lie down. During the day I remained there, and toward evening my fever returned still more violently. D. had gone to the hotel after my blankets, and it becoming dark he had considerable difficulty in finding his way back through the mud and bushes. He then went for the Dr., who came and gave me some powders which succeeded in breaking the fever. Next day with D's aid I got to the hotel and applied to Mr. Brown for a berth in the sleeping room — but of course he had none for me, as he rented them for a dollar per night. After some time however, I succeeded in obtaining a mat on the floor under the berths. And this was Missourian hospitality — in fair keeping with their character generally. D. remained and took care of me until I began to mend, then much to our joy, he got a situation. In about a week, although I was yet feeble, I again began my duties, but only had been at them two days when the proprietor sold out, and as their successors did not wish my help I was again out of employment.

More fortunate than before I found another situation that same day. There I remained 8 days and might have remained longer if I had only been sufficiently servile and sycophantic to the 1st Steward, who was a haughty, insolent, and overbearing foreigner. This I could not and would not do, the consequence of which was I was discharged. In the meantime the rainy season had set in more than six weeks earlier than on the previous year, and people were not prepared for it — many had not their buildings finished, while hundreds were living in tents. People also came in from the mines in large numbers, seeking for shelter from the soaking rain. To make matters worse flour raised from 16 to 50 dollars per bbl., and all other kinds of provisions in proportion. The rain had made the roads impassible which caused a stagnation in business, not only making it impossible for the newcomers to get employment but also depriving those of situations who had them. Houses which but a few weeks before had been paying $300.00 per month could then be supplied with men who were glad of the chance to work for their board. Owing to the unavoidable exposure of the inhabitants — the damp, chill atmosphere, and poor water, the filthiness and bad condition of the city, there was a great amount of sickness. There appeared to be no sympathy or feeling for a sick and suffering man, except it was some particular friend; and it was really a painful sight to see them as they walked about the city pale and emaciated — looking more like ghosts than men! Many were the smart and enterprising young men who had come thither with high hopes and fond anticipations, but who met only with a stranger's grave and a stranger's burial, without even a single tear of sympathy! Such was the condition of things when I again found myself out of employment, and no place to go to! For two days I traversed the city from one end to the other in search of a place but found none — yet my proud American spirit would sooner let me beg than stoop to the insolence of an insignificant foreigner! Hitherto I had always taken up in favor of foreign emigrants, but now I began to change my mind. When I saw nearly every situation in the city filled by ignorant and insolent foreigners, whom the genius of our free

institutions had allowed to stand upon the same platform
with our own citizens to the exclusion of well educated
and industrious young Americans, who were thus thrown
out of employment and suffering for the comforts of life,
my very blood boiled with indignation! Our government
ought not to allow them to come and carry away the gold
so — it is robbing our own citizens — and turning the
gold into channels from whence we can receive no benefit
when we might have it ourselves.

◇◇◇◇◇◇◇

In the other diary, my great uncle George Wangersky talks about arriving in America: my grandfather was already in New Hampshire. "On
the next day, we began to land on Ellis Island. The customs agents were
inspecting everyone's luggage, but I had only the white bag, which
was almost empty. . . . We went through the immigrations inspector.
He said, 'Where are you going, and how much money do you have?'
At the time, everyone was supposed to have twenty-five dollars cash.
I had my money in a small bag on a string around my neck. I kept it
under my shirt. I pulled the bag out, untied it, and showed it to the
inspector. He counted it and said, 'Do they have a job for you as soon
as you come?' I said, 'I don't know.' He said, 'All right. Go ahead.'"

Three days later, he was working in a Claremont shoe factory, taking orders from a Polish-speaking boss: "The first day, he told me to
wipe the dust from the cases. Then two days later he showed me how
to size shoes. The shoes were coming in forty-eight pair lots, all mixed
up. I was sizing them before they went through a machine. I used to
earn one dollar a day, five and a half dollars a week." And his family in
Belarus? This, from when he was leaving; "And it so happened that as
soon as we came to the station, the train came, so we didn't have much
time. My father grabbed me, kissed me, and said, 'Do not forget me,
Sonny.' A stream of tears began to roll down his face. 'I said, Goodbye, Daddy. I will not forget you as long as I live.' And this is the last
time I saw my father."

I was up early, walking into the hills behind Placerville on a narrow stretch of road with no shoulder that alternated between heavy trees and long vistas of valleys of scattered cedar and dry sedge-brown soil. I was wearing a shirt I bought in Mexico, a guayabera, and jeans, and I was tanned brown. There were houses tucked unevenly along both sides, different styles but all basically one storey. I meet two pairs of seniors walking: one pair crossed to the far side of the road, while the other nodded a stern and dismissive hello.

I passed under the "Neighborhood Watch" sign, marvelling at the knuckled, pine-sap-oozing pinecones that had fallen, larger than the size of my hands bunched together. Until now, I hadn't seen signs on houses warning that people were gun owners, and that they would use their guns if necessary. Now, I did. A few cars passed by, but it was hot and still and mostly quiet.

As I passed some houses, I saw homeowners pull back from the windows.

The first time I saw a door ease open, with no sign of the people inside and an angry dog boiling out at me until it came up short, barking, just inside the fence, I didn't think about it. The second time, the dog bigger and the fence a buried electronic "invisible fence" so that I wasn't sure the snarling dog would stop before it reached me, I was more shaken than anything else. The third time, with the dog's owner sitting on the porch as his pet launched itself toward me, I was beginning to feel like an unwanted foreigner myself.

I turned around to head back, feeling less welcome with every step.

∞∞∞∞∞∞

December 4, 1849

While looking about the city I came across A. B. Hurd from Fond du Lac, who like myself was just recovering from a fit of sickness. He was residing at Coloma (The Mill) the place where the gold was first discovered, and had been doing a fine business, keeping boarders and packing, until he was taken sick. He urged me strongly to go home with him offering me $100.00 per month as he intended to commence a boarding house again. I gladly accepted his offer, hoping by getting higher up in the mountains to find a more healthy situation — nor was I disappointed — for my health improved daily from the time of my arrival there. I found on my arrival Mrs. H. confined with an infant daughter, and no person but him to officiate as nurse, although there were 20 or 30 women in the place! They had a house, one room of which was fixed up quite comfortably, and having nothing else to do I commenced making doors and windows for the others, and to prepare table and benches ready to keep boarders as soon as Mrs. H. should recover. At this and other work such as getting wood etc., I continued until two days before Christmas when I went on that and the succeeding day I packed a mule to Georgetown — distant 12 miles — and earned fifty dollars each day for Hurd. When I started back from Georgetown on the evening of the 24th it was nearly sunset — and during my walk of nearly 12 miles through those lonely mountains after dark I had full time for undisturbed meditation. Such a Christmas Eve I had never before witnessed, and how different was my situation then from what it had been on former similar occasions!!

Remember the scare I had at hearing the firing of guns, yelling and hooting when I reached the top of the hill about a mile above the town. I thought it was an Indian attack. It was the boys celebrating.

December 25, 1849

Christmas was a fine warm and pleasant day. It was celebrated by a grand ball at the hotel — but my time and thoughts were quite differently engaged. Mr. H. was attacked with the pleurisy a day or two before Christmas and Mrs. H. was not yet able to sit up. No nurse having been procured, mine was the task — whether pleasant or unpleasant — to take care of them, cook, wash dishes, bring and chop wood, hunt and milk the cow, and take care of the mule and "little one." This state of things lasted for near a week when he recovered so as to take my place.

At that place I found my friend Charles Chandler — Mr. Hazen and Louis. My health having improved much, and there being a chance to go digging with Charley, I wrote to friend Drury to come up, hoping that it might prove alike beneficial to his health.

◇◇◇◇◇◇◇◇

The fireworks have been over for an hour, the end of the El Dorado County Gold Week, the finale a sharp smacking rattle echoing off the hills. Meanwhile, out front, the party bus is disgorging gold panners, all in town for the 2016 World Gold Panning Championships.

In the lobby of the Cary House Hotel in Placerville, a white-bearded gold panner in a Tyrolean hat festooned with badges is saying his goodnights in German to an almost empty room.

We've headed outside so Leslie can have a cigarette, and we're watching the people step off the bus.

They may be gold-panning competitors, but they all know each other, most of them carrying custom-made pans over their shoulders in soft fabric bags, most of them also a few sheets to the wind. There's hugging, kissing, more German. Inside the bus, there are other panners, headed for their hotels. Just one stop on the championship circuit.

A young man with a look close to a surfer dude staggers out from a nearby bar and walks in among the panners, trying to beg a cigarette. We're on the sidelines, Leslie obviously with cigarettes.

The panners don't have any, or don't understand, fending him off with heavily accented English. The man calls out goodbye but gets no response. Finally, he sings out "Ricola!", the punch line to a commercial for a popular Swiss sore throat remedy.

Leslie topples against the side of the hotel, laughing, coughing, laughing again.

⟨⟨⟨⟩⟨⟩⟨⟩⟩

January 15, 1850

Last night was the coldest we had at this place — it froze quite hard — a thing not witnessed before but a few times. At Georgetown, 12 miles from here the snow is 14 inches deep — none has yet been seen here, except on the tops of the mountains near by. The weather is that of spring at home — it does not rain more than half the time, but the atmosphere is exceedingly damp. My own health is improving finely. I now weigh 166 — more than I ever before weighed by 16 lbs. Still I have not recovered from the bad effects of the trip. My bones appear weak and incapable of enduring fatigue. A very little exertion exhausts my strength. It is undoubtedly the result of the scurvy though it did not exhibit itself in any outward form.

At Sacramento City January 8th, there has been a great flood — the water began rising an hour after dark, and rose a foot an hour. The people were obliged to flee for their lives, leaving their property behind — of which it was estimated that over two millions worth was destroyed. They had to pay as high as fifty dollars a person in some cases to get out of the city onto the high land near Sutter's Ft. Board was four dollars a meal, and provisions rose very much in price. One man having gone upstairs to keep out of the water had to cut a hole in the roof to escape. The water was seven feet deep in the main street, so that the steamer came up it.

At this place, Sutter's Mill or Coloma, the south fork rose 10 ft. carrying away the bridge and a great number of gold washers. In attempting to ferry the river on Sunday four men got into the stream, and one of them, Mr. Lappham was drowned. His son had started the Friday before for the east, intending to bring his mother with him on his return in the spring. After having with Mr. Hurd one month and three days (earning one hundred and ten dollars) I left him, he not having anything more for me to do. He offered me a home there but I chose to work for something more than my board and consequently hired to Mr. Bent to assist him in making gold washers at five dollars a day and boarded. He was from Wisconsin, and is the first man I have seen in California who lives as he did at home. He does no labor on the Sabbath and lives a strictly Christian life. Both he and his wife are fine people, and much thought of here.

March 14, 1850

Been out "prospecting" with Doane and got nothing but a wet jacket for our pains.

◇◇◇◇◇◇◇◇

On the side of the American River, there's a muddy beach where the state park allows people to pan for gold in the same water that the miners worked near Sutter's Mill. We make our way down to the narrow stretch of gravel beach that is the only open part of the river. We pan: I find a small node of fool's gold. Leslie finds glittering mica. I get nothing but a sunburned neck for my pains.

◇◇◇◇◇◇◇◇

March 15, 1850

This day the same. Time passes very heavily indeed, nothing but rain — rain — Capt. Quay gone back to buy things for the new hotel. Everyone much astonished by the continued rain. Last year, Mr. Bailey informs us, there was not a drop of rain during March, but now it falls as

328

easily as though it cost a fellow 5 bits instead of five dollars a day to live.

March 16, 1850

Went prospecting again with Doane and O'Bryan 4 miles down the river, and found a little. Capt. returned — weather fine again.

◇◇◇◇◇◇◇◇

Almost 500 panners are in Placerville from 23 different countries. The World Goldpanning Association has 16 pages of competition rules. No one knows how many gold flakes they're looking for in the 15-to-20-pound buckets of sand and gravel. They're trying for the best time, and every panner is videotaped in case there are protests. What was survival is now sport.

◇◇◇◇◇◇◇◇

March 18, 1950

Went down with Doane and worked — made $1.50. Rained again all afternoon.

March 19, 1850

Went prospecting again — found nothing in the shape of gold, but found myself badly poisoned again on my face etc., though I know not how, when or by what I was poisoned. Some there are who pretend to be satisfied with life in this country — but as for me I am not, nor can I imagine what kind of taste those have who are: for not a day — no nor hour, passes that we do not see every custom of home — every principle of morality and religion — every better feeling of our nature violated with the utmost indifference! None of the luxuries — but very few of the comforts — and a small portion only of the necessities of life are to be obtained here, while of good society — that greatest of earthly enjoyments — there is none! For others this kind of life may answer — but for me it will not; it falls far short of filling the ends and aims in life which I have formed. I love my home — my friends — my kind in general; and I desire to be where I can mingle freely with them — partake of their feelings and mingle my ideas and thoughts with theirs. I love the customs of my youth and my home, the principles which in early youth my Mother taught me, and I cannot bear to see them violated with a ruthless hand — much less can I join in the sacrilegious act. Gold may have its charms for the many: it hath charms too that command the body — the intellect — the soul — and all of man that is; yet strong as it may be it is not sufficient inducement to cause me to seek it at the expense of all my happiness — both temporal and eternal.

⬦⬦⬦⬦⬦

As we walk along the side of the hotel, there's a man leaning against the alley wall, having a smoke, dressed in the black T-shirt and pants favoured by back-of-house kitchen staff. He sees that I'm carrying a black plastic gold pan.

The place to go, he explains, is where there are fresh slides of earth along the riverbank. He finds lots of gold that way, he says. Lots of gold. We should try it.

Pansplaining.

⬦⬦⬦⬦⬦

March 26, 1850

Very hot day. Thermometer stood (it was said) 119. I am quite sick. Symptoms of fever and slight diarrhoea. Passed the day most miserably — earning nothing with the prospect of a summer's sickness ahead.

⬦⬦⬦⬦⬦

One of the things that we do find panning in the sand and silt along the edge of the river is a small lead fishing weight. It's a shot weight, almost perfectly round, with a slit through the middle so you can set your line in it and pinch the soft lead ball so it holds tightly in place — but it's not for fishing.

We discover later that having a weight like that in your pan helps you to know if you're panning properly: the lead is close in weight to gold, so if you can pan at the right speed to keep the lead ball in your pan, you are probably keeping any gold that you might have from washing out.

Panning makes you both meditative and on edge. In some ways, it's a lot like fly-fishing. Long stretches of the same rhythmic motion, the sort of thing that lets thoughts wander, while at the same time, the clear knowledge that the moment you let your guard down, something will happen: a fish will strike, a small bright fleck will flash in the sunlight and surge over the edge of the pan, falling irretrievably back into the fast water. For both, the big one is often the one that gets away.

∞∞∞∞∞

March 30, 1850

Quite unwell — bought a box of Moffat's pills for which I paid <u>four dollars</u> to a Dutch Jew.

March 31, 1850

Feel better this morning. Much cooler, cloudy and a little rain.

April 1, 1850

Election Day — fine weather and a great time. Mrs. Hurd unwell. Myself gaining a little.

April 4, 1850

Mrs. Hurd dangerously ill — not expected to live.

April 8, 1850

Up to this time I have not been doing much of anything
— not well — Mrs. Hurd died this forenoon. She had
been insensible for some time, but appeared to recognize
me this morning. Next day she was buried, I attending to
the digging of the grave etc.

◇◇◇◇◇◇◇

Placerville Hardware is packed with everything from necessary
plumbing parts to utility ladders to wind vanes, but it also veers to
gold-mining tourist goods, everything from sweatshirts to wood-
handled pocketknives with just about anyone's first name burnt into
the handles. The sign out front says, "The oldest hardware store west
of the Mississippi," adds that it was established in 1852. This whole city
has the feel of a tourist town banking hard on its gold-rush history: the
architecture, the old fonts on signs, the antique and gemstone stores.

Dodge's diary entries are stretching out more than ever, days apart
and mere sentences at a time. The wonder of the trip, the expectation
of the future, has fled. The story is winding down. I feel somewhat the
same way: I'm also not sure if my goals are even in reach.

◇◇◇◇◇◇◇

April 11, 1850
Very busy making a sheet iron rocker. Charles Chandler
intending to go up to Bird's where some new diggings are
reported to have been found, he and Ebon are very desir-
ous that I should go with him.

April 14, 1850

Started about 10 A.M. reached Spanish Bar that night —
worst hill I ever saw.

April 15, 1850

Started early up the steep hill & reached Bird's by 2 P.M.

We found about 5,000 persons there and no diggings of consequence. There had been 10,000 but were fast leaving.

My feet were a little sore when I started up, from the effects of the poison, and walking up here made them so bad that next day I was unable to walk. I paid a physician $2.00 for a little sugar of lead and remained 5 days trying to heal them, but getting no better and a chance offering to ride down for $45.00 I returned to Coloma on the 20th and stopped at Mr. Brent's. He intended to start for the mountains this week to open a boarding house and Ebon is going with him.

⬦⬦⬦⬦⬦⬦

The town of Coloma is essentially all state park: every scrap of what the town used to be like is long gone.

It's now interpretive displays of the different kinds of mining, reconstructed buildings, recreations of events. The ground has healed over all the scars of the mines, so that it looks a lot like any other day park. Unlike the burrowing shafts on the edge of the Black Rock Desert or the huge piles of overburden and waste rock from the massive modern mines, it doesn't look like the gold rush miners did much more than scratch the surface, and the surface has basically forgotten about the intrusion. Like every historic site we've been to, voices are kept low, reverential. Occasionally, a peal of laughter from children. But nothing like the rough and tumble, the drinking and violence, that there was.

⬦⬦⬦⬦⬦⬦

April 29, 1850

This day at noon I commenced clerking for N. Pauly at $250.00 per month. Weather fine. Ebon leaves tomorrow with Mr. Paddock.

April 30, 1850

Mr. Pauley leaves this morning for San Francisco to

purchase goods. Business very dull, but little doing in the mines. Gambling, drinking, fighting, and whoring has almost become the business of the day. It is surprising to see how much matters have changed for the worse since last fall.

May 8, 1850
Today the wind blows cold and chilly — every day people continue to arrive from the States — many of whom heartily wish themselves back there again.

June 29, 1850
I am very anxious to return to the States, but Ebon is not ready, and does not wish to go yet. The weather is exceedingly warm — the thermometer ranges at 108 degrees. Myself quite unwell. Symptoms of fever.

∞∞∞∞∞

Outside Courtroom #2 in the Eldorado County Courthouse in downtown Placerville, the rules are clear: "No tank tops, halter tops, shorts, food or beverages of any kind including chewing gum."

Upstairs, Judge James R. Wagoner is stewarding the courtroom through the regular churn of the judicial clock: setting dates to hear motions, to hear cases, to start trials. He's got a huge paper desk calendar, a desk piled with fat case documents. He comes into the court with a heavy mug of coffee clenched in one hand. He's the laxative in a constipated court system, keeping things moving, and it's clear he intends on doing just that. There are six inmates in the dock, five men, one woman, all in handcuffs and orange jail uniforms, loose tops, baggy pants. There are also a dozen or so other defendants, released on bail and seated in the courtroom. As the morning wends along, two more prisoners are led in.

It's a courtroom of dark brown panelling and blue chairs, with the judge's desk cutting across one corner of the courtroom.

There's a short bit of strife over delaying a vehicular homicide case until January 17, a full four months away, keeping the accused in jail until then. The case is a retrial, with a witness that will have to be brought in from Texas, complicated by the fact that she has two small children and her husband is just leaving for several months' work in Europe. There's also a motion to obtain Verizon cell phone records at the time of the accident.

The judge wants to keep things moving: "We've got to get this wave out so we can get the next wave in," he says.

The justice warehouse is alive and well in the U.S.

Sheriff's officers hand paper back and forth to have inmates brought back on the right days for appearances — the judge slides fat rubber bands off case files, deals with each case, and then snaps the bands back around the bulging file folders. Lawyers bob and dip at the prisoners' bench, talking to their clients, then agreeing to decisions on dates and appearances.

Michael Charles Phillips is there to plead no contest to his 5653 Fish and Game charge. The judge explains the case maximums, explains how a $1,000 fine will become $3,000 after law-imposed fees and levies.

It's a case about dredging for gold in protected waterways and can include up to six months of prison time. Phillips was caught illegally dredging on August 22, 2015, but the details aren't spelled out in the court, or in the court documents. Phillips has agreed to a deal that will see three years' probation and a ban on dredging for a year.

The no-dredging requirement becomes a stumbling point: when the prosecution makes it clear that they want it to mean no dredging anywhere, Phillips sighs an audible and drawn-out "Ahhh," as if that was something he wasn't expecting. He's wearing a felt shirt, dark blue jeans with no belt, and American flag suspenders.

He's a rangy man, the kind of skinny that makes suspenders stay taut, working for their keep. He has short, sandy hair, peaking to a point in the front, flattened down in a way that suggests it's usually unruly.

Judge Wagoner is not willing to impose the ban the prosecution wants, one that would essentially ban Phillips from dredging worldwide.

"What if he wants to go to Alaska, be on one of those shows?" Wagoner asks. "I only enforce California laws."

Phillips shifts from foot to foot. It's clear that he wants to take his vocation to a new frontier, at least to be able to continue gold mining somewhere else.

Eventually, the defence, prosecution, and judge reach a practical medium: since probation requires people to obey the law, Phillips won't be allowed to dredge at all in California for a year, and "nowhere in the world in an illegal manner."

During his three years of probation, Phillips, his home, and vehicle can be searched at any time, without warrant.

He has $220 in fees and levies to be paid and he asks if he can pay at the clerk's office downstairs.

The judge says yes, calls a 15-minute recess, and leaves with his coffee cup in hand.

<><><><><>

July 11, 1850

Left Coloma on the stage, for the city, intending if Ebon was ready to start home on the Steamer *Tennessee* on the 15, but he could not get ready in time, so I concluded to remain till the 1st of August. My health still feeble — not able to work though I have a chance in the "Times."

July 15, 1850

The weather here is exceedingly disagreeable although the days are warm and cloudless. One day the thermometer will be above a hundred and the next it will scarcely rise above 70. From midday it is extremely hot, and before morning one will be uncomfortably cold under three good woolen blankets. These sudden changes are far from being healthy or pleasant. On the bottom near the river the evenings and mornings are very damp, chill and disagreeable.

This is the Holy Sabbath — and though this is the city of thousands — having more energy and enterprise — more business and wealth than any other city of the same age in the known world — yet not a solitary peal of a "churchgoing bell" disturbs the morning stillness. They boast of their wealth and their growing greatness; yet how little do they think of him who gave it all! They boast that on the bosom of their river rides a hundred sail — that in their midst are men who count their fortune by hundreds of thousands — that in their city and among their edifices of but a year's growth are hotels and saloons of which any city in our mighty republic might well feel proud — and that all of wealth, taste, beauty, and magnificence are there combined, yet but one small solitary, simple, and unadorned <u>church</u> is to be found amid all their greatness and their wealth! While their gambling hells fitted up and adorned with all the luxuries and magnificence that art can devise or wealth obtain are filled to overflowing by men from every nation and people, but now and then one is seen slowly wending his way to the house of worship! While thousands congregate to indulge in bacchanalian glee, and sin of every kind and hue, how few — how very few — assemble to hear the word of God, and listen again to the instructions of their earlier days! 'Tis strange — 'tis passing strange how soon, and with what apparent ease men cast aside all the restraints and influences which from their infancy has been brought to bear upon them! — with what perfect carelessness and unconcern they adopt habits and customs directly antagonistic to those to which all their life they have been accustomed. Here is a school in which to study human nature — and this a subject worthy of the contemplation of every mind. Here Man is to be seen and studied as he is naturally. Stripped

> of all that restraining influence which in a moral commu-
> nity is always thrown around it, the human mind is here to
> be seen in all its naked deformity — and if there be a man
> on earth who doubts the natural depravity of the human
> mind, let him come to California — see and be convinced.

∞∞∞∞∞

The last part of the drive is an anxious one. We leave Placerville at 4:00 a.m., following handwritten instructions to the Sacramento air-port. It's dark, the pavement wet, and everyone else seems to know where they are going. Leslie's driving: she's always better at the big, fast roads.

There's only a light-blue sliver of morning horizon as we turn in Milligan at the rental agency — they sweep over the car with flash-lights and sign us out with no comment. We leave the coolers behind in the trunk and head into the airport.

We've gone 5,600 miles to follow Dodge's 2,000 or so. And once we take off, all of it falls away behind us in a few hours at 37,000 feet, the mountains and deserts and passes reduced to something that looks like the surface of the three-dimensional globes that used to be popular in the '80s. It makes everything big seem smaller, less important, more easily overlooked or forgotten.

In the seat in front of us, two women talk about visiting their kids at college, about how one has a homemade quilt to drop off, wonder-ing whether her son will like it, if she'll have to turn around and bring it back across the country in her luggage. A crossing that will take hours, not months.

As the country slides beneath us, I'm left with the thought of a chapter closing, of something done that I will not get to do again. Below the plane, whole mountain ranges slide by, an amazing sight. In the row in front of us, I don't think either of the women take the time to even look out the window.

July 20, 1850

Arrived at San Francisco at daybreak, and immediately engaged passage on the brig "R. W. Brown" to Panama for $75.00 — were told that she would positively sail that day, but when night came the Capt. had to hunt up some more men. The day was spent in heaving up the anchors both of which were got up without difficulty.

July 21, 1850

We were much surprised at the appearance of San Francisco. In the Bay were about 600 vessels of all kinds and sizes, ships, brigs, schooners, & steamers from the size of a skiff to a large ocean steamer — sloops and everything else all mixed together — some coming in and others going out and hundreds more lying idle — & two or three being wrecked and sunk on the island abreast the town. The city is built in a curve of the bay, partly sheltered from the ocean breezes by the high sand hills in its rear — upon a succession of the most barren of which I ever saw, it is built. It is decidedly a most barren, sandy, uneven, and lonesome looking place. Notwithstanding which from its situation and harbor — the largest and one of the best in the world — it is destined to be one of the first cities of the globe. During the afternoon of each day the wind from the ocean blows a perfect gale which makes it so cold and disagreeable that an overcoat is absolutely necessary. Although but a couple of years old it already contains 60,000 inhabitants. Large and beautiful ships, which at home would be worth from 20 to $30,000 lie there decaying and rotting for want of care — many of which will probably never leave the harbor again. When we were nearly clear of the fleet, the Capt. came on board, bringing another man — being still two hands short — and a breeze springing up, they hoisted sail and we were soon under way — the wind blowing fresh inland so that we were compelled to beat out. Oh how many and varied were the thoughts that crowded thick and fast upon my mind, as I stood upon the deck of that vessel with her prow homeward turned! That moment for which I had so long and anxiously looked, for which I had prayed and hoped so fervently, had at length arrived; and yet I felt not that joy which I felt should mark the moment of my departure to my loved home and living friends. I was happy — and yet sad. With my joy was mixed a feeling of regret for which I could not account, and yet could not drive away.

Chapter 17

Across the Continent

Neither Dodge nor I had found what we were looking for. Dodge, at least, left for home: I was still looking for it.

It doesn't come to me until much later, travelling again, on the northern tip of Newfoundland, at Raleigh. It's a different kind of almost-desert, a vast limestone barren where the only plants are small succulents and mustards and sedges that fight for every opportunity to grow in a windswept wasteland.

I started thinking, sitting in the cold night under the sharp stars, about boom and bust. And sheer luck. Everything. All the stories. Fort Kearney, Fort Bridger, this year's mountain pass route, motor hotels, door latches, immigrant hotels, riverboats, gold mines, steam locomotives, St. Louis nights, desert cars, festivals, almonds, hydro plants, army bases, goose hunts, peace and war, dairy and corn and bicycle races and forest fires and restaurants and alkali lakes.

William Castle Dodge.

And me.

Years in, and I was sure that I had failed to find my own fit. Thousands of miles, and I was no closer to home.

And then came Phoenix. And something as simple as the common, communal answering prayer known as the Eucharistic Preface. But I'm getting ahead of myself.

Three years after Sacramento and back on Dodge's trail looking for what seemed to be unfindable, Leslie convinced me we should visit my younger brother George and his wife Debbie in Phoenix.

I hadn't seen George in years, communicating with him and with my older brother, Charles, only by occasional email. I was apprehensive.

We landed at Sky Harbor International on a sticky night, wrestled with getting our rental car, followed confusing Google Maps instructions as Leslie drove us through a maze of planned community street names — East Tanglewood Drive, East Amberwood Drive, East Silverwood Drive — until we found his address.

George came out the door of one of a row of similar stucco houses — a rental with an unused basketball net out front from an earlier tenant — and was immediately, obviously, unmistakably George.

The house has three citrus trees along one side, and backs onto a manmade lake big enough for the neighbours to have boats. A fountain in the middle turns off at a set time every night and comes on again in the morning. George and Debbie warned us about scorpions. The night air in Phoenix is ridiculously still and pleasantly warm, even in November. Some of the houses across the pond were Airbnbs, and were inhabited only for noisy weekend events, sometimes with banquet tables. It was a completely different world to me.

A couple of nights in, George and I wound up sitting on the small square wharf behind the house just as the night came on, legs identically crossed under us.

A long, white pontoon boat tooled past several times, the husband at the wheel wearing a captain's hat, wife in the bow like an unnecessary lookout, the boat travelling a regular counter-clockwise circle with each trip.

I knew, all at once, as we sat there talking and then not talking, the sunlight fading through pink and orange behind the black silhouettes of a row of palm trees, that he and I were seeing and hearing the same things, processing them in similar ways. That everything is built on a foundation of shared experience and memory that still holds true, even if the routes we're taking diverge every single day.

I remember that the last time all three of us were together — my older brother Charles and George and I — we were in a Vancouver craft brewery eating small bratwurst sausages dipped in a selection of grainy mustards, drinking beer. We'd lapsed easily, effortlessly, into speaking a family shorthand of memories that came from our shared childhood, memories that only we have. And, with both our parents gone, a shorthand that is decipherable only to the three of us, even though we're spread across North America.

As we talked at the brewery, both of my brothers had reasons for me not to write this book.

As usual, they followed up that conversation with longer, more formal cautionary emails, just the way our father used to do in neatly handwritten letters on thin airmail paper, and the way Mom would do in sometimes urgent and serious tones over the phone. Family tradition.

As usual, I ignored the advice.

This time, I'm glad I did.

Because, finally, on the wrong trail altogether, I found what I was looking for, an understanding of where I fit, and why. It's my story — but it's also our story, Leslie's and mine. And that's the key. Fitting in is where stories interlock, where a handful of words suddenly light shared memory's stage, those few words unlocking untold miles of experience.

I'm not formally religious: I go to Quaker Meeting occasionally, like my mother did for years. I went to an Anglican school, and took part in the Eucharistic Preface, where the reverend and the congregation speak a rote prayer back and forth.

I hear it sometimes in the back of my head: "The Lord be with you," the reverend says. "And with your spirit." "Lift up your hearts;" "We lift them up to the Lord." Every time I hear it, I'm back in the school chapel in New Brunswick over 40 years ago and can see the school chaplain, who we just called "the Rev," lording over his small domain.

There are versions of the preface in most Christian faiths, and similar call-and-response prayers in other religions. For the Quakers, it's sharing a silence, eyes closed, waiting for the light and safe in your absolute trust of the silent others, the "Friends" around you.

It's not where you live, or daily contact. It's that sharing of the stories and knowing the familiar lines, particularly the stories we inhabit, that makes the family I was looking for. The thing that made me feel so much an outsider on a Manitoba farm was the very thing I sought. And in writing a diary he professed he didn't want people to see, what Dodge sought too.

The world and my place in it, even my place in our family, are, at the core, stories. Stories you — and others — remember together.

And it suffers from the risk of easy and wholesale erasure. It's what you lose when parents die, and you can no longer pick up the phone to confirm something you think you remember. With divorce, when a block of shared history is often closed off. With pull-up-the-stakes cross-country moves, when the easy comfort of being with friends is dislocated.

Months later, after we'd seen George and Debbie in their home environment, after I'd finally been able to set their space in my mind, they pulled up stakes again, heading for Virginia and a medical residency for Debbie.

Constant motion. But some things don't change.

They do beneath our feet, but between us, there's the bedrock comfort of the same ground.

Afterword

D odge's route from San Francisco, crossing the Isthmus of Panama and then taking a steamer north to New York, was supposed to be a shorter, quicker, and simpler route home. Becalmed for days and short of water, it had its own unexpected trials.

He returned to Fond du Lac, finished his law degree, and took up a variety of careers — from farmer to newspaper publisher to writer to inventor.

Dodge's obituary ran in *The Washington Post*, January 4 and 5, 1914, the crossing of the Great Plains summed up in barely two sentences.

INVENTOR DODGE IS DEAD

Man who improved old-time guns, victim of Pneumonia.

He was also gold miner, doorkeeper in House of Representatives, and Patent Attorney.

William Castle Dodge, well-known inventor, patent lawyer, and civic worker, who had been ill for the past two weeks at his home, 116 B street northeast, of Pneumonia, died at 5 o'clock yesterday afternoon. While Mr. Dodge had not been actively engaged in business for several years, his general health was good, and his death came as a great surprise to his friends.

Born at Solon, Courtland County N.Y. December 9, 1827, Mr. Dodge led a most eventful life. He was educated in the common schools of Solon, and later was graduated from Ithaca Academy. In 1846 he went to Wisconsin, where he took up the study of law. When the rush for gold was made to California in 1849. Mr. Dodge was among the first to cross the prairies in quest of the precious metal. The following year he returned to Wisconsin, and in 1851 was admitted to the bar. In 1854 he went to Minnesota where he settled near Winona and took up farming as a vocation. He introduced the first iron water wheel for mill use in that state. Four years later he went to St. Peter, Minn., where he conducted the *St. Peter Free Press*, then one of the largest publications in Minnesota. In 1860 Mr. Dodge came to Washington, where he bacame doorkeeper of the House of Representatives. The following year he bacame examiner in the patent office, where he served until the close of the civil war. It was the war which led him to consider the then imperfect firearms, and it was largely due to him that many improvements were made to the guns then in use. He was honored by several European governments for his work along these lines, and the Congress also compensated him for his services.

At the close of the war he also became a patent attorney and his business is still being run by his sons and grandsons. He was among those who founded the present Society of Associated Charities and was for many years a member of the board of trustees.

Mr. Dodge was first married in 1851 to Miss Jane Van Patten, of Schenectady, N.Y., who died in 1860. The following year he married Miss Elizabeth A. Schrivener, of Washington, who survives. He is also survived by three sons, Philip T., of New York; William W. and Horace A. Dodge, both of this city, and four daughters, Miss Jennie Dodge, Mrs. Thomas J. Johnston, of Brooklyn, N.Y.; Mrs. Clair Hillyer, of Chicago, and Mrs. J.W. Murphy of this city.

The Library of Congress has two short entries of his papers:

WILLIAM CASTLE DODGE

British letters patent for an improvement in firearms, being his device for ejecting empty shells from a revolver. Parchment, two sheets, with the Great Seal of England attached.

Presented in 1904, by the late William Castle Dodge, of Washington, D.C.

The National Capital, its Location and Government by William Castle Dodge. A volume of unbound manuscript sheets, 1817-1826. Gift, 1914, of the heirs of W. C. Dodge, Washington. D.C.

Later, I found a printed copy of his 22-page book titled *Breech-Loaders Versus Muzzle-Loaders or How to Strengthen Our Army and Crush the Rebellion with a Saving of Life and Treasure.*

In writing this book, I've used much of William Castle Dodge's original diary, with the exception of some short segments that, while of interest for those who follow western trail routes carefully, slow the narrative and add little more than the direction taken and distances travelled on particular days.

I have edited the diary lightly, leaving his original spellings and punctuation, but correcting a handful of small obvious errors. Some repetitive sections have also been removed.

I have, for clarity's sake, provided the full names for several rivers that he regularly shortened to initials after their first use, and have inserted full place names for abbreviated versions used by Dodge so that readers won't have to pause to figure out his intentions. I have also inserted full names instead of the initials Dodge favoured for identifying his fellow travellers whenever possible. Sections of his time spent at the goldfields — long, miserable, and often dogged by sickness as he moved from job to job — have also been abridged.

The end of the diary — Dodge's trip by ship from San Francisco to Panama, his crossing of the isthmus, and his subsequent ocean travel to New York — is also not included.

The last entry in the diary was made on September 20, 1850, just short of 18 months after the first entry.

It was simple, short, and to the point.

"Left for New York where we arrived at 4 P.M. on the 20th."

At long last, the constant questions that dogged William Castle Dodge throughout his trip — the simple availability of water, fuel, and grass — didn't matter anymore.

But the story still does.

Acknowledgements

No thanks are enough for my critical first reader, magical first editor, and absolutely fearless travelling companion, Leslie Vryenhoek. The book is much better not only because of her valuable literary insights and careful arguments about words, tone, and structure, but also because of her eyes, ears, and keen impressions throughout the several thousand miles of trail. There is, frankly, not one single person on Earth better to be lost with in uncounted acres of empty western desert. She took us cheerfully where I feared to tread.

Thanks to Susan Renouf, my excellent and smooth-tempered editor at ECW Press, who didn't lose faith and move to rope the story in as the page count rose, and whose editorial touch is both surgical and near-painless. (That is, by the way, a rare and rich combination.) Many thanks are also due to ECW Press, for taking the chance on *Same Ground* that every single nascent book is, especially during the unsettled times of the COVID-19 pandemic.

Heartfelt thanks to my long-time agent and friend, Shaun Bradley, who has helped me navigate the business of writing in more ways than she knows: her frank and steady counsel kept my eyes on the writing road as she deftly kept the necessary mechanics working.

Thanks also to ArtsNL, the Newfoundland and Labrador Arts Council, for their financial support of some of the travel costs involved in researching and writing this book — outside the writing world, it may not seem obvious, but that sort of investment in the arts makes things like this book possible.

To my brothers, Charles and George, thanks for your careful counsel and being the ones who also know and keep so much of our shared memories.

Thanks also to all the family members and employers who tolerate the time and attention I devote to writing projects.

Thanks, finally, to those who we met on the road, especially those who shared their stories with us, knitting us in a small way into the great big worldwide web of people, a web that has nothing to do with the internet, and everything to do with humanity.

Russell Wangersky is the author of seven books of fiction and non-fiction, including Burning Down the House — a finalist for the Hilary Weston/Writers' Trust Prize for Non-fiction, Canada's largest non-fiction award. For years a dual citizen after being born in the U.S., he is all Canadian now, and is often mystified by his southern neighbour. He has twice been nominated for the Scotiabank Giller Prize, for his short story collections The Hour of Bad Decisions and Whirl Away. His work has won the Rogers Non-fiction Prize, the BC National Award for Canadian Non-fiction, the Edna Stabler Award, and the BMO Winterset Prize multiple times. Formerly a columnist with the SaltWire newspaper chain based at the Telegram in St. John's, NL, he is currently editor in chief of the Saskatchewan Postmedia newspapers. He lives in Saskatoon with his spouse, fellow conspirator, and debate opponent, Leslie Vryenhoek. They have four children.

When not writing or editing, he might be metal detecting, fly fishing, or panning for gold — Russell maintains there are great similarities between all three, but that's something you'd have to ask him about directly.